The Third House

The Third House

Lobbyists and Lobbying in the States

Alan Rosenthal
Eagleton Institute of Politics
Rutgers University

PRESS

A Division of Congressional Quarterly Inc.
Washington, D.C.

Copyright © 1993 Congressional Quarterly Inc.
1414 22nd Street, N.W., Washington, D.C. 20037

Printed in the United States of America

Third Printing

Cover design: Paula Anderson

Library of Congress Cataloging-in-Publication Data

Rosenthal, Alan, 1932-
    The Third House: lobbyists and lobbying in the states / Alan Rosenthal.
      p. cm.
    Includes bibliographical references and index.
    ISBN 0-87187-671-X -- ISBN 0-87187-672-8 (pbk.)
      1. Lobbying--United States. 2. Pressure groups--United States.
   3. Parliamentary practice--United States. I. Title
JK1118.R676 1992
324'.4'0973--dc20   92-28705
                                                       CIP

To Patrick Cole Rosenthal

CONTENTS

PREFACE

When asked by friends and colleagues why I was writing this book, I usually explained as follows. I had studied and written about legislators for years, but legislators did not really appreciate my efforts. Then I wrote a book about governors and legislatures. To my dismay, I found that governors are oblivious to mortals who are not themselves governors, so no acknowledgment came from that direction either. It finally occurred to me that if I switched gears and wrote about lobbyists, I could at least expect free food and drink by way of appreciation. Some of my interviews with lobbyists—people who are alleged to be genetically programmed to pick up the tab—were conducted over breakfast, lunch, or dinner. It turned out, however, that I paid more often than they did. So much for my quest of acknowledgment!

While I wrote this book in part for acknowledgment, I wrote it mainly to challenge the conventional wisdom about lobbyists and lobbying. That is not to say that lobbyists do not buy legislators meals or entertain them in other ways. They certainly do. But there is much more to lobbying than that. Anyone who has spent as long as I have studying and consulting with legislatures would at some point have to become interested in lobbyists. The surprising thing is that my interest emerged only recently. One of my books, *Legislative Life*, was published about ten years ago, and it ignored lobbying almost entirely—an enormous oversight. My hope is that *The Third House: Lobbyists and Lobbying in the States* will redress this deficiency.

A few years ago I began to conduct, in collaboration with the State Governmental Affairs Council (SGAC), a program designed to enhance the professional skills of representatives of member companies and associations. This enterprise involved me in questions of direct lobbying, coalition building, grass-roots mobilization, and ethics. It also brought me into contact with many lobbyists. Instead of catching a dread disease, however, I became more and more interested in lobbying. Then, in 1990, I was appointed chairman of a commission on legislative ethics and campaign finance. The members of the commission (four of whom were legislators and five, citizens) examined the regulation of lobbying, among other matters, and made several recommendations for legislative action. My involvement with this commission further whetted my appetite for the subject.

The lobbying of state legislatures is in need of study. The media have a narrow, and even distorted, perspective on lobbyists and lobbying. The public's comprehension is likewise limited and unduly negative. In contrast, my first-hand observations and experiences have given me an appreciation for both the lobbyists I have met and the institution of lobbying. I have become one of the not-too-many people outside of the field itself who believes lobbying to be an honorable profession. But, then, I also believe politics is an honorable profession. If that were not enough of an admission, I confess to being a cheerleader for legislatures and an admirer of the legislative process. Readers should therefore be aware that a particular perspective is present in this work.

My account of lobbyists and lobbying in the states is based largely on interviews with about one hundred lobbyists in California, Colorado, Florida, Minnesota, New Jersey, and Texas as well as a few in Maryland and Washington, D.C. Lobbying life is described mainly from the point of view of lobbyists themselves. This vantage point is essential, I believe, for conveying a feel for the enterprise and for understanding what lobbying entails. But it is also important that we make judgments. Thus, I have endeavored to step back, acquire distance, and analyze the practices and effects of lobbying and its role in representative democracy.

In writing this book, I owe special thanks to individuals in five different communities.

The first is the community of political scientists, in which I claim membership. Political scientists have by no means been idle in this area. They have produced a substantial body of knowledge on lobbyists and on the interest groups lobbyists represent. Their writings have been extremely useful to me and their findings are reflected throughout this work. I am grateful to these colleagues and hope that this book contributes to the overall effort of the discipline. Several political scientists have been of special help. Allan Cigler of the University of Kansas and Clive Thomas of the University of Alaska read the manuscript and made a number of comments. Earlier Malcolm Jewell, Ronald Hrebener, and an anonymous reviewer offered their critiques of my proposal. I am happy that the reviewers liked what I had written, and I appreciate their suggestions for improvement.

Another community to which I owe a debt of gratitude is the state capitol community, consisting of legislators, legislative staff, lobbyists, and journalists from across the nation. These are the people with whom I have worked and about whom and for whom I've written. They have provided grist for my mill and are primarily responsible for my education—or miseducation—over these past years.

Without support from still another community—the Eagleton Institute of Politics, Rutgers University, and the State of New Jersey—I would not have been able to devote myself to state legislatures as I have. I still do not take for granted all of the privileges we academics have. Academics are a fortunate lot. The late Don Herzberg, my predecessor as director of Eagleton, afforded me my initial opportunity, recruiting me just when the state legislative modernization movement was getting under way. Since then, the university administration—deans, provosts, and presidents—has enabled me and the rest of us at the Institute to take advantage of many opportunities to engage in basic and applied research and public service. And New Jersey's political leadership has appreciated and supported our work.

I owe special and personal thanks to the Institute's faculty and administrative and secretarial staff, in particular, to Chris Lenart and Joanne Pfeiffer. As my administrative assistant, Chris runs the place when I'm preoccupied with writing a book. (She also runs it when I'm not so preoccupied.) Joanne typed and proofread this manuscript and, as usual, managed to put up with my impatience and to tolerate my moods. She is responsible for whatever errors of fact or interpretation can be found in these pages.

Naturally, the publishing community has also been helpful. I want to thank CQ Press, which I regard as the foremost publisher of books dealing with politics and government in the states. I trust that the present book will advance that enterprise, and not set it back. It has been a pleasure working with CQ's fine editorial staff—especially Brenda Carter, the acquisitions editor; Kristen Carpenter Stoever, the copy editor; and Nancy Lammers, the assistant director. Kate Quinlin, Jackie Davey, and the rest of the marketing staff were also quite helpful. If this book fails to succeed, however, they must all shoulder the blame.

Finally, I want to thank the most important and ultimately the most supportive community of all—family and friends. My children, who have taken on their own distinctive shapes, are a continuing delight and even inspiration. I appreciate them and I like them—John and Lisa, Kai, Tony, and Lisa. And Vivian, to whom pluralistic politics does not come easy, has been in my corner as well. She has broadened and deepened my perspective on life, while encouraging me to do my thing on lobbyists and legislatures. And so I have done it.

INTRODUCTION

The First Amendment to the U.S. Constitution guarantees the people the right to freedom of speech and also "to petition the Government for a redress of grievances." On that clause hangs the power of interest groups in America and their lobbyists in Washington, D.C., and in the states. "The right to petition" means that citizens and groups can appeal to the government for fair or even special treatment. Where petitioning government is guaranteed, so is the right to lobby.

Lobbying is simply the practice of attempting to influence the decisions of government. It employs a variety of methods, including but not confined to oral and written communications with public officials. The word "lobby" has been around for some time, having first appeared in the English language in the middle of the sixteenth century. The word then referred to the halls and corridors of the House of Commons. The first recorded use of "lobby" in U.S. legislative circles was in 1808.[1] Since then it has been part of the lexicon of American politics.

The people who lobby are known as "lobbyists." They are regulated by government at the federal and state levels and are thus required to register. Lobbyists today represent every conceivable interest and are active at every level of government. The primary arenas for their efforts are the U.S. Congress and the state legislatures, where they work to promote and defend clients and causes. They are integral to lawmaking. A legislative process without lobbyists, according to journalist Robert Dvorchak, "is like having a road map with only interstate highways. They are the access ramps, back roads, shortcuts, cutoffs and detours."[2] As evidence of their involvement and their influence, lobbyists in many places are known as the "third house" of the legislature. Along with the senate and the house of representatives, the lobby also has a role to play in the process by which a bill becomes (or fails to become) a law.

The Proliferation of Interests and the Growth of Lobbying

Thanks to a plethora of interest groups in the United States, there

Outland by Berkeley Breathed. © 1992, Washington Post Writers Group. Reprinted with permission.

are thousands of jobs for lobbyists. Writing more than twenty-five years ago, James Deakin described the interest-group scene in Washington, D.C.:

> There is an association, union, society, league, conference, institute, organization, federation, chamber, foundation, congress, order, brotherhood, company, corporation, bureau, mutual cooperative, committee, council, plan, trusteeship, movement, district, assembly, club, board, service or tribe for every human need, desire, motive, ambition, goal, aim, drive, affiliation, occupation, industry, interest, incentive, fear, anxiety, greed, compulsion, frustration, hate, spirit, reform and cussedness in the United States.[3]

Since then, even more groups have formed, so that an "explosion of representation" is reverberating throughout the nation's capital.[4] The level of political mobilization in the American system has risen dramatically, with an increase in the number and range of interests being represented and the number of issues being debated in Congress. Between 1960 and 1980, the growth in groups operating in Washington, D.C., was estimated to be about 30 percent. Many were formed in response to government initiatives. As government programs became larger and more numerous, organizations of recipients and service providers grew apace. This period from 1960 to 1980, moreover, saw new interests arise—civil-rights activists, consumers, environmentalists, and feminists.[5] Stimulated by Ralph Nader and the ineptitude of General Motors in its battle with the consumer advocate, public interest groups rose to prominence.[6] One group led to another, sometimes as a reaction and in opposition to, but also in emulation of the former's success.[7]

The states soon followed suit. In the past twenty-five years the states have seen a marked increase in the number of lobbying groups. In Iowa, for example, only the railroads, bankers, utility companies, and so forth used to be active in Des Moines. Now all sorts of groups are represented at the capitol. Frankfort has also witnessed the triumph of political pluralism. Kentucky government and politics are no longer dominated by a small group of special interests—coal, horse racing, liquor, and agriculture. As the economy of the state has diversified, so have organized interests.[8]

The expansion of interest-group organization and representation in the states results from a variety of developments. State governments have moved into new fields and become active in consumer affairs, the environment, the workplace, and other areas dealing with social issues. Meanwhile, the federal government—through the Nixon, Ford, Carter, Reagan, and Bush administrations—has been retreating from its earlier commitments to the states and localities. Federal deregulation has left a power vacuum for the states to fill. As a consequence, the states have started to impose their own regulations—on packaging, hazardous waste, automotive emissions, and so forth. Furthermore, with cuts in federal aid but no letup in federal mandates, the ante has been raised in state capitals. Even in good economic times, the states have had to consider new and higher taxes; and in economic downturns, their need for revenues has been the number-one priority.

With states both choosing and having to take on new and greater responsibilities, interest groups have targeted their capitals. The cry used to be, "We don't need state government, we'll go to Washington." Not anymore. Groups today have to make their appeals state by state. Although it is true that policy has become nationalized and issues spread quickly across state lines (the media abet this process), this actually makes it more important for a group to establish a presence in each of the states.

As in the federal arena, the range of interests has broadened. Groups concerned with social and public-interest issues are now active, as are single-issue organizations. They have been able to shape the agendas and policies of the legislature. With federal budget cuts and the advent of block grants, a number of the advocacy groups have to get their money from different coffers. Therefore, they are much more active at the state level than they once were.[9] Some of these groups, moreover, have not only challenged but also threatened the positions of more traditional groups.[10]

With the expansion of state government and/or the formation of new groups, business and professional interests have also grown. Due to the volume and impact of legislation affecting business in the 1970s, the state governmental relations efforts of business expanded significantly.[11] For example, a study by the American Society of Association Executives found that the percentage of associations monitoring state issues had grown from 35 percent to 70 percent from 1982 to 1987.[12]

Recently, too, many traditional interests have been fragmenting. Cities no longer leave representation solely to the municipal association. They represent themselves as well. Companies that once relied exclusively on their membership in business and trade associations are no longer inclined to do so. Because of keen competition and the differential effects of legislation on firms in the same industry, they are more likely today to provide for their own representation in addition to that furnished by an umbrella association. As a consequence, even more interests are being articulated in the states.

Any group that can be touched by state government cannot afford to be without representation. If groups do not realize the need for a lobbyist at the outset, they soon learn their lesson. For example, Florida's cities appealed to the legislature for the enactment of a program that would have facilitated urban development. The legislature was willing to accede but insisted that the cities come up with a revenue source to fund the program they wanted. Everyone searched for a source. They found it in the dry-cleaning business, one of the only groups without a lobbyist in Tallahassee. With no one in the legislature speaking against it, a sales tax was imposed on dry cleaning. Within a few days of the tax's enactment, the dry cleaners had gotten themselves a lobbyist.

Until the recession of the early 1990s, lobbying had been a rapidly growing profession. Take the increase in business lobbying alone, which some say has become the most significant function performed by business associations.[13] Therefore, associations have added to their lobbying ranks. Individual companies also have established their own lobbying capacity. A survey of four hundred firms found that about 72 percent lobbied at the state level.[14] Industries once represented by a single lobbyist are now fractured into different groups. Colorado banks are an example. They used to have one lobbyist in Denver. Then they hired a second. Soon the Independent Bankers Association added its own. Following that, several contract lobbyists were taken on. Finally, individual banks and out-of-state banks hired their own lobbyists.[15]

An Associated Press survey found that in 1990 there were more than 42,500 registered lobbyists at state capitals, an increase of 20 percent in four years.[16] That same year, New York registered almost 2,000 lobbyists, a 17 percent rise over the previous year. During the period from 1976 to 1986, the rise in Oklahoma was more than 300 percent, from 83 to 343.[17] From 1985 to 1990, lobbyists in California and New Jersey increased by almost 50 percent; and it was over 50 percent in Texas from 1982 to 1987. If one goes back further, the growth is even more dramatic. Minnesota's lobbyist corps, which in 1990 numbered about 1,200, representing 1,125 groups, almost doubled in a decade. Florida's lobbyists numbered about 5,800 in 1990 and represented 3,300 principals. A decade earlier, 4,000 lobbyists represented 1,800 principals; ten years earlier than that, about 900 lobbyists represented 1,100 principals. Over the span of the past ten years, the growth in registered lobbyists in Florida has been almost 50 percent. Over twenty years, it has been more than sixfold.

Today, lobbying is a far different enterprise. Its exponential growth is described by a lobbyist in Minnesota, whom I interviewed in October 1990: "Ten years ago you saw the same people day in and day out. It was like a small fraternity. Everyone had places where they stood around the rotunda. Now, I'm lucky if I know a fourth of the lobbyists." The styles and techniques of lobbyists at state capitals have also changed. State government relations at one time could be conducted with "a shake and a howdy," according to the vice president for government relations at Pennzoil. No longer is that the practice.[18] Long gone are the days when lobbyists set up card tables in the rear of the house chamber in Wyoming to pay for legislators' votes as they were cast.[19] Nowadays, lobbying is professional and sophisticated. New techniques have been developed, including coalition building, grass-roots mobilization, public relations and communications, and even polling; and the older techniques of relationship building, political activity, and direct lobbying have undergone considerable refinement.

Lobbying is different today because legislatures have changed so markedly. Lobbying could not afford to lag far behind. Since the late 1960s and the period of state legislative reform, legislatures practically everywhere have modernized. The expansion of professional staffing has increased their capacity. Moreover, they have developed a sense of independence and do not routinely accept executive leadership. They are much improved and far more capable. And as Jesse Unruh, the late speaker of the California assembly and state treasurer, said: "As legislatures improve, the third house tends to improve too." [20]

The action is at the state level. With legislatures developing, political careers and elections becoming more important, and partisan competition sharpening, the environment for lobbying has been undergoing further change. A New Jersey lobbyist, who earlier had served on the legislative staff, described this new environment: "There's just more lobbyist consumers because legislative staff has grown, because legislative agendas have become more encompassing, because legislators have gotten to be better politicians and focus more on the politics of it rather than the policy of it." Legislators nowadays introduce bills that are more aggressive, more wide ranging, and more headline grabbing. The process is far more driven by politics than it used to be. Lobbyists cannot remain aloof from this new reality because they are so integral to the process, a process that politicians, and not lobbyists, continue to command.

How Lobbyists Are Perceived

Americans are skeptical not only toward government and public officeholders but also toward those whose business is dealing with

government. The image in the American mind is that of special interests
having their way with representatives in Washington and with state
legislators, naturally at the public's expense. A typical view can be seen in
a book by Kenneth G. Crawford, a journalist based in Washington, D.C.:
"Since the founding of the republic, the democratic process has been
perverted to a greater or less[er] degree by cunning and powerful
minorities bent on serving their own interests." [21] Some evidence certainly supports this view of greedy special interests subverting democracy. The Southern Pacific Railroad dominated California government
until it was swept from power by the Progressive reform movement of the
early twentieth century. Standard Oil was so influential in Pennsylvania
that some claimed it had done everything to the Pennsylvania legislature
except refine it. Historical examples of interest-group power abound;
contemporary examples, while fewer and further between, are still not
that difficult to find.

Given such instances and their treatment in the media, it is not
surprising that citizens are concerned. A *USA Today* poll (August 1990)
found that 69 percent of Americans responding agreed somewhat or
strongly that special interest groups had too much control. A poll
conducted by CBS News/*New York Times* (October 1990) found, moreover, that 71 percent of the respondents thought most members of
Congress were more interested in serving special-interest groups than in
serving the people they represented. Also "special interest" is a pejorative
term just as "public interest" is a term loaded with positive meaning. For
most of us, the battle is between special interests on the one hand and the
public interest on the other. It is easy to choose sides in such a
confrontation.

The fact is that many people belong to or are represented directly or
indirectly by special-interest groups that are trying to get a fair shake, an
advantage, or a program from government or are trying to stop something
from being done that would adversely affect them. It is understandable,
therefore, that when people are asked about particular interest groups,
they are more favorably inclined than when they are asked about "special
interests" as such. A Gallup poll (April 1989) shows favorable views,
particularly with regard to groups that might not appear to have a special
interest. Of those responding, 93 percent felt positively about the
American Cancer Society, 82 percent about Planned Parenthood, 71
percent about the National Organization for Women, 58 percent about
the National Rifle Association, 55 percent the National Right to Life
Commission, 55 percent Handgun Control, and 54 percent the American
Civil Liberties Union. Only the Tobacco Institute suffered, with a mere
26 percent of the public positive in their views. Could it be that many of
those questioned knew little about these groups, but were responding to
labels!

The word "lobbyist" is also loaded. The attitudes of both the public and the press are very negative today. Lobbyists are too powerful; they are not to be trusted. Here, too, there is historical evidence to support current attitudes. Few lobbyists had the power of Artie Samish, who operated (some would say "governed") in California during the 1930s and 1940s. Samish was a newspaper cartoonist's dream, with his straw hat, large cigar, big paunch, and loud tie. What he is remembered most for today is an article in a 1949 issue of *Collier's* magazine, titled "The Secret Boss of California." The cover of the magazine was a color photo of Samish posed with a ventriloquist's dummy, "Mr. Legislature," in his hand.[22] The lobbyist was pulling the strings of the legislature.

Since the days of Samish, lobbyists in the states have not achieved the Californian's notoriety. But instances can be found, even in Wisconsin where ethical conduct is of the highest order, of lobbyists twisting arms, offering bribes, and seducing legislators. Recent scandals in South Carolina and Arizona mainly involved legislators, but lobbyists were also implicated. It is the media's business to report such messes. They are news, while honest legislators and lobbyists are not. The public therefore generalizes from the worst possible cases, not having heard about the best.

Just as Americans believe that special interests are a cause for concern, so 64 percent think, according to a *USA Today* poll (June 1990), that the role of lobbying in politics is either a "somewhat" or "very serious" threat to American democracy. A national survey conducted by Associated Press/Media General (September 1989) highlighted the negative attitude of the public toward lobbyists in the states. People do not like lobbyists' influence. Almost half think lobbyists have a great amount of influence (another 39 percent think they have some influence) in shaping laws that come out of legislatures. More than half feel that they have too much influence. Nor do they like the way lobbyists behave. More than half have an unfavorable opinion of their behavior; only one out of six consider their ethical behavior to be good.

The public, furthermore, does not trust state legislators to resist the blandishments of lobbyists. The same Associated Press/Media General survey found that four out of five citizens believed legislators were overly influenced by campaign contributions and three out of four thought legislators were overly influenced by gifts from lobbyists. California's citizens may be even more critical of legislators than people elsewhere. A *Los Angeles Times* poll (January 3, 1990) revealed that 53 percent believed that taking bribes is a relatively common practice among California legislators. And by two to one they agreed that most state legislators are for sale to their largest campaign contributors.[23]

The press is as negative as the public, but not as passive. Typical of the editorial press is a recent editorial from the *Star-Ledger* in New

Jersey. It declared that "the power of the lobbyists cannot be overesti-mated," and continued by setting up lobbyists as the enemy of the public interest: "Many lobbyists pride themselves not in the legislation that's enacted but in the legislation that's killed—particularly if it's legislation that would aid the public but hurt their clients." [24] When statehouse reporters write about lobbyists and lobbying, they fixate on campaign contributions and gifts. Recently the *St. Paul Pioneer Press* ran a seven-part series of articles condemning the system in Minnesota (one of the few places with public financing of legislative campaigns). Even in a state with squeaky-clean government, the newspaper alleged that the special interests had a tight grip on the legislature. A columnist, commenting on the series, wrote: "If you have been reading 'Bankrolling the Legislature' ... you know that the foul odor you have been smelling does not come from the Pig's Eye sewage plant, the Smith Street St. Paul stockyards or the garbage bins behind your neighborhood hamburger joint. The stench is coming from the hog wallow at the Capitol." [25]

The implication is that lobbyists, who represent special interests, are buying votes. Yet, except for campaign contributions, entertaining, trips, and gifts, other aspects of lobbying go unreported by the press. Even a series of articles on lobbying will deal almost entirely with what lobbyists contribute to or spend on legislators and what legislators allegedly do in return.

If, for example, Legislator A receives a campaign contribution of $1,000 from Lobbyist B and also votes in support of the interests of B's client, then it is implied that A voted the way he or she did because of the contribution. The possibility that A would have voted that way in any case, and that the contribution was designed to help a friendly legislator get reelected, is seldom entertained, yet surely deserves serious consider-ation.

An example of press interpretation (or misinterpretation) is provided by an incident that was well covered by Florida's capitol press corps in 1988. The press reported that lobbyists for Alamo Rent-a-Car hosted a dinner for legislators at an expensive restaurant the night before a legislative committee voted on an issue involving Alamo. The stories suggested that the free meal and the favorable vote for Alamo were linked. A few years later, the *Pensacola Journal* recounted the event, concluding: "The next day, Alamo's side won. Coincidence?" [26] Obviously the journalist writing the article did not believe so. The fact is, however, that Alamo had rounded up enough votes on the committee well in advance of the committee meeting, and the dinner itself had nothing to do with the outcome. Perhaps Alamo's significant economic presence in the state was the pivotal consideration. But that explanation received much less attention in the press than the dinner paid for by lobbyists.

Observing Lobbyists and Lobbying

If people observe lobbyists and lobbying at all, they do it through the media. The media view lobbying mainly in terms of the exchange of money for a vote—a quid for a quo. Lobbyists themselves talk about their striving to attain "access" simply so they can present their case. Some lobbyists go further, admitting to influence and hoping to reap benefits from their reputation. Legislators, who are on the receiving end, claim that most of what lobbyists do is provide useful information. They report that they are not swayed by lobbyists, although their colleagues may be.

There is a modicum of truth to each of these perspectives. Lobbyists are looking for something in return for their generosity. But it is not usually a vote. Lobbyists want and work for access, but they also want and work for more. Legislators do get needed information from lobbyists, but that is not all they receive. An exploration of lobbyists and lobbying must go further than these one-dimensional perspectives.

Political scientists, particularly in their studies of interest groups in America, have gone further. The explorations of Jeffrey M. Berry; Allan J. Cigler and Burdett A. Loomis; Ronald J. Hrebenar and Ruth K. Scott; Kay Lehman Schlozman and John T. Tierney, and Clive S. Thomas and Ronald J. Hrebenar are among the recent works that have proved very useful to this study.[27] They are cited throughout the present work. On lobbyists and lobbying, specifically, less has been done. But the early study by Lester W. Milbrath, and that by Harmon Zeigler and Michael A. Baer are still relevant today.[28] The political scientist who in recent years has done as much original research as anyone on both interest groups and lobbyists in Washington, D.C., is Robert H. Salisbury.[29] His work has informed that of all political scientists in this field. Other political scientists, practitioners, and observers have made their contributions, too; they are cited frequently in the following pages.

The Scope of This Study

The approach taken in this book is distinct from that of previous approaches. We are attempting, on the one hand, to cover a broad area and, on the other, to provide detail on lobbyists at work. Just what do lobbyists do? How do they do it? In these pages, we shall survey the scene, but we shall also probe into many of the subjects brought up. By examining the types of people involved, the techniques they use, and the jobs they do, we hope to convey to the reader a sense of the lobbying enterprise and its part in the legislative process. Of interest here are matters of timing, targeting, cultivating, strategizing, coalescing, mobilizing, educating, and justifying. To our knowledge, a study such as this one has not been done at the state level before.

Our examination of lobbying is located within the state legislative context. It is intended to apply generally, even though each state is not quite like any other and each legislative body in its particulars is unlike the rest. The present study, while meant to be generic, is rooted in the lobbying cultures and practices of six states—California, Colorado, Florida, Minnesota, New Jersey, and Texas.

Several important indicators for these six states are shown in Table I-1. The political cultures, as characterized by Daniel Elazar, include "moralistic" Colorado and Minnesota; "individualistic" New Jersey; Florida and Texas, which are primarily "traditionalistic"; and California, which combines the moralistic and individualistic strands.[30] The size of the legislatures varies, with senates ranging from 31 to 67 members and houses from 65 to 150 members. In four of the six states Democrats have controlled both houses of the legislature from 1983 to 1992, while in New Jersey control has been split, and in Colorado Republicans have been dominant throughout the period. During this time, four of the six states have had both Republican and Democratic governors, while California has had only Republicans and Colorado only Democrats. As far as population, these states overrepresent the larger ones. No small states are in the sample. Four of the six have had significant growth in the last decade.

The six states have legislatures that are more developed or professionalized than most. Karl T. Kurtz has categorized the fifty state legislatures on the basis of the length of their legislative sessions, the size of their staffs, the level of compensation to legislators, and the stability of membership. Of the eight in the very professionalized category, California is studied here. Of the twenty-five in the somewhat professionalized category, Colorado, Florida, Minnesota, New Jersey, and Texas are represented here. None of the seventeen legislatures in the least professionalized group are part of this study's sample.[31]

More specifically, New Jersey was chosen because the author has been a resident in that state and a student of its politics for many years. California had to be included because of its predominance, the professionalization of its legislature, and the complexity of its politics. Texas is another large state, and one with a free-wheeling political culture. Florida is like Texas, particularly as far as its culture is concerned, and it is also a place that the author has explored in his work with state legislatures. Minnesota, with its tradition of progressivism and its moralistic political culture, is the only midwestern state examined in this study. Like Florida, Minnesota for years has had a strong and effective legislature. So has Colorado, whose culture resembles that of Minnesota. Moreover,

Table I-1 Characteristics of Six States Examined in the Study

	California	Colorado	Florida	Minnesota	New Jersey	Texas
Population, 1990	29,760,021	3,294,394	12,937,926	4,375,099	7,730,188	16,986,510
Population rank, 1990	1	26	4	20	9	3
Population growth, 1980-90	25.7	31.8	32.7	7.3	5.0	64.8
Political culture [a]	Moralistic dominant; strong individualistic strain	Moralistic	Traditionalistic dominant; strong individualistic strain	Moralistic	Individualistic	Traditionalistic dominant; strong individualistic strain
Size of legislature						
senate	40	35	40	67	40	31
house	80	65	120	134	80	150
Partisan control of legislature, 1982-92	Democratic	Republican	Democratic	Democratic	Democratic/ Republican	Democratic
Partisan control of executive, 1982-92	Republican	Democratic	Republican/ Democratic	Democratic/ Republican	Republican/ Democratic	Republican/ Democratic
Professionalization of legislature [b]	Very	Somewhat	Somewhat	Somewhat	Somewhat	Somewhat

[a] The categorization of political culture is that of Daniel J. Elazar, *American Federalism: A View from the States*, 2d ed. (New York: Thomas Y. Crowell, 1972), 118.

[b] The categorization of professionalization is that of Karl T. Kurtz, "The Changing State Legislatures (Lobbyists Beware)," in *Leveraging State Government Relations*, ed. Wesley Pedersen (Washington, D.C.: Public Affairs Council, 1990), 23-32.

Colorado is one of a relatively few states in the nation where the legislature has been under Republican control.

These six states are by no means representative of the fifty; no six states could be. But they offer some variety and can reasonably serve as the basis for generalizations about lobbyists and lobbying.

In any study, it is necessary—and often difficult—to decide what to include and, more important, what to leave out. Our focus here is solely on the legislature, not the executive. We realize, of course, that the executive branch is also lobbied by lobbyists. Governors initiate programs and sign or veto bills enacted by the legislature. They are by no means exempt. Indeed, according to former Arizona governor Bruce Babbitt, "the ultimate lobbyist's coup is to plant an idea in a governor's agenda." [32] Few of them succeed, however. The access lobbyists have to governors is relatively limited. Departments and agencies, by contrast, receive an increasing amount of attention from lobbyists, particularly with the proliferation of rules and regulations that affect economic interests and other groups. Lawyer lobbyists, especially, devote substantial energies to the relatively invisible business of lobbying the bureaucracies.

Nevertheless, the legislature is still considered the stomping grounds for most lobbyists in the states. Normally, when lobbyists discuss their work, their conversations revolve around legislatures and not executive agencies. Most of their time is spent in the legislative arena. A recent survey of Kansas lobbyists, for example, found that about 70 percent of the respondents spent four-fifths or more of their time lobbying legislators, with executive activities concentrated among representatives of regulated industries and professions. A recent survey of Minnesota lobbyists found that roughly two-thirds of their efforts were directed at the legislature and only about one-fifth directed at state agencies.[33] Furthermore, lobbying the executive is not at all the same thing as lobbying the legislature. Executive agency lobbying deserves study, but this is not the place that we shall do it. Let the reader be warned, therefore, that although what lobbyists do on legislative terrain is a large part of the lobbying story, it is not all of it.

The Approach of This Study

The political science literature, the writings of practitioners and others, state political journals, and the newspaper press are all drawn upon in this endeavor. Yet the principal source of information for this study is lobbyists themselves. During the period from July 1990 to May 1991, the author conducted interviews with 105 lobbyists representing various types of practices. It was decided to focus on lobbyists themselves, rather than to interview legislators, journalists, and others as well. There simply were not sufficient resources to do it all and it seemed more important to concentrate directly on the subjects under study and thus be able to interview the different types of lobbyists in a number of states. Interviewees include contract, association, company, governmental, and cause lobbyists (who will be differentiated in chapter 1). All of the lobbyists who were interviewed were registered and spent either all or most of their time lobbying the legislature. Governmental lobbyists, for our purposes, were persons employed by counties and cities, but not legislative liaison personnel working for state departments and agencies. Again, a decision was made to exclude this category largely because the clients—the departments or agencies and ultimately the governor—were so very different from the rest. Legislators and legislative staff in the six states were asked by the author to recommend lobbyists who represented a range of clients and who had a substantial presence in the capitol. As many as possible of those recommended were interviewed. Only one refused outright; a contract lobbyist in California said he had a policy of not granting interviews. Another, who was on the state government relations staff of a large corporation, had great difficulty getting clearance from the legal and public relations departments, and the interview fell through. Several interviews that had been scheduled had to be canceled at the last minute because more pressing engagements arose for the interviewees.

Of the total number of interviews, thirteen were conducted in Sacramento with California lobbyists, sixteen in Denver with Colorado lobbyists, twenty-one in Tallahassee with Florida lobbyists, twelve in St. Paul-Minneapolis with Minnesota lobbyists, seventeen in Trenton with New Jersey lobbyists, and sixteen in Austin with Texas lobbyists. Three more were conducted in Annapolis with Maryland lobbyists. A number of government relations directors for associations or corporations, who had responsibility for multiple states, were interviewed at their Washington offices. Only two interviews were conducted by telephone; the rest were in person.

Most interviews ran about an hour; some were only half an hour. The interviews were unstructured since we were not testing hypotheses, focusing narrowly, or necessarily seeking comparative information. Different matters were therefore pursued with different lobbyists, depending on their activities and their interests. The author took notes during the interviews and wrote them up soon afterwards. The quotations taken from these interviews are not paraphrases but are accurate within a word or two of what the lobbyists said. At the outset, the author decided to assure interviewees confidentiality. Otherwise, it was believed, they would not have been able to talk candidly about their activities, their colleagues, their clients, and the legislators and legislatures with whom they dealt. Lobbying is a business where discretion is essential, and the risks of offending someone can be high. The lobbyists who are quoted, paraphrased, or who otherwise serve as a source in this book cannot be cited in the following pages.[34]

One objective in the chapters that follow is to put the reader in the lobbyist's shoes. That way the reader can see the process from the lobbyist's perspective. At the same time, it is important to keep in mind that although this book focuses on lobbying, the legislative process is not dominated by lobbyists. There are other influences at work, and in critical instances more important ones. Furthermore, the author's orientation is essentially positive toward, and understanding of, lobbyists and the lobbying process. That does not mean that critical analysis is absent in what follows. Another objective of the book is to analyze the behavior and practices of lobbyists as they interact with legislators, and to assess their role in the legislative system. The reader must decide whether these objectives have been met.

A Preview of the Book

After this introduction, the book is divided into two main parts before the conclusion is reached. The first part, consisting of four chapters, deals with the players, the practices, the issues and interests, and the settings. The second part, also consisting of four chapters, deals with the strategies and tactics of lobbying—what is done, why, and to whom.

We begin in chapter 1 with a description of the people who lobby. We consider the various kinds of lobbyists who operate at the capitol, who they are and what they are like, and why they are in the business that they are in. Chapter 2 focuses on state government relations as conducted by national and state corporations and associations. It also assesses the advantages (and disadvantages) of contracting out for lobbying services.

Issues and interests at stake are discussed in chapter 3. An important distinction is made between the larger public-policy issues and the smaller special-interest issues. How lobbyists keep track of issues and legislation is also described, as are the general battle lines when interests compete.

Chapter 4 goes on to explore the settings in which lobbying takes place, pointing out variations according to the rules of the game in each state. The structure of the legislature, the nature of the legislative process, and patterns of politics and power all make a difference. So does the capital culture and the ethical climates of each state. One of the principal techniques employed by lobbyists, that of building relationships, is the subject of chapter 5. Relationships develop both naturally and by careful cultivation, and they undergo trial in legislative combat. The concepts of "access" and "connection" are considered here, and an assessment is made of how relationships benefit both legislators and lobbyists.

The involvement of lobbyists in political campaigns is another principal technique, which is explored in chapter 6. Lobbyist and PAC contributions and just what money can and does buy are addressed here. So is the more active participation of lobbyists and interest groups in political campaigns.

Chapter 7 explores the three major techniques used by lobbyists to generate widespread support. One is that of building coalitions, which is easier said than done. Another is that of grass-roots mobilization, which is being used by more and more groups. The last is use of the media and public relations, the first resort of some groups and the last resort of others.

In the final analysis, lobbyists have to make their case in the legislature issue by issue. In chapter 8 we consider certain tried and proven principles of direct lobbying, differences between being on the defense and taking the offense, and the various targets of lobbyists in the legislative process. Most significant in direct lobbying are the education and information lobbyists provide members of the legislature and the functions that are thereby served. A discussion of the importance of compromise completes the chapter.

Chapter 9 concludes the book with an assessment of the influence of lobbyists, the power of clients and causes, how interests are represented in the American states, and the relationship of lobbying to representative democracy.

Notes

1. James Deakin, *The Lobbyists* (Washington, D.C.: Public Affairs Press, 1966), 54.
2. *Salt Lake Tribune,* July 1, 1990.
3. Deakin, *Lobbyists,* 34.
4. Bruce C. Wolpe, *Lobbying Congress: How the System Works* (Washington, D.C.: Congressional Quarterly Inc., 1990), 4.
5. Jack L. Walker, "The Origin and Maintenance of Interest Groups in America," *American Political Science Review* 17 (June 1983): 390-406; also Jack L. Walker, *Mobilizing Interest Groups in America* (Ann Arbor: University of Michigan Press, 1991).
6. See Martin Ryan Haley and James M. Kiss, "Larger Stakes in Statehouse Lobbying," *Harvard Business Review* 52 (January-February 1974): 125-135;

and Ronald G. Shaiko, "More Bang for the Buck: The New Era of Full-Service Public Interest Organizations," in *Interest Group Politics,* ed. Allan J. Cigler and Burdett A. Loomis, 3d ed. (Washington, D.C.: CQ Press, 1991), 112-114.

7. Jeffrey Berry, *The Interest Group Society* (Boston: Little, Brown, 1984), 44-48.
8. Malcolm E. Jewell and Penny M. Miller, *The Kentucky Legislature: Two Decades of Change* (Lexington: The University Press of Kentucky, 1988), 275.
9. Harold Wolman and Fred Teitelbaum, "Interest Groups and the Reagan Presidency," in *The Reagan Presidency and the Governing of America,* ed. Lester M. Salamon and Michael S. Lund (Washington, D.C.: Urban Institute Press, 1985), 314.
10. Clive S. Thomas and Ronald J. Hrebenar, "Nationalization of Interest Groups and Lobbying in the States," in *Interest Group Politics,* 3d ed., 66-67.
11. See Seymour Lusterman, *Managing Business-State Government Relations* (New York: Conference Board, 1983).
12. W. John Moore, "Have Smarts, Will Travel," *National Journal,* November 28, 1987, 3022.
13. Charles S. Mack, *The Executive's Handbook of Trade and Business Associations* (Westport, Conn.: Quorum Books, 1991), 76.
14. Public Affairs Research Group, *Public Affairs Offices and Their Functions* (Boston: School of Management, Boston University, 1981).
15. Randy Welch, "Lobbyists, Lobbyists All Over the Lot," *State Legislatures,* February 1989, 18.
16. *Salt Lake Tribune,* July 1, 1990.
17. David R. Morgan, Robert E. England, and George G. Humphreys, *Oklahoma Politics and Policies: Governing the Sooner State* (Lincoln: University of Nebraska Press, 1991), 145.
18. Lusterman, *Managing Business-State Government Relations,* 2.
19. Haley and Kiss, "Larger Stakes."
20. Donald G. Herzberg and Jesse Unruh, *Essays on the State Legislative Process* (New York: Holt, Rinehart, and Winston, 1970), 18.
21. *The Pressure Boys: The Inside Story of Lobbying in America* (New York: Arno Press, 1974), 38.
22. Charles G. Bell and Charles M. Price, *California Government Today* (Homewood, Ill.: Dorsey Press, 1980), 132-133, 140-141.
23. Cited in Charles G. Bell, "Cynical Californians: Politicians on the Take," *Comparative State Politics* 2 (February 1990): 20-23.
24. August 31, 1991.
25. *St. Paul Pioneer Press,* special reprint section, April 1992.
26. July 1, 1990.
27. Berry, *Interest Group Society;* Cigler and Loomis, *Interest Group Politics,* 3d ed.; Hrebenar and Scott, *Interest Group Politics in America,* 2d ed. (Englewood Cliffs, N.J.: Prentice-Hall, 1990); and Schlozman and Tierney, *Organized Interests in American Democracy* (New York: Harper and Row, 1986). By Hrebenar and Thomas there are "Interest Groups in the States," in *Politics in the American States,* ed. Virginia Gray, Herbert Jacob, and

Robert B. Albritton, 5th ed. (Glenview, Ill.: Scott, Foresman/Little, Brown Higher Education, 1990), 123-158; *Interest Groups in the American West* (Salt Lake City: University of Utah Press, 1987); *Interest Groups in the Midwestern States* (Ames: Iowa State University Press, forthcoming); and *Interest Groups in the Southern States* (Tuscaloosa: University of Alabama Press, forthcoming).

28. *The Washington Lobbyists* (Chicago: Rand McNally, 1963); *Lobbying: Interaction and Influence in American State Legislatures* (Belmont, Calif.: Wadsworth, 1969).

29. "Interest Representation: The Dominance of Institutions," *American Political Science Review* 78 (March 1984): 64-76; "Washington Lobbyists: A Collective Portrait," in *Interest Group Politics*, ed. Allan J. Cigler and Burdett A. Loomis, 2d ed. (Washington, D.C.: CQ Press, 1986), 146-161; "Who Works with Whom? Interest Group Alliances and Opposition," *American Political Science Review* 81 (December 1987): 1217-1233; "Who You Know Versus What You Know: The Uses of Government Experience for Washington Lobbyists," *American Journal of Political Science* 33 (February 1989): 175-195; and "Putting Interests Back Into Interest Groups," in *Interest Group Politics*, ed. Cigler and Loomis, 3d ed., 371-384.

30. The "individualistic" political culture emphasizes the centrality of private concerns, conceives of government as limited, and regards politics as a business. By contrast, the "moralistic" political culture stresses the idea of commonwealth, with government pursuing the public good and politics centered on the notion of the public interest. The "traditionalistic" political culture, which applies mainly to the southern states, is rooted in a paternalistic and elitist conception of society. See Daniel J. Elazar, *American Federalism: A View from the States*, 2d ed. (New York: Thomas Y. Crowell, 1972), 93-102.

31. Karl T. Kurtz, "The Changing State Legislatures (Lobbyists Beware)," in *Leveraging State Government Relations*, ed. Wesley Pedersen (Washington, D.C.: Public Affairs Council, 1990), 23-32.

32. Remarks to Pharmaceutical Manufacturers Association, Washington, D.C., November 4, 1991.

33. Allan J. Cigler and Dwight C. Kiel, *The Changing Nature of Interest Group Politics in Kansas* (Topeka: Capitol Complex Center, University of Kansas, June 1988), 21-23; Craig H. Grau, "Minnesota: Labor and Business in an Issue-Oriented State, in *Interest Groups in the Midwestern States*, ed. Ronald J. Hrebenar and Clive S. Thomas (Ames: Iowa State University Press, forthcoming).

34. Generally speaking, unless a book, journal, periodical, or newspaper is specifically cited, the source of information (but not my own analysis) is one of the lobbyists I interviewed. This is not the first time that a political scientist, in order to acquire sensitive information, has assured a respondent anonymity. Nor is it the first time that the reader will have to trust in a scholar's integrity to report and use interview information accurately.

CHAPTER 1

The People Who Lobby

All of us have considerable experience lobbying (and being lobbied), at least in the general sense of the word. Nearly everyday we try to persuade someone to do what is in our interests or, conversely, *not* do what is contrary to our interests. Some of us have even lobbied government officials, our representatives in Congress, or the state legislature. We wanted them to act or vote in a particular way, again, because it was in our interest for them to do so. However skillful we may be at lobbying, very few of us do it for a living—in the sense that we lobby in the state capital regularly, professionally, and officially.

Only a relative handful of people meet the legal definition of lobbyist. These individuals are required to register with the secretary of state, attorney general, secretary of the senate, or clerk of the house, depending on the state. Just how many people are required to do so by law varies enormously from state to state. Just how many people do register is a function both of the number of organized interests with policy agendas within a state and of the state's specific lobbying requirements. In Arizona, for instance, 6,000 lobbyists are registered; California has only 788. In Florida, 4,600 are registered; in Texas only 800; and in New Jersey only 631. The principal reason for disparities, which do not reflect the size of the population or the economic development of the states, is the definition of who lobbyists are according to how much time they devote to their jobs. In states where the definition is very narrow and does not include part-time volunteers for hundreds and hundreds of organizations, fewer individuals have to register. Other states prefer to be on the safe side, requiring registration of anyone who comes close to active lobbying. In places where any person having relatively few contacts with legislators is legally defined as a lobbyist, the registration lists tend to swell. Florida statutes, for example, require the registration of all persons who seek to encourage the passage, defeat, or modification of any legislation (with the exceptions of legislators and legislative staff). Moreover, several states, Florida included, require state and local officials lobbying in their official capacities to register also. This also adds to the rolls.

One must proceed cautiously in making comparisons among the states on the basis of lobbyist registration figures. Who a lobbyist is depends on when and where he or she is lobbying. Statutory definitions change from time to time. New Jersey lists relatively few lobbyists, for example, because only those who are compensated and spend a certain amount of time lobbying are required to register. Many of those who register, moreover, are not full time. For instance, a recent survey of lobbyists in California found that 60 percent of those responding said they did not consider lobbying to be their full-time occupation. Some were managers of associations, others practiced law, some ran businesses, and a number engaged in other occupations altogether.[1]

Most important, of those registered, only a few are considered "featured players" in the legislative process. Of five hundred lobbyists in Colorado, for example, only about a hundred show up every day the legislature is in session. Out of six hundred registered lobbyists in New Jersey, only sixty to seventy spend a good deal of time in Trenton and wield real influence. An even smaller proportion of them are "major players"—individuals who are involved either in a few issues that have statewide significance or in many issues of much narrower import. In this book, we shall be dealing mainly with registered lobbyists who have become very involved in the legislative process in the states.

Who They Are

The term "lobby agent" made its way into the language of the New York legislature in Albany in the early 1800s and was soon shortened to "lobbyist."[2] Since then, other terms have also come into use. Given the American system of federalism and the nature of statutory language, it is hardly a surprise that lobbyists today are known by a number of appellations—legislative agent, legislative counsel, legislative advocate, professional advocate, and so forth. In the world of organized interests, they may be known as state governmental relations professionals, public affairs consultants, state counsels, or (whatever the capital city happens to be) representative.

Despite the variety of names, just about every lobbyist can be defined as "a person designated by an interest group to represent it to government for the purpose of influencing public policy in that group's favor." [3] The lobbyist's principal role is to represent a group's interests. Groups can reap gains or suffer losses at the hands of state government. As a consequence, they must be attentive to what the legislature is doing, or might do, to them or for them. One Texas lobbyist notes that, in his state, "groups such as bass fisherman, midwives, pawnbrokers, as well as oil and gas, utilities, truckers, chemical companies, and environmentalists are all represented by lobbyists." As one contract lobbyist explained, "I'm trying to present a point of view for a group of people in a better way than they can do themselves."

Lobbyists are professionals who by virtue of knowledge and experience advise and represent clients. Another contract lobbyist describes his role as follows:

> A lobbyist is an advocate for his clients just like a lawyer. If he signs on with clients, he signs on to help them achieve their interests. It could be that they only want to protect themselves against adverse legislation. They are affected vitally in their daily lives and their welfare by what happens across the street [at the statehouse].

Just as individuals turn to attorneys for help on legal and other matters and to financial consultants for counsel on investments, so they turn to other professionals, that is, to lobbyists, when they require assistance in dealing with government.

As representatives or advocates of interests, lobbyists have as one of their principal roles that of communication. That is the thesis of one of the most significant and seminal studies of Washington lobbyists. This study defined lobbying as the "stimulation and transmission of a communication" by someone other than a citizen acting on his own behalf, with the hope of influencing a governmental decision. [4] In the business of lobbying, however, communication is a two-way street. The traffic runs from client to legislature and from legislature to client, as we shall explore further in chapter 2. One lobbyist explained: "I have a client on my left and the legislature on my right. I am the guy in the middle."

Although communication is an important part of the process, lobbying is not simply the transmission of information. The purpose of the endeavor is persuasion. Legislators must be persuaded to support the particular position being presented by a lobbyist. Persuasion is not necessarily conversion, however. "You don't change minds," explained a California lobbyist, "You find ways to make them think they agreed with you all along." Friendship, assistance, pressure, along with argument and information, are among a lobbyist's repertoire of persuasive techniques. As we shall see, although many factors are taken into consideration, the bottom line in the relationship between lobbyist and client is success. And success depends, at least in part, on the lobbyist's ability to persuade.

Lobbyists are a truly diverse lot. Frances Oakley, the widow of a New Jersey fireman who died in 1957, is also treasurer of the Police and Firemen's Widows' Association of New Jersey and has concentrated her efforts on getting survivor pension benefits raised. Harold Hodes, a former chief of staff to New Jersey governor Brendan Byrne (D), is principal partner in Public Strategies, the largest independent lobbying firm in Trenton, representing about fifty clients. Both of them are New Jersey lobbyists.

Lobbyists in Florida also vary—from former house speaker Don Tucker, who earned $500,000 for guiding a bill to lengthen the racing season through the legislature, to Charles Lee of the Florida Audubon Society. There are also Marion Hammer of the United Sportsmen of Florida, who persevered for years to get a gun decontrol bill through the legislature, and Harry Landrum, who represents among other groups the powerful Florida Realtors Association. They are joined on the lobbyist lists by Karen Woodall, who until recently headed Florida Impact (she now is on her own as an independent lobbyist), which lobbies for the impoverished, and Jon Shebel, who heads Associated Industries of Florida, the state's largest business group.[5]

Jackson, Barish & Associates is the top money-maker among California lobbying firms, with earnings of $1.6 million in 1988. Clay Jackson, the principal, is said to be in demand because of his clout, not because of his policy analysis. An entirely different operation is the California Children's Lobby, a low-budget advocacy coalition represented by Sherry Skelly.

As the preceding examples show, lobbyists are a varied species indeed. The press pays greater attention to contract, or independent, lobbyists because of the size and variety of their clientele, their typically generous campaign contributions, and their reputation as lavish entertainers. Yet several other kinds of lobbyists are active in state capitals and must therefore also be taken into account. Thomas and Hrebenar, for example, have placed lobbyists in five categories. They have also estimated the proportion of each group in the state capital lobbying community: contract, 15-25 percent; in-house, 40-50 percent; government and legislative liaison, 25-40 percent; citizen or volunteer, 10-20 percent; and private individual, 5 percent.[6] Others have made use of similar categories.[7] The groupings used below differ in some respects.

Contract lobbyists are also known as independent lobbyists, "guns for hire," or state counsel (for national corporations or associations). What distinguishes these individuals is that they are not employees of a single organization, but instead have a number of clients, ranging from a half-dozen to thirty or forty. A few may even represent fifty to one hundred clients. Contract lobbyists may be sole practitioners, partners in larger firms, partners or associates in law firms, or members of other multiservice organizations. In this text, they are typically called contract lobbyists, although from time to time they are referred to as independent lobbyists.

Association lobbyists are just that. They represent business, labor, professional, and trade associations. These in-house lobbyists work for a specific organization, although they may have duties that extend beyond lobbying. National associations headquartered in Washington, D.C., or sometimes New York (e.g., Pharmaceutical Manufacturers Association and the American Petroleum Institute), and state associations, located in the various capitals of the states, both employ full-time professionals who are responsible for dealing with legislation and the legislature.

Company lobbyists, like their cousins, association lobbyists, work for a single organization, usually a business. A company may have interests in just a single state, as do utilities, hospitals, many banks, and smaller corporations. Or it may have interests within a number of states and facilities in a few. In some cases—Anheuser-Busch is an example—a business will have interests that extend nationwide; but the larger the state, the greater a company's concern. Companies have their own personnel but are also likely to be represented by one or several business and trade associations.

Governmental lobbyists are employed by associations composed of local governments, including county and city officials, school boards, property appraisers, tax collectors, sheriffs, water districts, clerks, and other public officials. Also in this category are those who lobby for particular jurisdictions, such as Anne Arundel and Prince Georges counties in Maryland or the cities of Dallas and Houston in Texas and Tampa and Miami in Florida.

Cause lobbyists cover a broad spectrum of groups. They include public-interest (or "white hat") lobbyists and those representing nonprofits and single-issue groups. Their clients normally have no commercial, material, or governmental interests—rather, they are philosophical and ideological. They generally appeal to moral principle. Among the most visible groups in this general category are those generally labeled "public interest," the focus of which is good government. The League of Women Voters, Ralph Nader's Public Citizen, Inc., and Common Cause are prominent examples. Also visible and active here are the environmentalists, such as Audubon and the Sierra Club, and the various state public interest research groups (PIRGs), whose agenda includes consumer as well as environmental issues. Hundreds of nonprofits are registered to lobby. Impact, for instance, is a Florida coalition sponsored by twenty-nine religious denominations to attend to social, economic, and poverty-related issues. In New Jersey the Council of Churches, Association of Jewish Federations, and Catholic Conference all have interests in legislation. In two-thirds of the states, groups, such as the California Children's Lobby, monitor children's issues.

Somewhat different are the groups with more ideological and, hence, controversial programs. They include organizations on the left: state affiliates of the National Organization of Women, National Abortion Rights Action League, and the American Civil Liberties Union. They also include organizations on the right: California's Right to Life League, Christian Action Council, and Concerned Women of America; Florida's Eagle Forum, Minute Women, Pro Family Forum, and Clean Cable Coalition are other examples.

The Business of Lobbying

Individuals on an organization's payroll need not be concerned about selling their services. As shall be discussed in chapter 2 below, they have other, equally pressing, concerns—dealing with an executive or chief executive officer, interpreting and helping to shape association or company policy, educating the membership, and employing and supervising independent lobbyists if they are needed. But these in-house lobbyists have essentially a single client. For them, lobbying is not a business, but an adjunct to some other enterprise. The independent or contract lobbyist, by contrast, is in a business, either as a sole practitioner or a member of a firm. This type of lobbyist must sell his or her services to a number of clients. Some of them are year-round, continue over time, and generally pay a basic retainer. Among other things, they want a watchdog at the state capital. Others employ the lobbyist on a one-shot basis to handle a particular issue during a certain legislative session. In some places, a few lobbyists will work bills for a contingency fee, taking a downpayment with a promise of more if they succeed. In other places, contingency fees are illegal. There are almost as many arrangements as there are lobbyists.

The differences among these types of lobbyists are marked. Although they all are charged with promoting or opposing legislation, they vary in approach, style, and techniques because of who they are and who they represent. The challenges they face are not at all the same. Indeed, the differences among contract, association, company, governmental, and cause lobbyists are substantially greater than the differences among lobbyists from various states. That is to say, contract lobbyists in Minnesota resemble contract lobbyists in Florida much more than they resemble cause lobbyists in their own state.

Types of Practice

Although the business of contract lobbying has grown larger and more complex, the sole practitioner is still the norm. Because the overhead is low, lobbyists can hang out their shingles when they have only a few clients lined up. Many of these independent lobbyists work for six or seven groups—the chiropractors, a medical center, travel agents, horse breeders, the burglar and fire alarm association, or a city in their state. Some carry as many as thirty clients. A few specialize in certain kinds of issues or issue areas, but the large majority are diversified and carry mixed portfolios. (Occasionally, sole practitioners share suites of offices and secretarial support and may collaborate in the referral and handling of clients.) In Colorado, for example, of the 395 lobbyists registered in 1982, only 33 represented two or three interests and only 18 represented more than three. In Texas only about 10 percent had five or more clients, and another 10 percent had two to four.

More and more lobbyists of late have been entering into group practice with partners or working for lobbying firms. Significant advantages are offered by scale. First, multiple services can be offered a client. New Jersey's Nancy Becker Associates, for instance, can assist clients with research, budget analysis, bill drafting, grass-roots organizing, legislative and regulatory monitoring, workshops, receptions, media and newsletters, and association management. Second, greater support services are available. Maryland's Bruce Bereano and another attorney do all the hands-on lobbying for about ninety clients who run the gamut from large supermarket chains, vending-machine operations, court reporters, coin collectors, nursing homes, realtors, to Weight Watchers International. But Bereano has several assistants who specialize in arranging social events and assisting the lobbyists on specific issue areas and keeping in touch with clients.

Third, the lobbyists in a firm can more easily conduct "team lobbying," backing one another up with a senior lobbyist taking the lead on strategy. The Florida firm of Haben, Culpepper, Dunbar & French illustrates the point. The partners include a former house speaker, a former counsel to Governor Bob Martinez, and a former member of the legislative staff with more than fifteen years of lobbying experience. "The first thing [the merger of lobbying talent] brings is an aura as much as anything," said John French, one of the partners. "When people see me, they know I've got Ralph [Haben] and Pete [Dunbar] backing me up." [8] All three have to know each of the issues. Fourth, a group practice permits better coverage of legislators. The more lobbyists, the broader their contacts with legislators are likely to be. One lobbyist may have close relationships with members of the house, another may have better relationships with members of the senate. Fifth, a larger firm will, generally speaking, have the reputation for greater clout and therefore be more attractive to potential clients. A firm with a large staff, a formidable list of clients, and a war chest in PAC contributions has special appeal.

A relatively recent development is the entry of large law firms on the scene. In many state capitals today, one can find a full-service law firm with the added service of lobbying. In some cases, lobbying has been in the repertoire of the firm from its establishment because of a founding partner's experience and interests. Joel Sterns had served as counsel to the governor of New Jersey and been involved in Democratic politics throughout his adult life. When he left public service in 1969 and opened up offices on West State Street across from the New Jersey State House, lobbying and law were both natural activities for him. In most cases, however, the phenomenon of law-cum-lobbying postdates the emergence of the New Federalism and additional power being wielded by the states.

A law firm based in one of the larger cities of the state might locate an office in the capital. For example, the Miami-based firm of Steel, Hector & Davis in Florida also maintains a large operation in Tallahassee, just a few blocks from the capitol. Seven lobbyists, working in teams, represent a prestigious list of clients. Or a law firm, such as Faegre & Benson, has offices in downtown Minneapolis, not too far from the state legislature, as well as in Washington, D.C. It did not enter the lobbying field until 1983, and then did so somewhat reluctantly. But clients wanted a full-service law firm. The chief lobbyist at Faegre & Benson does a substantial amount of work for about eighteen clients, a number of whom are members of the Twin City corporate community, other business associations, and the City of Minneapolis and Hennepin County.

The law-lobbying phenomenon appears to have advanced furthest in Texas. In 1984, with the field getting crowded and competition stiffer, two prominent contract lobbyists, independently of one another, saw the future as being with law firms. The appeal of a law firm was that it could furnish administrative and secretarial support that contract lobbyists were unable to provide on their own. Moreover, a large law firm already had a clientele from which lobbying clients could be recruited. Finally, lobbyists were promised greater security; or as an early convert put it, joining a law firm was "a method of extending one's useful life."

After two Austin law firms brought on lobbyists, others quickly felt the competitive pressure to offer their clients similar service. One firm after another brought on a lobbyist, and as the competition continued, their cadres of lobbyists expanded. Now, most of the highly influential lobbyists have arrangements with law firms, and the large, prestigious Austin firms dominate not only law but also lobbying. However, the current system in Texas may not last much longer. Some of the lobbyists have not had their expectations fulfilled for a number of reasons.

Legal work and lobbying work generally do not overlap. And mainstream lawyers do not understand the profession of lobbying; like the public, they generally look down on it. The law-firm environment is not at all political and therefore not hospitable to those engaged in

political work. Furthermore, lobbyists do not feel that they have benefited financially from their affiliations. The firms supply few clients and
lobbyists themselves must continue to act as the rainmakers. Add to that
the financial difficulties encountered by some of the major firms, and
lobbyists are beginning to think about moving outside again. If a few go,
others will likely follow, and the marriage of law firm and lobbyist will
have run its course in Texas.

Among the newest developments in the business has been the
emergence of the Washington-area combined-service firms that have
begun to sell lobbying wares in the states. Burson-Marsteller, Ogilvy &
Mather Worldwide, APCO Associates (as a lobbying arm of Arnold &
Porter), and Jack Bonner of Bonner & Associates all have sought to
expand their business by going to the states.[9] Hill & Knowlton, a
Washington firm with more than two hundred people in its employ, has
also gotten on the bandwagon. It offers one-stop shopping with management consultants, researchers, direct-mail experts, grass-roots specialists,
public relations professionals, and lobbyists.[10] In 1990 it opened up
offices in Tallahassee, Albany, Sacramento, Springfield, and Austin.
However, the Washington firms still have not made a great impact in the
states, where the action continues to be primarily local.

Competition and the Marketplace

Although contract lobbyists maintain friendships with one another
and share professional norms, they are in a very competitive business.
Although it is a friendly competition, it is competition nonetheless. Even
in good times, there is just so much business to go around. When it comes
to wooing deep-pocketed clients, one lobbyist gets the contract and the
other loses it. In Austin, for example, no more than two-dozen lobbyists
dominate the marketplace and control the most profitable accounts.
They are the power-brokers, who have arranged a virtual cartel. Small
lobbyists, who live precariously, resent the "big boys" who compete
among themselves and share the spoils while keeping others at arm's
length. Trade association and corporate lobbyists also appear to envy the
hired guns, who make a great deal of money. In addition, individual
members of associations employ their own lobbyists, and this causes some
concern to association directors.

Some lobbyists advertise their services, targeting mail to a select
industry. The top lobbyists, however, seldom seek out clients in a public
way but depend on their reputations, contacts, and friends. It ordinarily
takes a few years to establish oneself, with clients coming slowly as the
word gets around. Lobbyists themselves make referrals to one another if
their plates are too full or if the interests of a potential client threaten to

conflict with those of a current one. And lobbyists do look out for their colleagues when it does not interfere with their own practices. Occasionally, if a client of theirs has an issue to push, they may alert friends, who then seek to be hired by the other side. They expect like treatment in return. It is reported in some places that here and there an issue is generated by lobbyists themselves as a way to stimulate business. There is always a legislator or two willing to introduce a bill that will send an industry or group scurrying for help.

In some instances, too, when it is late in the legislative session and too many balls have to be juggled at one time, a lobbyist may subcontract a piece of the action to a colleague. In fact, as the session proceeds with hundreds of issues rising to the surface, more groups and organizations emerge seeking representation. Under these circumstances, friendships count. If an influential legislator advises a group that "it would be a good idea to hire X," the message is seldom misinterpreted. This practice occurs in many states, although relatively few members engage in it. Up until about ten years ago, the governor of Kentucky recommended certain lobbyists to the major interests in the state, which then quickly retained them.

Those lobbyists with experience in the capital, particularly former legislators and legislative staff, have established themselves and their credentials over the course of years. They would maintain, along with a one-time member of the Colorado General Assembly, that "people have sought me out; I didn't go after clients. They knew my reputation." In lobbying, reputations grow over time, and certain lobbyists become known for their client lists, contacts, and clout. In lobbying, as in other domains of life, the rich get richer and the poor have trouble breaking in.

Lobbyists will take on one-shot clients, those who need something done at that session and perhaps the next. But they are generally seeking long-termers as well—"anchor clients." These are companies, organizations, and groups that, in the words of a Colorado lobbyist, "want you to cover their tail." They form the core of the lobbyist's business and give it greater stability.

Many lobbyists take most anything that comes their way. After all, bills must be paid. But others try to shape their practice. It is not easy to do. Some lobbyists are typecast, as are two women in Colorado whose experience was with advocacy groups and social service issues. Their initial clientele were the homeless, family doctors, and small pharmacists. They are now trying to expand beyond the ranks of the powerless and do-gooders, and are slowly succeeding. Other lobbyists shape a specialized practice from the outset. A lawyer-lobbyist in Tallahassee, who represents developers among others, has managed successfully to focus on relatively narrow environmental issues. A husband-and-wife team is just as successful working the other side of the street. They represent

Florida's canoe liveries and outfitters, Audubon, the Trust for Public Lands, Environmental Education League, Fish Watch, and also voluntary hospitals.

Other contract lobbyists in Tallahassee also manage to choose clients with discretion. One lobbyist turned down a bid from the tobacco industry, with which she had philosophical disagreements, and an oil company, which in her opinion had failed to clean up its act. A former legislator is similarly selective. He balances his list, keeping a corporate base, but still gets one-third of his clients and 10 percent of his income from nonprofits. Another Floridian, who both lobbies and practices law in a larger firm, prides himself on not having to take on clients with whom he feels uncomfortable. Lobbying is only part of his living, and the other, legal, part affords him a measure of independence. One of the most highly touted members of Tallahassee's lobbying community has developed his practice by picking and choosing. He was particularly careful at the beginning not to take on clients—such as the pari-mutuel industry—whose reputations were tainted.

Why People Lobby

Students in college, graduate, or professional schools will think about careers in law, business, medicine, teaching, accounting, journalism, the arts, and government and politics. They often pursue a course of study that leads in one direction or another, and then respond to opportunities as they present themselves. But hardly anyone entertains the idea of lobbying as an occupation or as a career. There is no course of study that trains one for an entry-level position as a lobbyist. And it is not at all like going into the family business, something that may be in the back of one's mind. Yet this too can happen. For example, Frank Hays, Sr., a former lieutenant governor of Colorado in 1975 established what has become one of the largest contract-lobbying firms in the state. His son, Frank, Jr., a while later, went into partnership with his father.

More than twenty years ago Harmon Zeigler and Michael A. Baer noted that lobbying was a marginal occupation, characterized by ambiguous behavior and no clear images. Those who became lobbyists did not make a predetermined choice of profession but had drifted into the field.[11] The career path of most lobbyists has changed little since they wrote.

The Career Paths of Contract Lobbyists

Different types of lobbyists tend to come to their jobs through different routes and for different reasons. The career paths of most contract lobbyists, and a number of the other types as well, are through government and politics. Until recently, government and politics, at the higher levels at least, have been a preserve of white males. Thus, a relatively small proportion of lobbyists in the states have been women; an even smaller proportion have been black. But in the past decade the number of women in the field has increased dramatically. A California survey shows that none of those registered as lobbyists before 1972 were women, but in 1983 one-third of the new registrants were female. By then, women comprised 14 percent of the total registrations in Sacramento,[12] and today the figure is undoubtedly higher. Colorado's legislature has one of the highest percentages of female members, 31 percent; similarly, almost a third of the state's registered lobbyists are women. Fewer women lobby in a state like Texas; but even so, 17 percent of the contract lobbyists in Texas who have five or more clients are women.[13]

Some of these female lobbyists represent public-interest groups and nonprofits, a number are in-house lobbyists for corporations, and quite a few are with associations. State government relations personnel headquartered in Washington, have a particularly large proportion of women in their ranks. Some of the contract lobbyists are also women but, with occasional exceptions, the heavy-hitters in this field are still men.

Government and politics are the training ground for lobbyists, particularly for the so-called hired guns. In his study of Washington lobbyists, Robert Salisbury found that half of them had previously been employed by the federal government.[14] The California survey, mentioned above, showed 36 percent of the lobbyists there having state government experience, with 21 percent recruited from the ranks of legislative staff and about 5 percent from among legislators themselves.[15]

These are people who aspired to enter political life and hold public office, or who caught the bug along the way. A former chairman of Minnesota's Independent Republican party, California governor Ronald Reagan's legislative liaison aide, the chief of staff to New Jersey governor Brendan Byrne, a top aide to Florida's governor Reuben Askew, the legislative assistant to Colorado's governor Richard Lamm—these are the kinds of individuals now lobbying the legislatures of their states. Some lobbyists have acquired expertise in a specific area of public policy. For example, a Florida lobbyist known as "Mr. Insurance" worked for two insurance commissioners and for twenty years has been lobbying for the insurance industry. A few lobbyists have journalistic backgrounds, such as the Trenton contract lobbyist who worked as a reporter for the *Newark Evening News* (and also as press aide to Governor Richard Hughes) and his one-time partner, who had been an editor on the *Trenton Times*. The latter had intended to take the knowledge he gleaned from lobbying back to a career in journalism. He got to like lobbying, however, and recently set up his own firm. An assistant city editor at the *Minneapolis Star* had his appetite for politics whetted, went on to law school, then handled legislative affairs for the attorney general, and finally went into lobbying.

Members of the legislative staff have a special affinity for lobbying. Nonpartisan research staffs are inclined to make a career of legislative service, or move over to the executive (what one of them refers to as "going into government"). But political and partisan staffs are more likely to see opportunities in the lobbying enterprise. A Maryland contract lobbyist served as an aide to two senate presidents and then began lobbying. In Texas, one of the contract lobbyists had gotten involved in politics right after graduation from college and took a job first on the staff of the house and then for one of the standing committees. Another was an aide to a house speaker and one was house parliamentarian through five speakers. In Florida, the staff director of a house committee and subsequently chief of staff to the speaker, became a partner in a practice with his legislative boss after he had completed his speakership. Another Florida committee staff director also teamed up with his former chairman when the latter went into lobbying.

Former legislators are among the most effective lobbyists in the state capital and are certainly perceived to be among the most influential. But like everyone else, lobbying was not in their game plan when they ran for the legislature. A few years ago, Florida's representative Sam Bell stood at the doors of the house chambers. Looking at the throng of lobbyists, he said to himself: "If that ever happens to me, shoot me." But in 1988 he lost a bid for reelection and, then, in 1991, after the two-year hiatus required by law, Bell was beginning to lobby. He was standing outside the same doors of the house chambers, waiting to buttonhole members on their way in and out. "I may say the same thing," Bell now said. "If I ever go in again, shoot me." [16] "Lobbying was the last thing on my list," recalled a Texas legislator turned lobbyist. "As a house and senate member, I was tough on lobbyists." But he has been in lobbying for more than ten years and plying his trade in a law firm for six. A former member of the Florida house, who was defeated in an election for Congress, joined a law firm in Tampa. Two years later the firm opened an office in Tallahassee, with one $5,000 contract. The former legislator handled that client and went out on his own when the law firm split up. His timing was good because the sales tax on services was the principal issue before the governor and the legislature. With all the groups fighting the tax, it could be considered a full-employment act for Tallahassee lobbyists.

The legislature is a natural training ground for lobbyists in many states. More than twenty former legislators, including two house speakers and a senate president, are registered in Colorado.[17] A similar situation exists in Florida, where four out of seven of the last speakers, among other former legislators, are in practice. In Texas, too, more members wind up as lobbyists, and two former speakers are now in the business.

Legislators are also overrepresented, proportionate to their ranks, in California and Minnesota. Only in New Jersey, among the states explored for this study, are legislators relatively few and far between in Trenton's "third house" (although a former president of the senate recently joined a group of lobbyists). That may be because a number of legislators who lose elections or drop out are subsequently appointed to well-paying jobs in the executive branch or on boards and commissions.

Legislators, and others who are members of the capital community, like politics. Some love it—are consumed by it; more than a few are addicted to it. A former staffer in the Texas legislature, who now lobbies for an association of local governments, commented: "It's all I do, all I really know—politics." Bruce Bereano, another former legislative staffer and now one of Maryland's premier independent lobbyists, does not drink or smoke, has no hobbies, but is an avid sports fan. He functions on four or five hours of sleep a night, devoting the rest of his time to work. Lobbying is his life.[18] A New Jersey lobbyist for teachers grew up in a political family, had an uncle who ran for Congress, and has a passion for politics. Although she has been a classroom teacher, she has also spent most of her life dabbling in the political arena.

A number of these people have a consuming interest in public policy. They want to affect policy, and lobbying is one way to do so. Some have a thirst for knowledge about issues and problems, and lobbying affords them an opportunity to continue learning. Many of them, of course, like power, and that is one of the reasons they went into government and politics in the first place. Nearly all of the lobbyists enjoy the game, although the women appear to be less infatuated with this aspect of lobbying than men. A New Jersey contract lobbyist put it tersely: "I love the action. I thrive on it." A lobbyist for a Florida city describes the addictive quality of the work: "When you get what you want, it feels so good; you want to go back for more." There is little better, said a lobbyist for New Jersey's business community, than "getting something through or blocking something or knocking PIRG's block off on a clean water bill." And Bereano is described as having "a desire to have his finger in every pie."[19]

Lobbyists exude exhilaration during the closing days and hours of a legislative session. This is their last chance to get something through—and also their opponents'. It is possible for them to win or lose. This is the lobbyist's moment of truth. Movement, action, and winning have special appeal for these political animals.

Lobbying is an appealing trade because political practitioners want to stay in politics and legislators and legislative staff want to continue playing roles in the process. Moreover, as legislatures and legislators have become more full time, members tend to sacrifice their outside occupations. No longer can they pursue two paths, as in earlier years. If they decide to, or have to, leave the legislature, there is nothing for them to return to as there was for the citizen-legislators. Still, some members are defeated. And others, with growing families or college tuitions in the offing, can no longer manage on a legislative salary. Where can they go, what can they do? Their greatest attributes are knowledge of the legislative process, familiarity with the issues, and friendship with many of the players. A number may be shocked that there is not widespread demand for their talents. Lobbying is, perhaps, the only endeavor that will put their talents to full use, and pay money besides.

Money is an important part of lobbying's appeal. Upon leaving the California senate, one individual was offered $350,000 by interests in Los Angeles to lobby a bill. How could he turn down such an offer? He discovered he liked lobbying and realized, as he put it, "I'm getting rich again." Another former legislator in Florida felt he was still involved in the legislative process. The difference was, in his words, "I used to do it for practically nothing, now I get paid well for it." One of New Jersey's presiding officers, who had announced that he was retiring from the legislature, was asked by a statehouse correspondent whether he intended to take up lobbying. The leader responded that he was tempted. "I think it would be very lucrative," he said. "The only problem," he added, "is that I would have to pay for the dinners, and I'm not used to that."

Not everyone cashes in; the competition is usually tough. But there are big dollars to be made, at least for a few—perhaps no more than the top five to ten lobbyists in a state capital. Maryland's Bereano had earnings of more than $1 million in 1989 thanks to his sixty or so clients and his twenty-hour days. The best lobbyists in Florida make over $500,000 a year. The very top lobbyists with the Austin law firms keep about 85 percent of the more than $1 million that they bring in. A number of their colleagues gross over $300,000. Incomes are not nearly as high in Colorado, where in 1988 one contract lobbyist reported $200,000, another reported $150,000, and three others passed the $100,000 mark. But most made between $20,000 and $50,000.[20] The highest-paid lobbyist in Little Rock, Arkansas, takes in $200,000, while a number of others have incomes ranging from $50,000 to $100,000.[21]

The Career Paths of Other Lobbyists

Association lobbyists are less likely than contract lobbyists to have political backgrounds, although some of them do. Most come to their present positions from other associations. That is because so many of those who lobby for smaller associations also have other responsibilities as executive directors. They recruit members and provide them with services; lobbying therefore claims only part of their time. Of fifty executive directors of state associations of certified public accountants, for example, the majority have association backgrounds, while nine or ten come from the accounting profession and a few, such as Bruce Allen in California, once served on the staff of the legislature. Typical is the case of Tommy Townsend of Texas, who earlier represented the realtors for thirteen years and has been with the trial lawyers for the past several years. Some individuals with associations come from lobbying positions with companies in the state.

Lobbyists for teacher associations illustrate a different career path. The large majority of them have prior experience as classroom teachers. Paul Hubbert, the executive secretary and "political genius" of the Alabama Education Association (AEA), started as a classroom teacher, became a superintendent in a small town, and then took over AEA in Montgomery.[22] Becky Brooks had sixteen years of classroom teaching, served as president of the Texas State Teachers Association, and then came to Colorado, where she has been lobbying for the Colorado Education Association. Dolores "Dee" Corona, a New Jersey classroom teacher, soon became active as president of a local chapter. Within a few years, she had a position as organizer with the New Jersey Education Association, and soon after that became its lobbyist and director in 1985. In some places, the education association recruits a person with a political, rather than educational, background to head their lobbying corps. Gene Mammenga taught at a state university, served in the Minnesota senate, and worked for the St. Paul School District before going to the Minnesota Education Association. The lobbying effort of the California Education Association is headed by Alice Huffman, who is more in the political than in the teacher mode. Her principal experience was in state government, and she had ties to a number of the Democratic leaders of the legislature.

Many of those who work in state government relations or who lobby for companies also come to their jobs from politics. For example, Hank Fisher spent fifteen years in Minnesota politics. He chaired the Democratic Farmer Labor party, served on the staff of Walter Mondale, and ran a gubernatorial campaign for Wendell Anderson. When the savings and loan industry, which had been fighting legislation on a usury ceiling, asked him to take on their case, he contracted to do so, representing the industry and a few other clients for five years. In 1980 he was hired to head the public affairs division of a Minneapolis bank that was encountering problems with community groups. Tom Hagan of Texas is another good example. He had worked for lieutenant governors Ben Barnes and William Hobby and then for U.S. senator Lloyd Bentsen as a legislative assistant in Washington. He came back to Austin in 1981 to take charge of state and federal relations for Central and Southwest Utilities.

Overall, most lobbyist personnel in corporations come from other departments in the company, not from outside. The pharmaceutical industry is illustrative. The national association's lobbying staff comes by way of government or association work. By contrast, the personnel of corporate members of the Pharmaceutical Manufacturers Association comes mainly from within the companies themselves (except in a few cases, such as Johnson & Johnson). Many are attorneys because the state-relations function often began in law departments and sometimes still reports to these units. There is a corporate belief, moreover, that lawyers are best suited for the job because they have been trained to interpret the language of legislation.[23] Those who do not make their way to lobbying from legal departments come from the corporation's marketing, sales, or human resources departments. They know the company and its products, and some think this knowledge may be more important in state government relations than an understanding of the legislative process and legislatures. This makes sense. Frequently the person responsible for a corporation's government relations does relatively little direct lobbying, but instead contracts out to independent lobbyists in target states. The median 1988 salaries of corporate state government relations executives was reported to be about $92,000.[24]

Lobbyists for county and local governments and their associations have varied backgrounds. A few come right out of politics or government. They may have budget and fiscal experience. A number go from city to municipal association or from one association to another. Some have training in public administration and have been employed by local government. Michael Sittig's father was director of the Florida League of Cities, and since high school the son worked for the league. He grew up in the business and practically inherited it when his father left. the top position.

Cause lobbyists have taken very different routes, arriving at their positions by way of involvement in movements or with issues. Some are active in or have served on boards of the organizations that they later are hired to direct. They have generally confined their work to advocacy groups. Dolores Phillips, for example, was a nutritionist employed by hospitals. She took on being director of the New Jersey Animal Rights Alliance and now lobbies for the New Jersey Environmental Federation. Briggs Gamblin, who is now at the national headquarters of Common Cause in Washington, started with the Colorado Open Space Council, went with COPIRG a few years later, and then to Colorado Common Cause. What distinguishes many of the good government, environmental, feminist, and even nonprofit lobbyists is that they are dedicated to a cause, a cluster of issues, or a vision of how society should function.

Not all the cause lobbyists continue in the same field. A few make a transition from organizational constraints to independence. Karen Woodall of Florida is an example. She spent from 1980 to 1990 as director of Florida Impact, serving the needs of the disadvantaged and homeless for a coalition of religious denominations. Now she has her own lobbying firm but for the most part continues to represent the same types of clients on a contractual basis. Nikki Beare of Florida provides a slightly different example. A housewife, she joined the League of Women Voters and became a community activist. She came up to Tallahassee to lobby the issue of equal pay for equal work and then increased her lobbying efforts on behalf of the Equal Rights Amendment. When various groups noted that she was spending time in the capital, they would approach her and ask if she would watch a bill for them. In return they would pay her way to Tallahassee. Pretty soon she was getting paid for her work and some time later was lobbying for business as well as nonprofit and advocacy groups.

Qualities and Styles

No two lobbyists are identical in personality or in the qualities they bring to their jobs. There is clearly no single set of characteristics necessary for effective lobbying. People who range widely in their personal qualities all may ply their trades effectively. Yet there seem to be a number of qualities that are desirable if one hopes to be successful in this enterprise. Some of the qualities noted here apply far more to contract lobbyists at one end of the continuum than to cause lobbyists at the other end, but they are relevant across the board.

Characteristics of Lobbyists

Experience is important. The longer lobbyists are at it (up to a certain point), the more they seem to know. Furthermore, it takes time for integrity and honesty to be demonstrated, for victories to be won, and for reputations to develop. A New Jersey lobbyist, who had worked earlier as a reporter and for the Republicans in the legislature, put it simply: "Hanging around for twenty years gives you a lot of valuable experience." In the 1960s, Zeigler and Baer found that lobbyists averaged from eight to twelve years' experience in the four states they were studying.[25] Because of the growth of their industry, many contract lobbyists are relatively new to the scene. But the principal figures have ten to twenty years in lobbying, and prior political and governmental experience before that. In this field youth is a disadvantage, and being a young woman may entail a special burden.[26]

Like everyone else, contract lobbyists age and retire, and some burn out. A former Florida legislator insists, "I will do this as long as it's fun."

By the closing weeks of every legislative session, he says, "I don't want to do this anymore." But he stays on because of the satisfaction he derives from doing good for clients, winning battles, and earning a nice income. Another lobbyist, from Minnesota, is about ready to leave. "You get worn out by banging into this stuff," he said. Another, who earlier had served in the Minnesota legislature, is less infatuated with the process than he used to be and leans on his colleagues a little more. However, voluntary departure by those who are successful is rather low (as it is in the legislature). The tenure of association and governmental lobbyists also appears lengthy. That is of particular benefit to the single client being represented in each case. It provides for continuity and memory, which give reassurance to legislators. Like the rest of us, legislators prefer stability in their relationships and, thus, a bit more predictability in their lives.

In their study of Washington lobbyists, Robert Salisbury and his colleagues found that experience provided knowledge about issues, familiarity with the decision-making process, and contacts.[27] Experience, in other words, leads to knowledge—of issues, process, and people.[28] These are not separate commodities but warp and woof of the same fabric: "Everything in government . . . is interconnected," writes a folklorist who was working in the Delaware legislature. "Each new event, each new policy is connected to past events and the old boys have been around long enough to know the strands are woven together."[29]

Along with experience and knowledge as requisite qualities, "people skills" (as a Florida lobbyist dubs them) are essential. Few lobbyists can survive without a sense of and enjoyment in dealing with people. There are exceptions, such as one individual who represents an environmental group and lacks what we have come to call "interpersonal skills." But he has a client who cannot be ignored, advocates issues with political appeal, and works hard. So, he manages to survive. Intuition and instinct are also key. One observer has written that the chief stock in trade of the lobbyist is an intangible quality called "feel."[30] It certainly is. Also fundamental is the ability to figure out what path is best to take. An Illinois lobbyist expressed it succinctly: "I get hired for political judgment." Another pointed out that judgment is critical in the processes of negotiating. "You have to know how to close a deal," he said, "[and] what they are willing to buy."

Other attributes that seem to count are a willingness to work hard, tenacity, and persistence. Some people argue that a sense of humor is important, particularly the ability not to take oneself too seriously. Others, the lawyer-lobbyists, maintain that legal skills are important because, as they see it, "he who writes the language of a bill has control." Moreover, those who have learned to read statutory language "can make mumbo-jumbo arguments about legal problems that might arise from proposed legislation." Such arguments are difficult for laypersons to counter.

Intelligence is also required, particularly nowadays. Lobbyists often must have command of substance as well as of process. Contract lobbyists, who represent many clients and take on a range of subjects, have to be quick studies. Many of them are.

As important as any other quality is a lobbyist's attitude. It has to be positive. It helps tremendously if lobbyists think highly of their clients, like legislators, and respect the process. To effectively represent a client it helps if a lobbyist can communicate a belief in that client's position. Indeed, it helps to believe in the client. Ginger Gold, a Rutgers University student, interned for Nancy Becker, a lobbyist who represented New Jersey's cable television industry. Ms. Gold embarked on her Trenton experience with negative feelings toward the industry, but as part of her internship had to put together a report on cable's positions. She soon came to defend the industry and observed in a paper that she wrote, "I guess that lobbyists must love their clients or learn to love them to do the job effectively." [31] For lobbyists, work on an issue can produce attachment, if not commitment, to a cause. It is not difficult. Practically every client can make a reasonable argument for his or her case. Even if clients cannot, a lobbyist is likely to believe that everyone deserves representation. Either way, it is possible to sincerely advance clients and their causes.

For contract lobbyists in particular, the main thing is how they feel about the people and the process. "You generally have to like legislators and the legislative process," according to a Florida lobbyist. People who do not tend to exit relatively soon. Most genuinely like legislative politics and politicians. A lobbyist for one of Florida's cities explains that on one hand, "I spend a lot of my energy just trying to find something I like in each member" and, on the other, "I try not to *not* like people."

Corporate lobbyists may feel less ardor and their demeanor may be more formal. But if they are to manage state relations, their attitude must also be positive. Corporate lobbyists must have regard for the legislature and for legislators. "If they are disdainful or critical," a lobbyist for a major pharmaceutical firm suggested, "legislators will sense it and their effectiveness will be limited." Lobbyists therefore have to take the side of politics and politicians. Specifically, they must understand and acknowledge the legitimacy of their points of view, even if they and their company are opposed to their positions.

The qualities that count most in lobbyists are thought to be those normally possessed by legislators themselves. This is one reason why former legislators are among the most effective and influential members of the lobbying corps in the state capital. They know the issues, the process, and the people as well, or better, than anybody. They have built up relationships and friendships, which takes time and requires proximity. For relationships to develop, people must be in close touch, as we shall discuss in chapter 5. More than others, former legislators have established reputations for trust and credibility. A few, of course, may have made more enemies than friends, but most of those who go into lobbying have emerged from the legislature in good personal shape. Moreover, legislators have a perspective that is useful in a lobbying career. It derives from their experience negotiating, compromising, and usually settling for somewhat less than they would have liked.

The transition from being a legislator to being a lobbyist is not easy, however. A period of adjustment is required. A former member of the Florida legislature had to learn how to get a note to a lawmaker on the floor. He had always been called out of the chamber to talk to lobbyists, but now the shoe was on the other foot. He had difficulty getting to see a few legislators; it was frustrating. But he was able to manage the transition because he enjoyed the process and was being paid handsomely.

There is always the question of whether the ego can adjust, especially if, as many admit, ego is 50 percent of life in public office. A former leader in Colorado is perceived to have handled things very well: "I found out I didn't have a vote and I didn't have a parking place. You learn to be humble and you learn to wait." The pace of his life changed, and his wife suggested (in jest, one would believe) that he take up needlepoint. The adjustment is tougher for others. Some assume they are still insiders even though they are not. Some try to "wing it," not mastering the issues they have to lobby. The most frequent criticism of former legislators, in fact, is that they are not used to working on detail and depend on relationships rather than substance. The most skillful and adaptable, by contrast, use their previous relationships but do not rely on them. Indeed, the less they rely on them, the more useful they are.

The Styles of Lobbyists

Various attempts have been made to categorize the styles of lobbyists. Among political scientists, Samuel C. Patterson distinguished among Oklahoma lobbyists as follows: the "contact man," who conceives of his job in terms of acquaintanceships and friendships with legislators; the "informant," who prepares information to support a client's case; and the "watchdog," who monitors the calendar in order to alert a client.[32] Among journalists, Lex McKeithen divided Florida lobbyists into four basic categories: "Pocos," the little guys with idealistic clients; "Cosmos," the bigger guys whose clients—doctors, lawyers, and accountants—have plenty of money; "Full-Court Pressers," the powerful lobbyists who represent organized industries or professions—such as realtors and optometrists—who take their legislative involvement very seriously; and "Big Boys," who have relationships with legislative leaders and make good use of campaign contributions.[33]

While acknowledging that the styles of lobbyists are highly individualistic, dependent largely on a person's peculiar personality and unique experience, it is still useful to differentiate among them. McKeithen's categorization is helpful because it distinguishes lobbyists principally on the basis of the clients they represent. For us, that is key, since the principal difference that can be observed among lobbyists is with respect to their identity. Contract or independent lobbyists have their own individual identities; in-house lobbyists mainly take on the identities of the company, association, government unit, or cause that employs them.

For the contract lobbyist only, influence is primarily personal. Legislators can identify the lobbyist first and foremost, the issue next, and then the client. "Unless you have had a big fight," said a New Jersey lobbyist, "probably half of them do not even know who you represent." That is partly because a contract lobbyist's client base may change over time but mostly because lobbyists represent twenty, thirty, or more clients during the course of a legislative session. On a single day, the lobbyist may concentrate on one specific issue rather than on others. "Today, I'm wearing my Blue Cross/Blue Shield hat," a Colorado lobbyist commented. Or on a single day, the lobbyist may focus on several issues for various clients. For instance, another Colorado lobbyist had represented as many as four clients before noon on a day early in the session. Even in a single conversation with a legislator, a lobbyist may deal with different issues, and on behalf of different clients.

It is no wonder, then, that legislators can identify the lobbyist more easily than they can identify the group that has contracted the lobbyist's services. To further strengthen their identities, contract lobbyists are more likely than others to develop relationships with legislators by means of entertaining, socializing, and engaging in political activity. Their interests are personal, extending beyond any client's. Their well-being in the business of lobbying depends on their connections with legislators even more than on their ties to any client.

To say that a contract lobbyist has his or her own very personal identity is not, however, to specify its precise nature. There are the "good ol' boys," whose modus operandi is the three Bs—bourbon, broads, and beefsteaks. Their approach is that of the "fixer." They are also "full service" lobbyists because they try to take care of the various needs of legislators. This "good ol' boys" breed is on the decline, although some pure types are still extant. In the ascendant nowadays are the "good new boys (and girls)," who make greater use of information and analysis, facts, and figures, but whose entertaining is more circumscribed than that of their predecessors. Even among the new breed, there are varying types. Some lobbyists are flamboyant types like Maryland's Bereano, described as a "consummate stroker, holding doors open for people, patting them on the back, buying them drinks." [34] He welcomes publicity, as do many of his colleagues. Others in Maryland prefer quiet and privacy. In Texas Neal T. "Buddy" Jones is described as "a fraternity man in the corridors of power" who "lobbies lawmakers like it was rush week." But Texas also has Rusty Kelley, low-key and friendly, Don Adams, who neither smokes nor drinks, and Dick Brown, who deals primarily in information. [35]

Association and company lobbyists, who are on the payroll of a single organization, are a very different lot from the people they refer to (somewhat derogatorily) as "hired guns." They are known by the companies that keep them, and not by who they are. IBM, Johnson & Johnson, the chiropractors, dentists, trial lawyers, and retailers all are more identifiable than the persons who handle state governmental relations for them. Take an AT&T lobbyist on the subject of entertaining legislators, for instance. The purpose, she points out, is for them to "get to know us better as a company and leave them with a feel-good sense of AT&T." That is not the purpose of entertaining done by contract lobbyists, who are intent on strengthening personal—not company—relationships.

Companies and associations are in it for the long term; their issues are around session after session. In-house lobbyists are loyal to those who employ them. They have to be. Company lobbyists have to concern themselves with top management, while association lobbyists have to please the officers, an executive board, and the general membership. Contract lobbyists have divided loyalties, to legislators as well as to clients. While they have to worry about their clients, they are not dependent on any one of them. Even more important to them than clients are legislators and their web of capital relationships, upon which they depend for cooperation, success, a reputation for effectiveness, and further clients.

Those who lobby for counties, cities, special districts, and governmental groups resemble the in-house association and company lobbyists in many respects. Their identities are a function of their governmental affiliations. Moreover, they are even weaker when it comes to political and social relationships. They do little entertaining, have no PACs, and do not play favorites, although they do evoke political constituencies consisting of local government officials. The style of their lobbyists tends to be straightforward and straight-laced and not overtly political. There are exceptions, of course. The lobbyist for the Texas Municipal League is totally involved with the legislative process, has a distinct political personality, and operates much like hired guns.

The cause lobbyists are the antithesis of contract lobbyists. Their identities are shaped by the causes they espouse—Common Cause and campaign-finance reform, PIRG and the environment, NARAL and choice on abortions, ACLU and the First Amendment. People who represent these groups tend, more than other lobbyists, to be true believers. Theirs often is a fight for truth and justice. Often they disdain compromise. How can one compromise the environment! They are willing to go to the wall for their beliefs and are less concerned than others about relationships with legislators now or in the future. Instead, in the critical words of one who represents the other side, they are "armed with a bucketful of righteousness" and a file folder of editorials.

Most of these lobbyists prefer to pursue "outside" strategies. They favor conducting research and dealing with the press and are, in the words of one cause lobbyist, uncomfortable with buttonholing legislators and "in-your-face" lobbying. Their personality types are different from that of the hired guns. There are, of course, exceptions. The public-interest lobbyists in Colorado play an inside game that is partly a function of their personalities and partly a function of the Colorado legislature's culture.

Some of the cause lobbyists, especially those working for fringe groups, are not well regarded by legislators. One such lobbyist, for example, tends to harangue legislators, as if her outpouring of words could turn the tide. For the most part, these lobbyists and groups rely on the correctness of their arguments, the press, and veiled and not-so-veiled threats that legislators will be punished at the polls. They fear being co-opted by the system, so they try to stay at arm's length. As a lobbyist in New Jersey explained: "One of the dilemmas in public-interest lobbying is the more successful you become and the more you get included in the system, then the more people expect you to play by the rules of that system." And that was not what he would have wanted to do. There are exceptions here, too. The lobbyist for the Texas Consumers' Union is described as aware of "when to hold a press conference and when to go into the back room." He can, and does, play the inside game as well as the outside one. Yet, as James Q. Wilson has pointed out, whereas most organizations have to conserve access and influence for a variety of policies, a single-issue group does not have to.[36] And cause groups are less likely to do so.

Notes

1. Jerry B. Briscoe and Charles G. Bell, "California Lobbyists—Preliminary Report" (Davis, Calif.: Institute of Government Affairs, University of California, Davis, n.d.). See also Allan J. Cigler and Dwight C. Kiel, *The Changing Nature of Interest Group Politics in Kansas* (Topeka: Capitol Complex

Center, University of Kansas, June 1988), 21.

2. Public Affairs Council, *The Third House: An Informal Survey of Corporate Lobbying at the State Level* (Washington, D.C.: The Council, 1973), 4.

3. Clive S. Thomas and Ronald J. Hrebenar, "Interest Groups in the States," in *Politics in the American States,* ed. Virginia Gray, Herbert Jacob, and Robert B. Albritton, 5th ed. (Greenview, Ill.: Scott, Foresman/Little, Brown Higher Education, 1990), 148.

4. Lester W. Milbrath, *The Washington Lobbyist* (Chicago: Rand McNally, 1963), 8.

5. Roland Stiteler, "Influence Peddling," *Florida Magazine, Orlando Sentinel,* May 29, 1988.

6. Thomas and Hrebenar, "Interest Groups," fig. 2; also see Malcolm E. Jewell and Penny M. Miller, *The Kentucky Legislature: Two Decades of Change* (Lexington: The University Press of Kentucky, 1988), 258.

7. Paul Brace and John A. Straayer, "Colorado: PACs, Political Candidates, and Conservatism," in *Interest Groups in the American West,* ed. Ronald J. Hrebenar and Clive S. Thomas (Salt Lake City: University of Utah Press), 55; Keith E. Hamm and Charles W. Wiggins, "Texas: The Transformation from Personal to Informational Lobbying," in *Interest Group Politics in the Southern States,* ed. Ronald J. Hrebenar et al. (Tuscaloosa: University of Alabama Press, forthcoming).

8. *Miami Herald,* May 19, 1991.

9. W. John Moore, "Have Smarts, Will Travel," *National Journal,* November 28, 1987, 3020.

10. Carol Matlack, "Dead in the Water?" *National Journal,* May 18, 1991, 1160.

11. Harmon Zeigler and Michael A. Baer, *Lobbying: Interaction and Influence in American State Legislatures* (Belmont, Calif.: Wadsworth, 1969), 46-48.

12. Briscoe and Bell, "California Lobbyists."

13. John A. Straayer, *The Colorado General Assembly* (Niwot, Colo.: University Press of Colorado, 1990), 186. Also see Cigler and Kiel, *Interest Group Politics,* 21; Hamm and Wiggins, "Texas."

14. Robert H. Salisbury, "Washington Lobbyists: A Collective Portrait," in *Interest Group Politics,* ed. Allan J. Cigler and Burdett A. Loomis, 2d ed. (Washington, D.C.: CQ Press, 1986), 153.

15. Briscoe and Bell, "California Lobbyists."

16. *Miami Herald,* May 19, 1991.

17. Straayer, *Colorado General Assembly,* 184-185.

18. *Evening Sun* (Baltimore), December 27, 1989.

19. John W. Frece, "Bruce on the Loose," *Baltimore Magazine,* February 1983, 58.

20. Straayer, *Colorado General Assembly,* 187; *Rocky Mountain News,* October 23, 1991.

21. *Arkansas Democrat,* June 24, 1990.

22. Alan Ehrenhalt, "In Alabama Politics, the Teachers Are Sitting at the Head of the Class," *Governing,* December 1988, 22.

23. Seymour Lusterman, *Managing Business-State Government Relations* (New York: The Conference Board, 1983), 27.

24. Charles S. Mack, *Lobbying and Government Relations: A Guide for Execu-*

tives (New York: Quorum Books, 1989), 58.

25. Zeigler and Baer, *Lobbying,* 61.

26. Others believe young women have an advantage because access to male legislators may be easier. If one can tolerate "honey," "sweetie," and an occasional condescending or familiar remark, the burden may be bearable.

27. Robert H. Salisbury et al., "Who You Know Versus What You Know: The Uses of Government Experience for Washington Lobbyists," *American Journal of Political Science* 33 (February 1989): 175-195.

28. Larry Landry, "The Art of State Government Relations," in *Leveraging State Government Relations,* ed. Wesley Pedersen (Washington, D.C.: Public Affairs Council, 1990), 87.

29. Kim Rogers Burdick, "A Folklorist Looks at Lobbyists" (College of Urban Affairs, University of Delaware, May 1990), 22.

30. James Deakin, *The Lobbyists* (Washington, D.C.: Public Affairs Press, 1966), 154.

31. Ginger Gold, "Lobbyists: A Love Story" (New Brunswick, N.J.: Eagleton Institute of Politics, Rutgers University, May 14, 1990).

32. Cited in Zeigler and Baer, *Lobbying,* 77.

33. "Third House Holds Capitol Power," *Gainesville Sun,* December 7, 1987.

34. *The Sun* (Baltimore), March 13, 1983.

35. *Dallas Morning News,* March 29, 1987.

36. James Q. Wilson, *Political Organizations* (New York: Basic Books, 1973), 315.

CHAPTER 2

State Government Relations

The relationships between contract lobbyists and their clients (or "principals," as the groups that employ lobbyists are known) are mediated by the numbers of clients they represent and their distance from them. The in-house lobbyists, by way of contrast, have but a single "client" and little if any distance. They are company men and women, not hired guns, and they have considerably less freedom of action. Their relations with top management, boards of directors, and organization members therefore receive nearly as much attention as their efforts at lobbying the legislatures. For them, lobbying and communications are two-way streets.

In-house lobbyists refer to their profession as "state government relations." Their ranks include vice presidents for public affairs, directors, and managers in the case of companies, and presidents, vice presidents, and, more commonly, executive directors and government relations directors of associations. In this chapter, we shall explore the role of these professionals within their organizations rather than their activities in the legislature. Their externally oriented tasks of direct lobbying, grass-roots lobbying, coalition building, public relations, and political action are all vital. But just as vital are their internally oriented tasks of helping to fashion organizational policy, communicating to executives and members, developing the necessary capacity, and building support within for the state government relations function. We shall also examine how these in-house professionals seek outside assistance from contract lobbyists and the ways in which contract lobbyists, their in-house cousins, and organizational clients all interact. The emphasis here is on (but not confined to) business and professional organizations—interests that are present and active in virtually all the states.[1]

The Culture of the Corporation

Corporations vary tremendously in the support they provide for their state government affairs department. Much depends on the type of industry, the size of the company, and the public-policy questions involved.[2] Some companies have particularly close relationships with state and local communities; the utilities, telephone, and gas and electric are examples. These kinds of companies devote substantial resources to government affairs and community relations. Their approach would appear to be "go along and get along." "We don't get excited over little annoyances," were the words of a telephone company lobbyist who is adept at cultivating legislators. "We love them all," he says, "We have no enemies." Companies that are deeply affected by state regulations also tend to opt for involvement. Indeed, they cannot easily avoid it. Even top management of these businesses may spend time and energy on lobbying to the state.

Andrew Baker is chief executive officer of MetPath, a subsidiary of Corning Inc., which operates clinical laboratories across the nation. As he explained to a group of in-house lobbyists, "We're at the mercy of regulation, so I spend roughly one-third of my time involved in governmental affairs."[3] The level of government doing the regulating also matters. The liquor industry offers an illustration. Beer is regulated at the state level, spirits primarily at the federal. Beer companies are well organized for working in the states because they have to be. Among spirits companies, however, only Seagrams has its own state government relations capacity. The others rely on their trade associations.

Companies may see state government relations as a way to improve profitability; they may consider it a way to minimize government interference with the functioning of the market mechanism; or they may view it as a means of accommodating the interests of business to the wider society. There are a number of reasons for corporations to pay attention. Yet a large number would prefer to avoid involvement with state government if this were at all possible. Although top management feels obliged to make some effort, its heart is not in it. This lack of support is evident to corporation lobbyists, relatively few of whom expressed satisfaction with the level of commitment demonstrated by management.

There is little incentive, however, for chief executives and senior management to become involved in government affairs. They have many other obligations. Some shy away from lobbying altogether because of their distaste for government. Others are willing to pay some attention to government relations at the federal level, where public officials have higher status and Washington offers hotels and restaurants not far below the levels of those in New York. This is known as the "Rose Garden syndrome." [4] IBM's Thomas Watson, Jr., recognized the need to cultivate politicians in person but concluded that the worst way to do so was with a Washington office staffed with professional lobbyists.[5] Nonetheless, IBM has a Washington office with its cadres of federal and state government relations personnel.

Relatively few business leaders engage themselves at the state level. Albany, Sacramento, Tallahassee, and Trenton have little appeal, and state legislators are too peculiar a breed. Top management is structurally and dispositionally removed from the political fray and, for the most part, not very accessible to the corporation lobbyist, who is likely to report, instead, to a general counsel or deputy general counsel within the company's legal department or to a vice president for public affairs.

In order for companies to go about their business with as few regulatory restraints and as light a tax burden as possible, state governmental relations staff is expected to defend company turf. Few companies have the luxury of thinking proactively. Instead, theirs is a holding action aimed at keeping government at arm's length. It is important, therefore, for their agents to monitor the political environment, be aware of threats, and design suitable defenses. Emphasis is on *not* making mistakes. Company strategies therefore tend to be conservative and cautious.

Of those companies surveyed by the Conference Board in the early 1980s, nearly half reported important interests in one state only; these included utilities and banks. Most of the remainder had an interest in fewer than five states. Three-quarters of the largest companies, however, had an interest in ten or more states.[6] Depending in part on the intensity and extent of their interests, these larger companies organize their state government relations function in different ways. Targeting a single state is comparatively easy to do—fewer choices have to be made. The person employed by the company to be responsible for lobbying can simply be based in, or spend considerable time at, the state capital. If necessary, he or she can be supplemented by another staff member or by a contract lobbyist.

Companies with substantial interests in a number of states, by contrast, have to decide how to cover them all. In this respect, MetPath's state government relations efforts are instructive. Like many other companies, MetPath first established its presence at the federal level. Then it had to decide how to achieve influence at the state level. The challenge for management was to get representation in the states without spending huge sums of money. First, MetPath had to identify key issues and states. Second, it had to hire someone to run the company's state government relations operation. Third, it needed to devise a strategy for monitoring legislation. Management therefore posed two questions: "What legislation will hurt us?" and "How do we get into the act early enough?" MetPath knew it would not be possible to monitor every state, so it decided to keep an eye on New York and California, bellwether states, and to a lesser extent Michigan, Illinois, and Massachusetts. The final task was to hire on a retainer basis contract lobbyists in the targeted states, bring them to the company headquarters in Teeterboro, New Jersey, and let them "see, touch, and feel" the business.

Comparatively small companies like MetPath may have a one- or two-person government affairs office and rely on contract lobbyists in selected states. Frequently, they will count on line management—plant and facility managers—to play a part in their lobbying campaigns. Larger companies usually employ regional state government relations professionals, as is the case with AT&T. The regional directors in turn may employ contract lobbyists. Larger companies also tend to have larger staffs in their headquarters—five, ten, or more professionals. Johnson & Johnson, for example, has six full-time staff members in its government relations department. These people shoulder responsibility for all fifty states but concentrate on fewer than half. But the pharmaceutical giant's main interests are in New Jersey, which its in-house lobbyists handle, and about fifteen other states where contract professionals are hired on retainer or as the need arises.

Anheuser-Busch, headquartered in St. Louis, offers another example of a company that takes state government relations quite seriously: its in-house state affairs group is supplemented by a network of independent, or contract, lobbyists in practically every state.[7]

Companies with little or no in-house government relations staff rely on trade associations; business associations also are relied on, though to a lesser extent, to represent their interests. The 1983 Conference Board study showed that about one-fifth of the companies surveyed, primarily smaller firms, reported reliance on associations.[8] Larger corporations also use trade and business associations. If their interests are more extensive than their government affairs budgets, they will not be able to retain contract lobbyists wherever they may be needed. They therefore have little alternative but to look to their associations for representation. Johnson & Johnson, again, is illustrative. Although it has in-house capacity, it also operates in its home state through the New Jersey Chamber of Commerce, the New Jersey Business and Industry Association, and the New Jersey Health Products Company Group. It pays dues to industry associations in California, Illinois, Massachusetts, and other states. Nationally, it works through the Pharmaceutical Manufacturers Association, the Health Care Industry Manufacturers' Association, and other groups.

Even if companies could lobby an issue on their own, on some matters they may prefer the cover provided by an association. A lobbyist for a telephone company, for instance, chose not to wage single-handed combat with the legislature on the issue of parental leave; he let the state business association handle it. "There is no sense," he explained, "in having a battle of Armageddon over this policy," despite the strong views management had on the issue. Another national corporation had opposed the sales tax on professional services, which was passed by the Florida legislature in 1987 and repealed shortly thereafter. But because this company did not want to be identified as a strong opponent, several associations served the company's interests and permitted it to remain in the background. Corporations that take strong positions on certain issues run the risk of a boycott of their products. The director of state government relations for a Minnesota bank summed up: "To the extent that the trade association can deal with common issues, we support the industry and don't lead the way." That attitude is not uncommon.

Inevitably, however, companies will need to act independently of their trade associations. A large Minnesota bank could not depend on its association, which was dominated by all the small banks that were members. A large liquor company, with its own line of wines, was leery of the Wine Institute, which it believed was driven by the Gallo company. Another national company had doubts about its trade association, which it thought represented the lowest common denominator of membership and, thus, reacted defensively to governmental change instead of seeking to shape it beforehand. These companies, and many more, use their associations but reserve the right to act independently.

The Organization of Associations

Although most companies cannot afford to put all their eggs in the association basket, business associations, which are multi-industry groups, and trade associations, which are single-industry groups, still play an important role in the representation of interests.[9] Several groups represent broad business constituencies in each state. In California, for example, business has membership in the following state organizations: Chamber of Commerce, Manufacturers Association, Business Alliance, Council for Environmental and Economic Balance, and Taxpayers Association.[10]

In addition, in each state there are hundreds of trade associations of every conceivable variety. Florida, for instance, lists among other associations the following:

Air Conditioning Contractors   Food Service
Air Transport   Funeral Directors

American Insurance
American Pet Products
American Publishers
American Service
Auto Dealers
Bankers
Beer Wholesalers
Broadcasters
Broker/Dealers
Cable TV
Cemetery
Chemical Industry Council
Community Bankers
Credit Management
Direct Selling
Electronic Industries
Energy Pipeline
Entertainment and Dining
Financial Services

Home Builders
Independent Gas Dealer
Independent Petroleum
 Producers
Industrial Cogeneration
Manufacturers
Marine Manufacturers
Mortgage Bankers
Municipal Electric
Pawnbrokers
Property Owners
Realtors
Recreational Vehicle Trade
Rental Dealers
Restaurants
Retail Grocers
Rural Electric Cooperative
Securities Industry
Transportation Builders

The array of associations with a lobbying presence in Tallahassee and other state capitals is staggering. Small wonder, then, that lobbyists are abundant in the legislative halls.

Associational Bases

Some associations are state based, others operate out of Washington but have interests in most of the states. Among the latter are the American Petroleum Institute, which has a large Washington staff, including regional managers, as well as a year-round presence in two-thirds of the state capitals. A much smaller organization is the Direct Selling Association, consisting of about a hundred member companies such as Avon, Tupperware, and Shaklee. This association manages to cover all fifty states with three professionals traveling around the country from Washington, and without any contract lobbyists. Many of the association's members, however, have their own state government relations capacity. Another example of a Washington-based group is the seven-hundred-member International Franchise Association, which includes as members Dunkin' Donuts, I Can't Believe It's Yogurt, MacDonald's, 7-Eleven, and H&R Block. The association, which deals only on matters specifically related to franchises, employs three professionals who have to cover federal and international as well as state government relations.

The Pharmaceutical Manufacturers Association is illustrative of large national trade associations. PMA was established twenty years ago and currently has a Washington staff of six state relations professionals, including a director and five persons responsible for various regions of the country. (A separate regional office, covering seven western states, was opened up in California in 1990.) These individuals travel to the states, get things organized, coordinate team efforts, and engage in "critical point" lobbying for the industry. Meanwhile, PMA provides information, resource support, and public relations for the industry nationwide. Regional staffers work with the twenty-five member companies, which also have their own state governmental relations departments, placing major emphasis on twenty states with the largest markets. Medicaid occupies about 85 percent of the association's time, with other issues such as generic drugs, tort reform/product liability, and animal research also on the agenda.

Although they may have Washington connections, the vast majority of associations are indigenous to particular states. Their activities encompass more than legislation and lobbying, with much of the staff time spent on membership services and the dissemination of information. Among the myriad of associations are the New Jersey Business and Industry Association, with seven lobbyists, the California Chamber of Commerce with twelve, and the Minnesota Chamber of Commerce, which has more than ten. The principal trade associations in Austin, Texas, are the trial lawyers, doctors, realtors, and automobile dealers.

Certified public accountants are organized state by state throughout the country. Of the CPAs' fifty state societies, only two lack lobbyists. In some the executive director lobbies; in others the lobbyist is the director of governmental relations; contract lobbyists do the job in a number of states; and in a few volunteers do the lobbying. In each of these associations a board of directors or comparable body has the responsibility for deciding on legislation.

State teacher associations, which are affiliated with the National Education Association, are major players practically everywhere. The New Jersey Education Association exemplifies these organizations. It has six full-time lobbyists, who have to advance the interests of 117,000 members. New Jersey's Public Interest Research Group is one of twenty-five state PIRGs. This group has seventy thousand members, about half of whom are students and the rest citizens signed up through an outreach program. PIRG's thirty-member staff in New Jersey includes several lobbyists. Organizations representing the interests of local-government officials also have state-relations expertise for lobbying the legislature. The California County Supervisors Association has five lobbyists, the Florida League of Cities six, as does the Texas Municipal League. By contrast, New Jersey has only one full-time lobbyist for the association of counties, in addition to the executive director, who lobbies part time. In Colorado there is only one lobbyist in-house, while two independent lobbyists serve the counties on a contractual basis.

The associations mentioned above are well endowed compared to most groups organized at the state level. The latter typically have just a single professional whose duties range widely. The California Children's Lobby is such a group. The organization's director not only tracks more than eighty bills on child care, health and safety, and other issues, but she also monitors four different budgets in two state agencies and handles the group's press, workshops, and fund-raising. The Sierra Club is another group short on lobbyists, relying heavily on volunteers. But recently it has managed to engage at least part-time lobbyists for the legislative sessions in all the states.

Internal Politics

Although the state government relations directors of associations are outward looking, they cannot neglect cultivating internal relationships. They have to attend to the overall views of the membership, the role of committees with which they work, and the organization's leaders to whom they relate on a regular basis.

The policies of business associations are made by a board of directors, usually on the advice of a legislative affairs committee. Staff members have considerable say in the policy-making process. Typically, they will explore the issues that the committee and board will be deciding. What is the issue about? How does it affect members? Who will gain and who will lose? Who are the supporters, who are the opponents? Are there other ways of dealing with the problem? What are the options—support, oppose, change? What priority does the issue merit?[11] It should be noted that most of the issues that come up in the legislature are not new; they have been around for a while. As a consequence, an association will frequently not need to adopt a position; it already has one.

Within limits established by their board, staff members have considerable leeway in interpreting and implementing organizational policy. They will usually touch base with a certain committee or check out strategy periodically with the board of directors. But during the course of a legislative session, staff has—and requires—freedom to act and react to events without requesting approval. Bills and amendments that suddenly arise may be inimical to association interests. Therefore, a rapid response often is necessary.

Other associations do not differ fundamentally from the business groups in how they make policy and oversee the conduct of state government relations. For municipal and county associations, a board of directors or the executive committee normally establishes the position. The staff must then advance that position and be given a relatively free rein. A group such as PIRG operates in a similar manner. Its board determines policy, but the staff makes recommendations to the board and then has discretion in following through on the board's position. Teacher associations encourage the broadest involvement in the development of policy. Their delegate assemblies decide on the recommendations of committees (on pensions, finance, etc.). Then the government relations committee, which is made up of local representatives, takes over. It establishes legislative priorities and formulates an action campaign. Strategy and tactics are up to staff, but staff keeps the committee informed through bulletins, meetings, and other contacts.

Despite the flexibility they have in advising on and carrying out organizational policy, state government relations personnel must attend to the care and feeding of leaders and members, whose confidence in them is essential. In most associations, the elected leadership turns over regularly, requiring the director of state governmental relations (and/or executive director of the association) to build confidence among newly elected leaders on an annual basis. Sometimes that may mean that one's every move must be measured, as in the case of an executive director who lamented, "You have to ask leadership if you want to cross the street." But if the director cultivates younger members of the organization at an early stage, he or she will have won their confidence before they ascend to leadership posts.

In many organizations, membership indifference has to be overcome. If an association has lost too many battles, members may withdraw from any activity. As strange as it may seem, occasionally the problem is that an association has lost too *few* battles. "I have a lot of trouble getting my board of directors' attention," commented the director of a Washington, D.C.-based association, "because they have become complacent." Involvement would probably increase if the organization were to suffer a loss. Without some threshold of interest, members cannot be mobilized and the potential power of a group cannot be harnessed and directed. That is why considerable time is spent communicating to members by newsletter, action brief, and special report. By personalizing issues, staff members have a better chance of persuading and mobilizing members.

For those predisposed to buttonholing legislators, it is frustrating to have to deal with key association members who do not understand the issues of politics. But that is what they must do. They have to return their phone calls and initiate calls of their own. Whenever possible, too, they will travel through the state, visiting with leaders in their home communities instead of waiting for scheduled meetings or relying on the telephone.[12] Although staff must educate members and persuade them that their participation makes a difference, they must also refrain from raising their expectations unrealistically. They must, moreover, mediate between the self-interested and parochial views of the organization and the imperatives of the legislative process. This is especially true for the cause groups, whose leaders demonstrate great zeal and intensity and may not adapt to the bargain-and-compromise patterns of legislatures.[13] For example, leaders of one California organization, wanting to maintain an inviolate image in the gay-lesbian community, view compromise as being synonymous with evil. Their lobbyist has been engaged in a constant educational campaign to get his members to "understand how the process works and what is probable, feasible, and impossible."[14]

Lobbyists understand that the legislature deals in increments, not big bites; but members of their associations want big bites. The state governmental relations staff of teachers associations provides a good example of this dynamic. One teachers' lobbyist described her challenge as getting the association to compromise. "I'm in the middle," she explained, "My job is to keep the two sides working together." There are times, in her opinion, when teachers have to be understanding, but there are also times when she cannot ask them to compromise. "There are not many showdowns, but they are well selected," is how she described the relationship between her association and the legislature.

When an association is united on an issue, the lobbyist's problem may be in restraining members. A bigger problem occurs, however, when an association's members cannot agree on issues because their interests diverge. The sad fact is that fragmentation and internal conflict are frequently natural conditions of organizational life. Local banks and those aspiring to regional or nationwide status do not coexist comfortably within a single association. Nor do industries that emit pollutants or those that manufacture environmental equipment.[15]

Frequently, large organizations are unwieldy. For example, the California Chemical Council's membership is highly diverse, ranging from Dow to small companies, and this tends to make agreement on organizational policy difficult. Among Florida's retail food stores are Albertson's and Waldbaums, each with more than two hundred stores, and about five hundred small, independent retailers. "Outside of taxes, this industry cannot agree on anything," declares one lobbyist in Tallahassee. A group like the CPAs ought to be homogeneous; but that is not the case. Accountants differ in the services they provide. They differ in where they work; half the members work in industry, while the other half are independent practitioners. The latter are split between those in large firms and those in small ones.

The oil industry, which is organized into state petroleum councils, may seem strong but it is actually weak in all but the few states where oil is produced. Its members are a diverse lot, who are not affected similarly by the issues. The major companies have interests that differ from the smaller refiners. Likewise, the refiners and jobbers frequently have opposing interests. Service station dealers have their own views on franchises, hours of operation, and rents, as do the oil companies. Because of their present image, the majors cannot take the lead on any issue, although they try to have their interests represented by other council members. In view of its fragmentation, the oil industry simply cannot define a course. "We're always on the verge of being neutralized," is how one petroleum council lobbyist described the industry's plight. In one state, oil faces a major fight, but the industry is so internally divided that even with a number of top-flight lobbyists in their employ they can do nothing. The lobbyists themselves are frustrated, waiting for marching orders. In the opinion of one of those involved, "It is like running with a bungee cord tied to your legs." Although citizens perceive oil interests to be large and powerful, at the state level the industry tends to be an ineffectual giant.

Also illustrative of fractionated groups are the associations of county and municipal government officials. The Texas Municipal League represents all the state's cities, but on certain issues Austin and Houston and Dallas will each go its own way. In New Jersey the split is between urban and suburban municipalities or urban and suburban counties, and also between the northern and southern parts of the state. The internal divisions of Maryland's association of counties reflect the differing legislative structures and roles within each of the state's twenty-four counties. That leads to varying local-state relationships, with members bringing substantially different perspectives to their association.

The resulting heterogeneity and lack of cohesion among members are burdensome for the staff. The disunity also limits the organization's effectiveness. In order to achieve a consensus, some associations will adopt positions that reflect the lowest common denominator of membership views; or they address the issues in the broadest, most general terms so that exception will not be taken. If associations go too far in one direction or another, they risk losing members. Cigarette companies, for instance, pulled out of the New Jersey Business and Industry Association because of its support for antismoking legislation. (They later came back in.)

Unless the membership is cohesive, an association is likely to adopt a compromise at the lowest common denominator. Another possibility is stalemate, whereby the association tries to adopt a position but simply cannot because it is internally rent. Among New Jersey's convenience stores, for instance, members who did not sell gas tended to support legislation authorizing self-service gas stations. Others, who sold gas but would have been at a disadvantage competing with the large service stations, were opposed. Their association could not take a position because of the split. On another issue, Public Service Electric and Gas Company backed a bill that would have taxed cogenerators, but most other members of the New Jersey Business and Industry Association were opposed. The association could not take a position. Indeed, it rarely took a position that favored one segment of its membership over another.

Contracting Out

Even companies and associations with in-house state government relations staff contract out to independent lobbyists for a good deal of the work. In this regard, the in-house professionals have the job of determining whether, when, and where contract lobbyists are required; employing them; and overseeing and assessing their work.

The Benefits of Employing Contract Lobbyists

The use of outside lobbyists has grown over the years, particularly among business companies and associations, but also among other groups as well. The reasons are several.

First, as we noted earlier, a national company or association may have a small staff and still have to cover many or all of the states. It will therefore allocate a percentage of the state relations budget for hiring independent lobbyists. Companies and associations within a single state may also seek outside help because their own staff is spread thin. Societies of CPAs, for instance, the one in Florida, do all the lobbying themselves. Many of the smaller societies, however, use contract lobbyists because their executive directors cannot carry the load.

Second, if in-house capacity exists, it may lead, not to self reliance, but to seeking outside support. According to the Conference Board survey, the more state-relations professionals in a company, the greater the likelihood it will hire contract lobbyists.[16] This is partly because the size of the in-house staff reflects the company's or the association's acknowledgment of how important lobbying can be. Thus, the more—up to a point—the more.

Third, a presence in the state capital is desirable, if not requisite. "It helps," said one state-relations professional from Washington, D.C., "if you live with them [legislators] and drink with them." Not all national organizations are situated in the U.S. capital; the same is true of some single-state organizations. Again, the CPAs provide an example. Although most state societies are located in the capital, some still are not; however, several have moved there in recent years. The Florida society used to be in Gainesville; but the CPAs decided this made no sense.

"We'd better be located where the action takes place," was the feeling expressed by one lobbyist. In 1980 the society took up quarters two blocks from the capitol building in Tallahassee. The in-house lobbyists, who "parachute in" when the legislature is in session, are also at a great disadvantage, not possessing the kind of relationships with legislators and their staffs that residential lobbyists develop. Moreover, by the time they arrive, the informal process is well advanced and the outcome may already be determined. Someone has to be on the scene all or most of the time.

Fourth, contract lobbyists are not only on the spot but they are also usually in the fray. By way of contrast, state government relations professionals tend to be more aloof and distant, sometimes taking on the semblance of bureaucrats. Independent lobbyists have greater standing as individuals and potentially greater influence. Indeed, as one state government relations professional observed, "Sometimes you need a well-connected lobbyist so that legislators will take you seriously." Retaining a hired gun signals the client's concern; the act resembles anteing up in a game of poker.

Fifth, if a state is critical for a national organization, it will require and retain counsel there. If an issue arises where no one is on retainer, the organization will employ a lobbyist on an as-needed basis and for the issue's duration. In New Jersey, for example, a proposal was introduced to ban the manufacture and sale of plastic tampon applicators because they washed up with other garbage on the beaches. Although it had its own staff, International Playtex hired two contract lobbyists in Trenton to kill the legislation. The latter devised the strategy and led the assault, while company staff lent support and, of course, paid the bill.

The disadvantage of engaging an independent lobbyist is that the principal loses much of its identity. Although the group may win in the short term, it has built little equity in the long. Some state government relations professionals therefore conclude that they have to do the lobbying themselves. This entails developing relationships with legislators, offering testimony, and establishing, insofar as possible, an organizational presence and, hence, an organizational identity.

Managing Contract Lobbyists

Once an organization decides to employ an independent lobbyist to represent its interests in a state, the government relations staff is then responsible for recruiting the individual. If they are not familiar with the state, they may employ on a consultative basis firms such as MultiState Associates or Stateside Associates, which have contacts throughout the nation. Such firms work for a fee, helping companies locate state counsel.

But state government relations staffers have their own networks by virtue of their company's or association's membership in the State Governmental Affairs Council (SGAC) and other such groups. It is not difficult to obtain recommendations, check out reputations, examine the client lists of contract lobbyists, and interview several, a few perhaps more than once.

Throughout the process the staff members must have in mind just what kind of lobbyist is needed for the task at hand—a former legislator? one of high or low visibility? a good ol' boy or one of the new breed? and so forth. An organization's reputation is shaped in part by that of the lobbyist it hires. Putting one of the most influential contract lobbyists on the payroll can provide instant status to an interest group. That may not be what a group has in mind, in which case one of the newer, less political lobbyists may be preferable. And there is always the problem of having to share time with a contract lobbyist's other clients, as was pointed out by a staff member of a Washington-based association: "The bigger the contract lobbyist, the more likely they have bigger clients. They have conflicts. And when push comes to shove, your interests get lost." From the point of view of the contract lobbyist, "You have to conserve chits; you can't use all your bullets." That means that not every client's interests can be represented equally, and certainly not at the same session.

In many cases—particularly in the more partisan states—a choice has to be made about employing someone with mainly Democratic or Republican contacts. A bank in Minnesota, for instance, retained a lobbyist with a Democratic background because it already had standing with the Republicans. Another example is the Greater Miami Opera, which first hired a lobbyist with Democratic credentials to lobby the Florida legislature. After a member of the opera board suggested hiring a Republican close to Governor Bob Martinez, a second lobbyist was also employed.[17]

Clearly, the more lobbyists, the more bases can be covered. Some interests therefore hire several lobbyists to represent them year-round. Others hire multiple lobbyists to represent them on key issues. Key issues usually involve fights between large companies or industries. In Texas they are known euphemistically as "blue bird" issues (as in the "blue bird of happiness") because so many contract lobbyists are employed on one side or the other, usually at substantial fees, resulting in happiness for them.

This large-scale lobbying gives rise to what is called "team lobbying," with five, ten, or more professionals on each side. Team lobbying permits a high degree of specialization. That is to say, the more lobbyists working an issue, the better the contact with members of the legislature. One lobbyist has close contacts in the senate, another in the house. One has an in with Republicans, another with Democrats. One knows the speaker well. Another has a long-standing relationship with the chairman of the standing committee that has jurisdiction. An African American lobbyist may have better access to African American members, and a female lobbyist may have greater rapport with women members.

Certain issues have generated battles between lobbying teams throughout the states. Tort reform and product liability, which involve business on one side and trial lawyers on the other, are such issues. Another fight between teams involves car-rental companies, with Hertz and Avis against Alamo and other smaller companies. The main issue here is that Alamo and its allies depend on collision damage waivers (CDW) for a large percentage of their business.[18] Hertz and Avis support legislation that would restrict the CDW practice, thus hurting their competitors. Although the fight has been waged in many states, perhaps the biggest battle was in Florida, Alamo's home base. Almost fifty lobbyists were involved, including a team of eighteen working exclusively for Alamo. Dayton-Hudson's contract-lobbyist law firm had fifteen lobbyists representing the company's interests on legislation that would have prevented a hostile takeover. One reason for hiring these lobbyists was so that they would not sign up with the opposition.

Team lobbying is used, to some extent at least, practically everywhere. But it is a prominent part of the legislative environment in Texas, where it came into style about ten years ago. In the period since, the automobile manufacturers have hired several lobbyists to pass a seatbelt law. Then tort reform and product liability engaged the services of a number of Austin's top guns, who were retained by the Texas Civil Justice League. The 1987 session of the Texas Legislature found AT&T pitted against U.S. Sprint and MCI, with thirteen lobbyists signed up on one side and twelve on the other.

One major battle was between Texaco and Pennzoil. Texaco came into Texas first and hired every major lobbyist in Austin but one; Pennzoil hired him. Before it was over, about twenty-five contract lobbyists were on the payrolls of the two companies. One prominent lobbyist commented in retrospect, "It was almost an insult not to be hired." Another remembered the experience clearly, "That was the biggest fee I ever made in my life." The lobbyists on each side would meet together regularly to compare notes and update strategies. "It was a zoo," recalled one of them, "like the bar scene in *Star Wars*."

Surely for those who do it, team lobbying has payoffs. Indeed, it has been labeled the "Lobbyists' Full Employment Act." And it may also be fun for lobbyists to share campaigns with colleagues, engaging in a form of lobbyist bonding. Given the connections each lobbyist brings to the enterprise, it can be effective as well, although one side can cancel out the other. Questions have been raised, however, about whether team lobbying has gone too far in Texas. Given the number of power-broker lobbyists involved, an issue may be receiving too high a profile. Furthermore, the amount of money being spent in fees may leave a bad taste with the press and public. Under such circumstances, team lobbying may become counterproductive.

Once companies and associations contract with lobbyists, they can choose either to direct and monitor their efforts closely or to trust in their competence and take a good deal on faith. The relationship varies by lobbyist and client. If a lobbyist has worked for a client long enough, a relationship of mutual confidence is likely to have developed, and the need for frequent contact lessens. Some clients are more politically astute than others and want to be involved, and the lobbyist acquiesces. The more bills clients have at stake, too, the more involved they are apt to be. Obviously, companies or associations that are located out of state have to limit their involvement. Their in-house lobbyists may want to be kept informed, but they are rarely on the scene. It is not likely that they will try to micromanage, and even less likely that they will be able to do so.

The situation tends to differ when the relationship between lobbyist and client is new. One of New Jersey's top independent lobbyists described his approach with a new client:

> We sit down in a room with a prospective client and we explain what our staff capabilities are. We first advise them on how we will handle the issue, on who will handle the account, and on who will take the lead. Then we ... try to get a feel for where the minefields will be and what resources we have to work with. Next, we break it down legislatively according to where our strengths and weaknesses are going to be.

Sometimes a company's concern is so great that top management involves itself in orienting a new contract lobbyist. That was the case with a bill, which was being pushed by Anheuser-Busch, to change Florida's regulations governing how beer companies conducted business with their distributors. Augustus Busch himself brought a Tallahassee lobbyist to St. Louis to tell him how important it was to the company. After that, it was up to the lobbyist to get the bill passed, and he managed to do so.

One of the principal jobs of the contract lobbyist is that of lobbying the client. "Communicating," "educating," "explaining" is how contract lobbyists describe their efforts. They keep track of what is happening, alert their clients to developments, and propose strategies of response or adaptation.[19] Their job requires setting the client straight and entails getting the client to think realistically about prospects. "Your position, A, won't sell. B, however, is possible. But, if you want a sure thing, go to C." That kind of talk is often necessary. Typically, the client wants to win, while the lobbyist realizes the value of compromise. One lobbyist described the fight between the engineers and the architects over professional turf:

> The engineers, who were one of our clients, would not compromise or change the bill that they wanted. We got the bill passed by both houses. . . . It was a crazy bill. They were lashing back at the architects, who they thought had wronged them.

The governor vetoed the bill. The lobbyist went back to the engineers and asked them to compromise. They finally agreed. But they could have held out and said, "We're paying you good money to get what we want done, and not what you want done." That would have been unfortunate for the client-lobbyist relationship.

Compromise is a major tool of a lobbyist trying to get a job done and to stay in the game to play another day. Those who depend on their relationships with legislators would much rather work things out so that everyone wins something and no one loses too much. The question, as posed by one lobbyist, is "When do you shoot the bullets?" The answer for most contract lobbyists is, "As seldom as possible." And given the legislative process, that is not only in the interest of the lobbyist but probably of the client as well.

Notes

1. See the categorization by Clive S. Thomas and Ronald J. Hrebenar, which is built on studies of interest groups in the fifty states. "Interest Groups in the States," in *Politics in the American States,* ed. Virginia Gray, Herbert Jacob, and Robert B. Albritton, 5th ed. (Glenview, Ill.: Scott, Foresman/Little, Brown Higher Education, 1990), 132-133.
2. Public Affairs Council, *State Government Relations: Results of a Survey of 55 Corporations* (Washington, D.C.: The Council, 1986), 16.
3. State Government Relations Institute, New Brunswick, New Jersey, July 12, 1990.
4. Seymour Lusterman, *Managing Business-State Government Relations* (New York: The Conference Board, 1983), 24.
5. Thomas J. Watson, Jr., *Father, Son and Co.* (New York: Bantam Books, 1990), 400.
6. Lusterman, *Managing Business-State Government Relations,* vii.
7. See Richard A. Armstrong, "Corporations and State Government Relations: An Overview," in *Leveraging State Government Relations,* ed. Wesley Pedersen (Washington, D.C.: Public Affairs Council, 1990), 9-12.
8. Lusterman, *Managing Business-State Government Relations,* 4.
9. Public Affairs Council, *The Third House: An Informal Survey of Corporate Lobbying at the State Level* (Washington, D.C.: The Council, 1973), 21.
10. Max Boot, "Business Associations—Big Names, Less Clout," *California Journal,* October 1988, 453.
11. Charles S. Mack, *The Executive's Handbook of Trade and Business Associations* (Westport, Conn.: Quorum Books, 1991), 79-80.

12. See also Kay Lehman Schlozman and John T. Tierney, *Organized Interests and American Democracy* (New York: Harper and Row, 1986), 143-146.
13. Marjorie Randon Hershey, "Direct Action and the Abortion Issue: The Political Participation of Single-Issue Groups," in *Interest Group Politics,* ed. Allan J. Cigler and Burdett A. Loomis, 2d ed. (Washington, D.C.: CQ Press, 1986), 28.
14. Kathy Beasley, "Low-Budget Lobbyists," *California Journal,* September 1988, 28.
15. Lusterman, *Managing Business-State Government Relations,* 8.
16. Ibid.
17. *Miami Herald,* December 11, 1990.
18. The waivers guarantee that the rental company will not sue customers if a car is damaged and add $12 to $15 a day to the cost of renting a car.
19. See Robert H. Salisbury, "The Paradox of Interest Groups in Washington— More Groups, Less Clout," in *The New American Political System,* ed. Anthony King, 2d version (Washington, D.C.: AEI Press, 1990), 224.

CHAPTER 3

The Interests at Stake

Studying the individuals who lobby, as we did in an earlier chapter, and their strategies and tactics, as we shall do in later chapters, is certainly important. But we must also examine the particular concerns of specific groups. "Without an adequate understanding of the interests involved," writes political scientist Robert Salisbury, "an analysis of institution, process, or policy choice will not get it right."[1] In line with Salisbury's advice, in this chapter we shall look more closely at the interests at stake, the issues involved, and the conflicts that arise.

Issues Big and Small

State government today makes major public policy decisions. These are no longer the exclusive province of the federal government. State legislatures have therefore come to play an increasingly important role. In the past major state policy was mainly the prerogative of governors; no longer. The distribution of taxes and tax rates, interstate banking, education reform, school funding, highways and mass transit, sentencing and prisons, Medicaid cost containment, economic development, and workers' compensation all are on the agendas of the states.

Take environmental issues, which are an increasingly important part of a state legislature's agenda. In the 1989-1990 sessions, thirty-five legislatures considered 1,126 different bills on recycling, forty considered 274 separate bills regulating the use of pesticides, thirty-five dealt with 226 bills restricting hazardous waste transportation, and thirty-six handled 238 pieces of groundwater legislation.[2] Environmental issues cut so many ways nowadays that the field has divided into segments, such as air, water, waste, and so forth.

There are also the so-called hot issues, emotional and moral questions that arouse special furor among competing groups and make legislators particularly uncomfortable. Abortion is the most obvious "hot" issue at present. But gun control, the death penalty, sex education, pornography, home schooling, and the use of animals in research are others. Such issues bring out groups that range from feminists and liberals on one side of the spectrum to the religious right and conservatives on the other, including such diverse groups as sportsmen, animal rights advocates, and the pharmaceutical industry.

The important issues mentioned above constitute some of the agenda of major items addressed by the legislatures of the fifty states. But other issues—and hundreds of other bills—are not major by any stretch of the imagination. How many of the 7,500 bills introduced in the 1988 and 1989 regular sessions of the California legislature were important statewide? Of the 1,200 introduced in Colorado, the 8,000 in Florida, 5,500 in Minnesota, 10,000 in New Jersey, and 5,000 in Texas, how many had significant implications for public policy? The answer is, relatively few.

Many of these bills are relatively inconsequential and do not attract the attention of any group.[3] More "housekeeping" than anything else, they are introduced in response to a request by an administrative agency. Or they are sponsored by legislators to please constituents of no organizational hue. Most will go nowhere. Beyond these, many others are promoted (and opposed) by interest groups, managed by lobbyists, and introduced by legislators on their behalf. A contract lobbyist in Texas categorized the legislation introduced at a typical session: about 100 had statewide implications and perhaps an additional 100 had impact on members' districts. "Another 4,800 don't appear on my radar screen at all," he said. From the perspective of statewide policy, these bills are minor; but from the perspective of one group or another, they are of tremendous import.

Generally, one-third to half the bills addressed by a legislature relate to "private" or "special interest" issues, but they will be debated in public-policy terms. These bills have only indirect relevance, however, to statewide policy. Although most everything has public-policy ramifications, they primarily affect the pocketbooks of various business and professional groups. These interests try to manipulate the regulatory environment, gain ground from their rivals, or put them out of business by seeking state intervention favorable to their cause. For every group looking for some advantage, some other group is resisting being taken advantage of. Moreover, if evidence of some abuse is brought to the surface, executive and legislative officials will seek to impose a remedy on their own.

Like individuals, groups have the constitutional right to petition their government. (Government, of course, does not have to give them what they want.) One contract lobbyist summed up as follows: "Frankly, the legislature in New Jersey exists for the lobbyist." What he meant was that the governor wanted five or six bills a year, legislators wished for one each, and the rest were desired by lobbyists and the interests they represent. "The fact is," he said, "that we are here because it is our right to be here." Lobbyists and their clients are the "squeaky wheels"; they expect to get the grease.

There is no way for groups to ignore the legislature entirely. The impact on interests large and small is too great. Corporations and associations can be affected by many of the bills that are introduced. A public utility company, such as gas and electric, is affected by almost anything government does. It is a big taxpayer, so a change in tax policy can be critical. Environmental legislation—water, air emissions, solid and hazardous waste—has important ramifications for its operations and balance sheet. Then there are bills on all sorts of strictly business issues. And the agenda for large companies has been expanding. For example, in the early 1980s Unilever had only eight issues on its list; by the 1990s there were more than sixty.

As an example, take the present situation of the nation's cemeteries and crematoriums. They are being challenged by those who question whether buried bodies could contaminate underground water or if cremation could be a source of toxic air pollutants.[4] The umbrella group representing the interests of crematoriums expressed concern because some states had environmental laws that lumped crematoriums together with other incinerators; that did not make sense. The issue for cemeteries and/or funeral directors was that, just as cremation was becoming popular (it is now used in about 17 percent of deaths), it began to suffer from antipollution laws. And the laws differed significantly from state to state.

The Conference Board survey found that in the 1981-1982 legislative sessions, 77 percent of the companies responding said they devoted significant time to tax issues; 60 percent of the respondents reported spending considerable time on legislation pertaining to right-to-know, plant closing, and corporate officers' liability. In addition, the companies said they spent a lot of energy on issues that grew out of the environmental and consumer movements, such as food labeling, drug formularies, one-way containers, clean air and water, transportation, and the storage of hazardous wastes.[5] Business associations in Minnesota have been focusing on workers' compensation, health care, environment, transportation, and taxes and spending. In California their focus has also included the unitary tax, tort reform, and the minimum wage.[6]

The 1988-1989 agenda of the New Jersey Business and Industry Association (NJBIA) is illustrative. The association took positions on legislation in eight general areas:

1. *Environmental matters.* Opposed or sought to amend seventeen bills increasing penalties for polluters, supported one of seven bills that would encourage the inclusion of plastics in the recycling waste stream, supported one and opposed four bills on Environmental Cleanup Responsibility Act (ECRA) reform, opposed fifteen bills on waste minimization, opposed twenty-one bills that would have delayed siting of new resource-recovery facilities, landfills, or transfer stations, etc.

2. *Industrial relations.* Supported or opposed five bills on labor, opposed or sought to amend ten bills on health, opposed three bills on the prevailing wage, and opposed five on workers' compensation.

3. *Corporate governance.* Supported three bills.

4. *Taxation.* Opposed two bills.

5. *Education.* Opposed five bills.

6. *Regulatory reform.* Supported one and opposed another.

7. *Development and planning.* Supported one and opposed another.

8. *Product liability.* Supported one bill.

Most of the bills that NJBIA opposed during the 1988-1989 legislative year were defeated. But a few passed, much to the consternation of association members, who would have to live with additional regulation. The executive director for the retail food association in one state pointed out that members were required to identify, label, and announce everything on their shelves. "We have more damned laws that require signs," she complained. "We are being regulated to death." New legislation can be overwhelming, as is frequently the case with the insurance industry. A lobbyist for a large company noted that at its 1990 session, the Florida legislature passed 140 measures affecting his company. He observed that "It will take the company six months to figure the legislation out. It will take the legislature a year to figure it out. But we'll have to start complying in two months." It is little wonder that business thinks it is under siege. Nor is relief in sight.

Legislative agendas are by no means confined to the business sector. Professional associations are also heavily involved. Certified public accountants, for instance, have a proprietary interest in educational requirements and the accountancy laws that license CPAs. They range further afield, alert to many other issues that can affect their profession—sales taxes on services, investment advisor regulations, real-estate-appraisal regulations, and legal liability and tort reform. Teacher organizations are also enmeshed in the process, depending as they do on the legislature for salaries and benefits, conditions of work, and collective-bargaining negotiations. Although teacher concerns are very focused, much that comes before the legislature can affect teachers and the schools. In Colorado, for example, of about six hundred bills introduced in the 1991 session, about seventy-five had implications for education, including one that would have abolished tenure.

Organizations of local public officials also have their hands full with all of the bills introduced in the typical legislature. The Texas Municipal League attends to more than a thousand bills during a typical session, not just monitoring them, as one lobbyist explains, but "really trying to screw with them." The County Supervisors Association of California has to pay attention to anywhere from two thousand to three thousand introductions during a session.

Keeping Track

The lobbyists' mill gets its grist in all sorts of ways. A few issues will come up once and then vanish from the scene. Many have been around for ages, however, and continue to crop up, year after year. Rarely can a group fold up its tent on the assumption that "this issue is won, let's move on to the next one." There is always the next session. Every bill that failed the previous year tends to be prefiled again, almost as a matter of course. An issues manager for one of the country's large insurance companies stressed that "issues tend not to go away; issues are around forever." This is because one or both sides are never fully satisfied with an outcome. Issues may be redefined as time passes, but in the struggle among groups, they are never truly resolved.

Initiating Issues

The bottle bill is one especially contentious issue that has been vociferously debated across the country for years. New York enacted a beverage-container deposit law in 1982 after a ten-year battle with the state's Food Merchants Association and the beverage industry suppliers. Opponents of the law have been unrelenting in their efforts to change it in the ten years since. California's bottle legislation still raises the question of which container type will benefit—aluminum cans or bottles. Every year, the bill undergoes a major fix as groups negotiate and battle.

Many issues are brought to the fore by a business or professional association in an effort to maximize advantage for itself or its members. Sometimes an industry will appeal for state regulation in order to eliminate the varying local regulations. Polystyrene as a packaging material has been banned by local authorities in a number of New Jersey municipalities. Because the industry lacks resources to contest the issue town by town, it has tried to get preemptive legislation. The tobacco industry is also seeking to have the legislature preempt local authority to limit smoking. That is because the antismoking movement has a great advantage at the local level, and "city and county councils are passing local restrictions," writes one journalist, "faster than the tobacco industry can count them." [7]

A number of initiatives come from the many cause-oriented groups. The environmentalists have been particularly effective in raising issues that lobbyists and their clients have been forced to confront. In addition, the issues will never be completely settled for the environmental groups; the cause and the issues are their raison d'être. [8]

Despite the intense involvement of various interest groups, however, it is incorrect to think that public officials merely respond to lobbyist initiatives. Governors, other state officials, and legislators raise issues of their own and take leadership in steering their passage. They have their own agendas, which are related to, but still independent of, those of business, labor, teachers, environmentalists, and the rest. Indeed, the more crucial the matter, the more important the role of public officials.

In 1990 newly elected governor Jim Florio proposed a restructuring of automobile rates. Insurance reform had been a promise of his campaign for governor the year before. The New Jersey Business and Industry Association opposed the shifting of costs that the legislation entailed. A Maryland securities commissioner initiated legislation that would have required CPAs to register and be regulated as financial planners. The local society fought the proposal. A few years ago, Minnesota's commissioner of commerce and attorney general undertook to regulate mortgage bankers. Predictably, they fought back. A New Jersey state senator for some years pushed an ethics code for local government officials. The New Jersey League of Municipalities expressed concern and did all that it could to waylay what it considered to be an unworkable plan, and one that would make life difficult for local public officials.

However issues arise, chances are that they will spread from one state to another. Solid waste, hazardous waste, recycling plastics all make the calendars of more than a few legislatures. Until recently, the bottle bill was an issue that had traveled widely. It has been enacted in a number of states but is now relatively dormant in others. As Common Cause succeeds with campaign-finance reform in certain places, its chapters elsewhere press especially hard.

Legislation tends to spread like wildfire because legislators today travel out-of-state to meetings and discussions sponsored by the National Conference of State Legislatures, the Council of State Governments, and other organizations. Legislators have their antennae out, constantly on the lookout for bills to introduce when they get home. Moreover, national organizations of public officials themselves suggest legislation by adopting model laws. For example, in 1990 the North American Securities

Administrators Association adopted a Model Franchise Investment Law. The next year, with the backing of state securities commissions, that proposal was introduced in several states. Public officials in one state will discuss possibilities with those in another. "What did you do? how much flack did you take?" they ask. If the answers are satisfactory, then they go for it.

Monitoring Issues

Given the numbers of bills introduced and the pace of legislative activity, how do lobbyists and state government relations staff keep track of what is going on? The answer is, not easily. Nevertheless, tracking legislation is a large part of what lobbyists do—in-house lobbyists and hired guns alike. They must be on the lookout for any bill that might affect their organization or client. One hundred, two hundred, or five hundred bills may need watching, although fewer are likely to have significant impact, and even fewer are likely to get very far. The lobbyist has to have a sense of whether a bill is going to move and whether it can go anywhere. A specialist in solid-waste management and government relations likened four thousand or so pieces of legislation to icebergs. Some can be nudged and they move away, "Others," he noted, "have a great deal of ice under them and can sink your boat if you're not careful." The image is apt. Legislation must be navigated with caution.[9]

State government relations professionals, who are not resident at the state capital, have to range widely in order to keep up with legislation that may affect their organization's interests. They subscribe to multi-state computerized information services, use their network of colleagues, and touch base with other organizations and associations. If they have contract lobbyists in specific states, they naturally depend on them for timely information.

The sheer volume of legislation makes tracking by computer particularly welcome. Most large companies and associations that are not in the states, and smaller groups that are on the scene, subscribe to one of the two major tracking services, the Commerce Clearing House and Public Affairs Information. Key words and phrases are provided by clients so that bills on these subjects can be identified and followed.[10] Procter and Gamble, for instance, uses Public Affairs Information. It receives and reviews about three thousand bills a year and then takes a position on two hundred to three hundred of them, while following another six or seven hundred.[11] Before the computer age, monitoring was a hit-or-miss proposition. It is now far easier to keep up with bills and amendments. All of this can be supplemented by other sources—association members, other associations, legislator allies, or lobbyists looking for business.

Some associations have developed their own computerized systems. Associated Industries of Florida (AIF) has one of the most advanced monitoring systems, which members and even nonmembers can use for a fee. Subscribers can search for key words and phrases and get a list of bills on the topic. AIF does not track every single bill, but more than 80 percent of them are tracked routinely.[12]

Lobbyists on the spot will try to identify bills of importance to clients as early as possible. Sometimes they can access everything on the legislature's computer system. Their job is to anticipate who has a stake in particular issues; and when, where, and how they are likely to push them. They are on the lookout for early-warning signs regarding crucial bills. "You have to have your ear to the ground," advises one contract lobbyist in Trenton. The worst thing that can happen is for lobbyists to be surprised by an issue they never thought would arise. But at every session each lobbyist is caught off guard by a bill or two. Inside sources are useful. One lobbyist visits a contact in the state attorney general's office to find out what issues will be coming up in his field. Another useful practice is to watch for indicators. For example, when Hertz started to hire a cadre of heavy-duty lobbyists in Tallahassee, Alamo knew an assault on its interests might be imminent.

In addition to scouting, lobbyists monitor the course of legislation after it is introduced. Although they may have computer systems to assist them, most lobbyists at the capitol have a hands-on monitoring operation. A Florida lobbyist describes his procedure:[13]

1. Preliminary screening
   - Reviews titles in presession interim calendars or journals.
   - Examines various legislative sources.
   - Watches for alerts by associations, legislators, legislative staff, and other lobbyists.
   - Checks with committee staff.
2. Review
   - Reads titles and summaries of printed bills.
   - Studies full text of bills on pertinent subjects.
   - Checks with clients for review and comments.

Moreover, when lobbyists are monitoring areas, their concerns are made known and legislators, legislative staff, and colleagues may alert them to noteworthy developments.

In Sacramento one lobbyist subscribes to a service whereby a copy of every bill is put into a box he rents at the capitol. He goes through all the bills, sorting them by subject. Bills he is not certain about are pulled and sent to his client organization, where attorneys and technicians analyze and otherwise ready them for a corporate decision. Another Sacramento lobbyist, employed by a cause group, cannot afford to subscribe to this service. Instead, she gets the weekly digest of bills, screening out the ones of no interest and reviewing the rest. She then fashions recommendations for her policy committee. An Annapolis lobbyist reviews every bill introduced in the Maryland General Assembly to determine which ones affect the interests of any of his fifty or so clients. This is a difficult feat, even for the most experienced lobbyist.

Lobbyists not only have to figure out which bills affect their clients, but they also have to determine priorities. How great an effect is a bill likely to have? What are the chances of its enactment? What should a client's position be? And what action should be taken?[14] If a lobbyist has determined that a number of issues affect a client organization, then he needs to decide what action, if any, to take on each. A Colorado lobbyist's rule of thumb is, "If it's going the way my client wants it to go, I stand back." A state government relations professional for a large New Jersey company says he makes careful calculations about when to intervene. Otherwise, he says, effort is wasted on legislators who can say: "We gave you that one, so we cannot give you this one." Lobbyists need to have a precise understanding of when to lobby an issue and how far to go with it.

It is said in legislative circles that there are bills for "show," bills for "go," and bills for "no." The first group of bills is introduced but is not meant to go anywhere. The second group includes those that the lobbyist wants to get enacted. The third group comprises legislation the lobbyist wants to defeat. Many more bills fall in the third category, particularly as far as business groups are concerned. Business is more apt to be on the defensive, its lobbyists constantly alert to bills that will impose taxes, regulations, or other hardships. Years ago, Zeigler and Baer noted that business lobbyists were inclined to define their role as one of stopping "bad bills" rather than pushing for passage of "good bills." [15] More recently Hamm and his associates, in a study of California, Iowa, and Texas, found that although groups generally were more likely to support than oppose legislation, business was the least proactive.[16]

The business community's major objective is to be left alone. It wants to keep state government from restricting its freedom of action. Whether fat and happy or lean and mean, business does not want government on its back (although it will appeal to government for subsidies of various sorts). Yet, in its view, the state legislatures are picking it to death. "Once the shark tastes blood," says Raymond L. Hoeving, president of the Public Affairs Council, "it keeps wheeling and looking for its target. I think governors and legislatures have tasted blood." [17]

Several examples illustrate the defensive posture taken by business. First, the liquor industry is in trouble because of the health and sobriety attitudes now pervading American society. It is also facing serious liability issues and feels it is being taxed to death. A Minnesota lobbyist who represents liquor put it this way: "They pound on you time and time again. It is futile to try to make major gains. I try to keep [the industry] from being destroyed." The tobacco industry is in worse shape, having been hurt severely by various bans on smoking in public places and increasing excise taxes. For tobacco lobbyists, too, the game is almost entirely a defensive one.

A giant company, which operates in Minnesota as well as elsewhere, is principally concerned with workplace issues. According to its contract lobbyist, the legislature is trying to solve social problems by regulating the workplace with respect to such issues as parental leave, drug testimony, and privacy. His job for this client is to keep government from interfering.

Contract lobbyists spend much of their energy defensively because most of their clients are from the ranks of business. A veteran New Jersey lobbyist estimates that about 70 percent of his work is defensive, but much of that involves monitoring legislation. A Florida lobbyist characterized his job as trying to protect the people he represents. "If nothing comes up," he says, "it's a victory."

Business is not the only group that wants to manage its own affairs without interference. Professional groups also want to limit government involvement, although they, too, depend on government for laws and regulations that benefit them. The certified public accountants were taken by surprise when Georgia passed a law requiring those who provided financial-planning services to register as investment advisers. The regulatory movement spread to other states because the financial planners, in order to professionalize, wanted to be regulated. The CPAs were already regulated. They claimed they provided only generic advice and sought an exemption in the law, but state securities commissioners resisted. The issue continues, with the accountants on the defensive.

County and local governments would like a larger share of state revenues, or at least the ability to raise some revenue on their own; otherwise, they too want to be left alone. In California more than a third of the bills introduced in a session affect county government. Most of them require a defensive posture by the association of county supervisors in an effort to "protect ourselves from the state's intrusion in our lives." The problem with the legislature, according to the Florida League of Cities, is its disposition to give employee benefits, particularly pensions that entail delayed costs to the cities. In the view of one in-house lobbyist, "the legislature runs out of money before it runs out of good ideas." Although money is not the primary issue in Texas, the situation is similar. The Texas Municipal League's emphasis is mainly defensive. In the 1991 session of the legislature, it was trying to get twenty-eight bills passed and about a thousand killed. "If we didn't pass a single thing and nothing bad passed," said one league lobbyist, "we would have a good session."

Given the nature of the legislative process, it is ordinarily easier for lobbyists to play defensive ball. But not always. Some measures have broad public appeal, making them difficult to oppose. A proposal for an indigent-care trust fund, paid for by a special tax on business, would have broad appeal. A business lobbyist could not oppose the principle of caring for the indigent but would probably argue that this was society's responsibility and should therefore be paid for out of general revenues. Some environmental and consumer bills are difficult for business lobbyists to oppose head on. But for the most part, the bills that lobbyists fight are of narrower scope and lesser interest to the public.

Lobbyists usually try to hold up the bills they oppose as long as possible so that they expire without final action by the time the legislature adjourns sine die. As the session progresses, the lobbyist's workload shifts; many of the bills are for all realistic purposes dead.[18] One lobbyist estimated that at the outset of the 1991 session of the Texas legislature, he had an interest in 150 to 200 bills, and was defending against 125 to 150 of them. By the time the session was drawing to a close, he was trying to get three passed and five or six killed.

Despite the importance of defense, particularly for those who desire to preserve the status quo, offense is also part of the lobbying game. Those who advocate a cause or who are seeking state support will obviously take a proactive stance. Environmentalists, for example, spend most of their time on the offensive. They can do so in part because of a sympathetic public and the press. For example, a Trenton contract lobbyist, who has as a client an environmental group, focuses on land-use issues that include the Pinelands (a protected area of the state), stormwater management, freshwater wetlands, farmland preservation, and funding. Her principle job is to develop and promote legislation. Throughout the state now, plastic-recycling initiatives are being advanced by environmentalists and opposed by the plastics industry.

Cities, too, from time to time have to go to the legislature for enabling authority. In Florida they sought a bill that would permit municipalities to levy a sales tax without resort to referendum. Then there are the groups that go on the offense in order to gain an advantage in the marketplace and/or to damage rivals and competitors. The nationwide push of Hertz and Avis to change the collision damage waiver system is one example. Another example is the effort of trial lawyers to limit protective orders, which protect the trade secrets of pharmaceutical companies during the discovery process in civil litigation.

Business, too, will take the offensive, either to prevent a governmental solution, modify regulations, preempt local action, or simply to be able to win a rare victory. In Minnesota, oil companies were able to cooperate with jobbers, dealers, and state agencies on a program to clean up underground storage tanks, whereby industry agreed to tax itself. Oil's attitude was that it had better clean its own house because a government-dictated alternative would be much worse. Tobacco has been under siege for years, unable to hold the line on taxes and regulation. Recently, however, it took the offensive in a number of states, sponsoring legislation barring employment discrimination against smokers. Among other things, the industry wanted an issue on which it could win.

A permanent defensive posture, furthermore, can be debilitating over the longer run. A Florida lobbyist, who represented human services groups making claims on the budget, said she had recently switched from being reactive to proactive. It gives a group greater stature, she said, "People learn that they have to deal with you." A national association of businesses also had traditionally assumed a defensive posture in order to maintain the status quo. But the goodwill others felt for the group, according to its state government relations director, seemed to be dissipating. The enactment of regulations adverse to his association's interests was, in his view, imminent. He therefore developed a proactive strategy that involved consumer education, support of enforcement of antifraud provisions, and alternative means of conflict resolution.

"If you continue to only play defense, eventually someone's going to kick a field goal right by you" observed the executive director of the Pennsylvania trial lawyers group.[19] Despite such advice, business is not normally proactive. One of New Jersey's top contract lobbyists encourages clients to be proactive, telling them to go through the laws and regulations that affect them and then come up with a wish list of things they want changed. This lobbyist's largest clients have yet to give him their lists.

Fighting It Out

An analysis of interest-group positions on legislation has found that there is no conflict on most bills introduced in a legislature. That is demonstrated by a 1960s study of Iowa.[20] It is also the case with respect to education and welfare bills in California, Iowa, and Texas.[21] But a more general study of Texas found that on about half the bills, only one group took a position and conflict occurred over approximately a third of them.[22]

In view of the hundreds, even thousands, of bills introduced each session, it is not surprising that many are uncontested. We have already seen that a number are sponsored by administrative agencies and pertain to narrow, housekeeping matters. Others are for the benefit (usually symbolic) of unorganized constituencies. And still others are being monitored, but have so little support that their chances of going anywhere are minimal. On these, lobbyists need not declare a position.

Moreover, many bills stimulate no opposition. James Q. Wilson refers to them as measures that concentrate benefits and distribute costs. They benefit a well-defined special interest but impose no visible costs on any other interests.[23] Each lobbyist will have more than a few bills to pass that are not controversial and have no opponents. On a minor matter, if no one objects, the legislature's tendency is to go along and satisfy the group. Perhaps also, as we shall see in chapter 8, the parties that had a concern reached agreement beforehand.

Occasionally, achieving consensus can be a fairly easy matter. An example of such a "consensual" issue is a 1988 bill that permitted New Jersey dentists to diagnose and treat patients in the hospital. The legislation was initiated because the New Jersey Department of Health prohibited dentists from taking medical histories or treating patients in a hospital setting. The bill authorized dental work as long as a physician was consulted and the dentist's credentials were approved by the hospital. Supported by the dental, medical, and hospital associations, the bill won unanimous approval in each house of the legislature.

Allowing for bills that are relatively inconsequential and those where consensus can be reached beforehand, there still remains much for groups to fight about in the legislature. Wilson refers to measures that concentrate benefits and costs, but not in the same place. These proposals, benefiting a well-defined special interest, at a cost to another equally well defined special interest, generate organized conflict.[24]

Group conflict on legislative terrain is by no means new. There has always been substantial conflict, at least as legislators view it. A 1963 survey of more than eight hundred legislators in the fifty states indicated that they perceived conflict in the areas of business, labor, liquor, and water resources, and less in health and education.[25] But the incidence of conflictual issues appears to have increased during the past ten to fifteen years as legislatures have enlarged their scope and more and more issues have been fought out. That is the experience of veteran lobbyists. According to Ralph Haben, a contract lobbyist in Tallahassee: "Ten years ago there was nobody on the other side, and now you can assume 90 percent of the time some other lobbyist will object to what you want to do."[26] A Maryland lobbyist holds the same view. He cannot think of one recent case where he was not competing with some lobbyist on the other side of an issue. Often, although there is no active and direct opposition, his client is competing with others—and even with members of the legislature—for budgetary resources.

It is important to realize that, even if competition is not always direct, group may still be pitted against group. Some groups make claims on the state budget, competing with other claims and constrained by finite revenues and the legislature's unwillingness to raise taxes. For these groups, the appropriations process is a principal target. But as much as they want budgetary benefits, groups also want to avoid paying more than what they consider their fair share of the bill. A good part of business's agenda, therefore, is related to the structure of state tax systems and the incidence of taxes on business.

Looking for Bucks

"The real action is in the budget," remarked a California lobbyist for a nonprofit association. A Colorado lobbyist had a similar perspective: "A lot of it is how to get money, where to get it, and who will pay." Pro-choice groups lobby to make funds available to family-planning clinics. The pharmaceutical industry lobbies in the budgetary process to ensure that money is allocated to Medicaid, particularly to pay for the drugs that the industry markets.

Groups, such as teachers, cannot ignore the budget, as is illustrated by the experience of the Colorado Education Association (CEA) during the 1989 legislative session. Discounting funds essentially committed by prior budgets, only $125 million of new money was available for all the state's needs. CEA wanted $81 million of that amount for education. It lobbied the joint budget committee, the legislature's most powerful body, but came away with much less than it wanted. So CEA appealed to the group that would determine the fate of the budget bill (the so-called long bill) in the house, the majority party caucus, with its thirty-nine Republicans. Sitting around the room at each of the open caucus meetings were not only lobbyists from the CEA, the rest of the education community, and some of the large local school districts, but also those for the counties, cities, and special districts, and those wanting more money for prisons, highways, mass transportation, and whatever else. The caucus room was crowded.

Local-government groups normally focus on the state budget. The New Jersey League of Municipalities is constantly trying to identify funding programs that will benefit its constituents by helping them to finance local programs. Moreover, the league has also had to be concerned with getting the state to fund the programs it mandates and thus reduce the burdens on local governments. With the economic recession of 1990-1992 and the gap between projected revenues and expenditures in three-fourths of the states, the question for local governments was not how to maximize gains, but rather how to minimize losses. California's association of counties, for instance, in the 1990 session of the legislature argued that no one segment of government should bear the burden and called for "sharing the pain." It wanted state tax increases; Democratic legislators agreed but the Republican governor refused a general tax increase. The result was that funds for counties were cut by about $700 million.

Avoiding the Bill

Everyone wants to avoid paying more taxes, and most of us would like to pay less. Those who have, or who generate, money are in greater and more frequent peril than the rest of us. That means business interests. A Florida legislator, addressing a gathering of state government relations representatives of large companies and associations, advised that when the state needs money "you are all at risk." Business groups agree; taxes are the major issue facing them. Here, they are not in combat with any other group but rather with government itself. Every year, according to one government relations specialist, the tax departments of major national companies "go crazy just analyzing the impact of tax legislation in the various states."

When legislatures are looking for ways to balance the budget, the so-called sin taxes on alcohol and tobacco are always leading possibilities. The affected industries will argue that the proposed hikes are not fair and, furthermore, that retailers will be hurt because neighboring states tax these commodities less. But the political risks of reaching into the pockets of these industries are negligible. The position of Anheuser-Busch, in a battle that took place in one state, was that alcohol should not be singled out, but the company would consent to pay more if the legislature wanted to increase the sales tax and put it on everyone. Increasingly, also, efforts are being made to increase taxes on alcohol and tobacco and then earmark the funds for social-welfare causes, such as drug abuse, alcohol education, and cancer research. Business lobbyists much prefer that taxes remain a revenue issue and not become associated with a cause.

Another revenue measure that has aroused the ire of both business and professional groups in recent years is the sales tax on services. Many groups fought the Florida tax on services fiercely in 1987 and succeeded in getting it repealed the following year. Since then legislatures have been leery but, because of the 1990-1992 recession and the decline in revenues, they have tried to extend sales taxes to additional goods and services. Attorneys, real estate agents, and certified public accountants all have engaged in battle. The CPAs, for instance, have tried to defeat taxes on services or to gain a provision, as they did in Massachusetts, exempting small business. In New Jersey, Governor Florio's 1990 sales-tax package included a 7 percent tax on telecommunications. The cable television association argued that it would have cost their 1.7 million subscribers an extra $25 per year, causing a decline in subscribers and harming the industry. One of the current issues confronting business is that of health insurance, with the prospect that legislatures will impose a payroll tax on business to finance indigent care. All of these issues ensure the continued employment of the most skillful lobbyists at the state capitals.

Just as groups seek to avoid greater tax burdens, they also look for tax breaks and exemptions wherever they can. It may be a tax break for art collectors or a box to be checked on a return that allows the taxpayer to earmark an amount for the homeless. Or it may be a tax credit for solar-electricity producers in California, the principal beneficiary of which is an Israeli firm that is the largest solar energy producer in the world.[27] The Maryland General Assembly helped a trade association representing linen and uniform rental companies, exempting it from paying a sales tax on cleaning materials and equipment.

Local officials are strongly concerned about tax policy, as well as budgets. In Texas the big issue for cities is taxes because the state provides so little local aid. Whereas the per capita national average of state aid to cities is more than two hundred dollars, in Texas it is about three dollars. With respect to taxes, however, the situation in the Lone Star state is different. Property, sales, and franchise taxes all are at the top of the Texas Municipal League's legislative agenda.

Getting an Edge

Groups are engaged in a never-ending quest to pull even with or gain ground on their competitors. If possible, they would like to force them off the field entirely. The legislature is being asked to decide between competing private interests, cloaking its decision, whenever possible, in terms of broader values, such as equity or the public interest. Whatever the rationalization or rhetoric, however, the underlying issue is that of group advantage. Local Bell telephone companies endeavor to get from under state regulation; AT&T wants them to remain regulated. Florida tracks compete for racing dates for pari-mutuels; whoever gets the prime dates comes out ahead.

Oil jobbers press for legislation requiring retail marketing divorcement, which would force oil companies to give up local dealerships they own. The measure would weaken big oil. The petroleum industry is opposed. On the other hand, the New Jersey Petroleum Council continues to press for repeal of the ban on self-service gasoline stations in the states. An underlying reason is that conversion to self-service would force many of the independent stations out of business, thus strengthening the position of the large oil companies. The New Jersey Gasoline Retailers Association, as might be expected, strongly supports the ban.

The biggest running battles by far of recent years is that over tort reform, insurance, product liability, and workers' compensation, with the trial lawyers on one side and business, insurance, and doctors on the other. These issues have been at the top of the agenda in many states, including Florida, Minnesota, and New Jersey. The ongoing conflict has been described in Texas as one in which the trial lawyers have managed, through their strength in the legislature, to preserve a civil justice system to their liking. It has benefited their plaintiff clients in personal injury, medical malpractice, product liability, and other civil cases. It has also benefited trial lawyers themselves, who collect contingency fees of up to 30 percent of jury awards to their clients. Most recently, business and organized medicine in Texas have effectively challenged the trial lawyers. In 1989 the issue in conflict was the increasingly costly workers' compensation system. The business effort to revise the system was portrayed as an assault on "the rights of victims." It was also an assault on "the pocketbooks of their lawyers." [28]

As we noted earlier, one of the fiercest economic battles to be fought in recent years was that between car rental companies—Hertz and Avis versus Alamo and some of the smaller firms. Known to lobbyists as "Car Wars," the principal issue was the collision damage waiver (CDW), a contract provision in which the rent-a-car company waives its right to recover damages against the renter. Alamo and the smaller companies, which rented mainly to individuals, profited from the fees for such waivers, while Hertz and Avis, which dealt mainly with self-insured companies, had less of an investment in the practice. If they could have CDWs prohibited, their competitors would be put at a disadvantage.[29] The Hertz-Avis onslaught was nationwide. Legislation to abolish CDWs was proposed in at least thirty-five states, passing in Illinois and New York and taking effect in 1989. Elsewhere either Hertz and Avis were repulsed or, by way of compromise, car rental companies were limited in the amount of money they could charge per day. In Florida much of the top lobbying talent was hired to represent one side or the other. Yet legislators neither understood nor cared about the issue. It could hardly be called a public policy question of great moment. It was nevertheless highly political, and the factor that probably determined the outcome in favor of CDWs was that Florida was Alamo's home base. Since the first battle in Florida, the combatants have continued and are still, in the words of one of Tallahassee's lobbyists, "trying to stick it to one another." In California the battle between car rental companies was also intense; and it included issues besides CDW. As in Tallahassee, practically every top contract lobbyist was retained. Legislation to ban collision damage waivers was suggested by Hertz and Avis, initiated by the state attorney general, and carried by a reform-minded member of the assembly. It passed the assembly, but the opposition had organized by the time the bill reached the Senate judiciary committee. Hertz and Avis maintained that the consumer was being ripped off by CDW; their opponents framed the issue in David-and-Goliath terms. Hertz and Avis, their lobbyists suggested, were simply trying to kill off the competition. They argued, moreover, that if the bill passed, car-rental rates would go up because collision damage would be included in the regular rate. The outcome was a compromise—caps on collision damage waivers.

These past few years, Hertz and Avis have also attacked on issues of airport-access fees and advertising. The two largest companies are usually located on airport grounds, for which they pay a premium. They supported legislation requiring that companies not similarly situated pay a special access fee for transporting car renters to and from the terminals. Hertz and Avis won the round. They also challenged Alamo on its advertising, declaring its rates were misleadingly low because their ads did not truly reflect the charges. They won here as well.

Combat between professions over turf may not match the car wars insofar as the number of lobbyists employed. But they do provide relatively permanent employment to some of the capital's lobbying corps. Competing professional groups seek to expand or defend their economic turf. A classic battle, one that has been waged just about everywhere, matches optometrists against ophthalmologists, with the former asserting claims to administer prescription eye drops and the latter objecting. Lobbyists call this particular dispute, somewhat predictably, "Eye Wars." Another face-off finds the orthopedic surgeons on one side of the line and podiatrists on the other. The struggle is over ankle injuries, and the issue is whether or not podiatrists should be permitted to work on ankles. Critical to their practice is the definition, established by law, of where the foot stops and the ankle begins. When the issue was fought out in Colorado, the medical association was distracted by the other, numerous items on its agenda. In contrast, the podiatrists had the ankle high on their priority list. The podiatrists prevailed; the law that was enacted defined the ankle as part of the foot. Recently, dog groomers have started battling veterinarians, trying to acquire the right to brush a dog's teeth. If this conflict goes the way others have, we can look forward to seeing "Canine Wars" in various states.

A group seeking to establish itself professionally will normally seek the sanction of the state through regulation. Groups such as acupuncturists and massage therapists can achieve recognition if the legislature enacts a law regulating them. And they can gain greater control of their own destinies rather than be controlled by doctors on a board of medical examiners.[30] When groups such as these turn to the legislature for help, other groups rise to defend their domains. The battle is joined. As one contract lobbyist describes the situation: "The toughest legislation to get passed is legislation that annoys another group. The engineers annoy the architects, the occupational therapists annoy the physical therapists." These controversies, in this lobbyist's view, have little to do with the good of the public in general. Therefore, he contends, most of the bills that lobbyists support do not bear on public policy issues. "The public," he concludes, "is not the consideration."

Notes

1. Robert H. Salisbury, "Putting Interests Back into Interest Groups," in *Interest Group Politics,* ed. Allan J. Cigler and Burdett Loomis, 3d ed. (Washington, D.C.: CQ Press, 1991), 383-384.
2. Robert H. Malott, "The Emerging Importance of State Legislation." (Remarks by chairman and CEO of FMC Corp. to American Legislative Exchange Council, November 30, 1990.)
3. Keith E. Hamm, Charles W. Wiggins, and Charles G. Bell, "Interest Group Involvement, Conflict, and Success in State Legislatures: A Comparative Assessment." (Paper prepared for the Annual Meeting of the American Political Science Association, Chicago, September 1-4, 1983), 13.
4. *New York Times,* August 27, 1991.
5. Seymour Lusterman, *Managing Business-State Government Relations* (New York: The Conference Board, 1983), 8.
6. Max Boot, "Business Associations—Big Names, Less Clout," *California Journal,* October 1988, 454.
7. Kathleen Sylvester, "The Tobacco Industry Will Walk a Mile to Stop an Anti-Smoking Law," *Governing,* May 1989, 37.
8. See Bruce C. Wolpe, *Lobbying Congress: How the System Works* (Washington, D.C.: Congressional Quarterly Inc., 1990), 34.
9. Tom Watson, "Dale Florio: A Lobbyist's Middleman Who Helps Business Navigate State Capitol Halls," *Governing,* February 1989, 32-34, 37-38.
10. It is important to specify all the possible codes, otherwise something will be missed. A lobbyist for a telephone company, for example, keys the word "utilities" because such bills can also be amended to apply to telephone companies.
11. Randy Welch, "Lobbyists, Lobbyists All Over the Lot," *State Legislatures,* February 1989, 21.
12. *Tallahassee Democrat,* September 15, 1991.
13. A draft was provided to the author by Wade Hopping, a Florida lobbyist.
14. See Lusterman, *Managing Business-State Government Relations,* 48.
15. Harmon Zeigler and Michael A. Baer, *Lobbying: Interaction and Influence in American State Legislatures* (Belmont, Calif.: Wadsworth, 1969), 134.
16. Hamm, Wiggins, and Bell, "Interest Group Involvement," 16-17.
17. Watson, "Dale Florio," 34.
18. Still, anything can happen practically anytime, as long as amendments are in order on the floor or conference committees are still meeting.
19. Kathleen Sylvester, "The Chastening of the Trial Lawyers," *Governing,* February 1991, 28.
20. Cited in Charles W. Wiggins and William P. Browne, "Interest Groups and Public Policy Within a Legislative Setting," *Polity 15* (Spring 1982): 550-551.
21. Hamm, Wiggins, and Bell, "Interest Group Involvement," 25.
22. Charles Bell, unpublished paper, July 25, 1984.
23. James Q. Wilson, *Political Organizations* (New York: Basic Books, 1973), 333-334.
24. Ibid., 335-336.

25. Wayne L. Francis, "A Profile of Legislator Perceptions of Interest Group Behavior Relating to Legislative Issues in the States," *Western Political Quarterly* 24 (December 1971): 706-707.
26. Welch, "Lobbyists, Lobbyists," 19.
27. James Richardson, "Special Interests Dominate Legislative Session," *California Journal,* November 1990, 529.
28. Sylvester, "Chastening of the Trial Lawyers," 26, 28.
29. Hertz undertook its lobbying campaign against CDW after it pled guilty to federal charges in 1988 that it had defrauded customers by charging inflated and sometimes fictitious collision-repair costs. *Wall Street Journal,* February 8, 1990.
30. One of the reasons for the plight of the massage therapists was that they were listed in the yellow pages of the telephone book along with massage parlor therapists, a profession of a somewhat different order. In Iowa, for example, the former speaker (and now working as a lobbyist) is shepherding a bill through the house that would distinguish legitimate massage therapists from so-called massage parlors, which, the therapists claim, are little more than houses of prostitution. *Des Moines Sunday Register,* March 29, 1992.

CHAPTER 4

The Rules of the Game

In a report offering advice to lobbyists, the director of state relations at the Sun Company wrote: "Every state capital has a personality all its own. Never go out on a limb until you know exactly how the game is played." [1] This is sound advice. Each capital, indeed, each of the fifty states, possesses a distinct political culture. Political scientists recognize the importance of political culture. One of the classic studies in the field, a comparative exploration of legislative systems, found it to be significant in determining the modes and styles of pressure politics in four states. The political cultures of the six states where we interviewed lobbyists vary significantly. [2] With a tradition of progressivism, California's state government is known for its professionalism and policy initiatives. Colorado has a more populist reputation, and this can be seen in its persistent distrust for big government and big business. Florida's cultural roots are traditionalist, but today it has no coherent identity. Progressivism and populism are at the core of Minnesota politics, and the sense of a civic community there, while weaker than it used to be, still remains relatively strong. By contrast, politics in New Jersey is characterized by individualism, pragmatism, and, until the 1970s, a localism that dominated state politics. The political culture of Texas is more individualistic, even Darwinian, with power relationships and hardball politics the mode of interaction among elites. Here politics are personalistic and government is limited. [3]

Just as political scientists differentiate states according to political culture, they also categorize them according to the strength of their interest groups. They no longer find one or two interests, such as the

Southern Pacific Railroad in California, running a state, although gaming is still very influential in Nevada, oil in Texas and Louisiana, and agriculture in a number of the farm states. Otherwise, political pluralism has been expanding, with interest groups sharing power among themselves and with others. Naturally, the impact of interest groups on government differs from place to place. According to a recent series of studies, their impact is greatest in Florida, somewhat less in California and Texas, still less in Colorado and New Jersey, and least in Minnesota.[4]

While political culture and interest group environment are rather abstract concepts, the state's economy is a more concrete phenomenon. Its effects on lobbying may be indirect, but largesse or budgetary constraint can be felt by almost everyone involved in the governmental process. The climate of looming deficits and shrinking budgets, particularly in places like California, Florida, New Jersey, and Texas, can dominate a legislature's agenda. Take the case of California. The 1980s was a decade of fiscal crisis, dictating everything the legislature and many interest groups did. Budget issues overwhelmed everything. In times of economic recession and fiscal stringency, legislatures have to consider ways of raising revenues. Invariably, this entails taxing many of the groups represented by lobbyists. Moreover, when budgets are tight, legislatures tend to regulate behavior instead of initiating programs. This, too, affects groups that lobby.

The frameworks established by a state's political culture, interest groups, and economy are important in this regard. How do they affect the work of lobbyists? In the states we are studying—California, Colorado, Florida, Minnesota, New Jersey, and Texas—how do these settings differ as far as lobbyists are concerned? How are they alike? What are the rules of the lobbying game, and how have they been changing?

The Legislative Arena

Lobbyists must adapt to a particular legislative environment. What works in the Colorado General Assembly might not work in the Texas legislature. Lobbyists must also adapt to peculiar circumstances, which change from session to session and vary with the change of personnel. That means that what works in the New Jersey legislature today might not have worked there five years ago. It means that Florida with Lawton Chiles as governor is quite different from Florida governed by Bob Martinez. The structure of the legislature, how the legislative process works, the patterns of politics, and the distribution of power all affect how lobbying is carried on in the states.

The Structure of the Legislature

State legislatures have changed. They were transformed during the legislative modernization and reform period, which began after the reapportionments of the 1960s and lasted through the 1970s. Legislatures added skilled professional staff, raised salaries for members, and improved facilities. As legislatures became more developed, their collective sense of independence increased. The legislative branch became more powerful vis-à-vis the executive. As legislatures became professionalized, legislative office became more attractive, and different types of people were recruited to candidacy.[5]

The professionalization of legislatures and the careerism of recent generations of members have had substantial effects on state politics and on lobbying as well. California, the first of the nation's legislatures to professionalize, became a full-time body with a large staff and a membership committed to careers in public office. In the 1950s, before the structural transformation, twenty-five full-time lobbyists stationed in Sacramento could visit members in their home districts. There was time and opportunity for the most personal interaction. Such relationships no longer exist, and today the dominant medium of exchange in California is campaign finance and fund-raisers.[6]

Professionalization and careerism are also influential in Colorado, Florida, Minnesota, New Jersey, and Texas, albeit to varying extents. In each of these states legislators are devoting more and more time to the job, especially if constituent service and political stroking in their districts are considered part of the job. Legislatures as institutions are spending more time in either regular or special sessions and more time between sessions, doing interim work through standing and special committees. In each of these states, many members are devoting from half- to full-time to their work as legislators and otherwise behaving like careerists. Of the six states under consideration here, only Colorado seems determined to maintain a citizen legislature and, so far, has managed to do so. The others have moved inexorably in the other direction.

Careerist legislators are intent on remaining in their current office, at least until they can run for higher office. With hanging onto their jobs as an objective, the guiding questions for them are: "How do I stay in office?" and "Is this going to cost me votes?" Thus, many legislators are almost always campaigning. All of this alters relationships that members have with one another and with lobbyists. Many legislators today—whether in Colorado or Minnesota, California or New Jersey, Florida or Texas—have less time to develop personal relationships than did their predecessors. Instead, they are concerned about who will be opposing them in the next election, what groups will be giving them support, and how the necessary funds can be raised.

The new breed of legislator tends to have held only government or political jobs. In California, for instance, one out of three members now fits this description. A good number of them have ascended to legislative office after having served on congressional or legislative staffs. Fewer attorneys sit in the legislature nowadays, and this has weakened the position of trial lawyers and their agents. There are also fewer people who work for large corporations or in business generally. This has not helped the agendas of business lobbyists in the legislature. Quite the contrary; business has been hurt by the change from a citizen legislature to a careerist legislature dominated by individuals having no other occupations and by school teachers and government workers, but few businessmen. In Minnesota, where this has been the trend, one contract lobbyist commented that he and his colleagues "can feel the difference in the working of the legislature."

The emergence of women in state legislatures during the past twenty years has also changed the environment. One consequence is that more women have been able to make their way as lobbyists. Another consequence is that the legislative culture has changed. Take Colorado, where one-third of the legislators are women. The "good ol' boy" atmosphere is practically gone in Colorado and is no longer as pervasive even in Florida and Texas, which now has a female governor. The emergence of minorities has also made a difference. African American and Hispanic legislators (the latter in California, Florida, and Texas) not only provide special access for ethnic lobbyists, but also, like women, have put new items on the legislature's agenda.

Although the Colorado General Assembly still officially maintains its citizen-legislature status, it has undergone substantial change, thus altering the environment for lobbying. Here, too, more careerists are serving. Here, too, legislators have come to spend quite a bit of time in Denver, both in session and on interim and ad hoc committees. The composition of the legislature's membership has shifted markedly. The ranchers, farmers, lawyers, and businessmen who used to predominate are no longer willing to sacrifice the time or income required by legislative service. Moreover, few companies are willing to underwrite employees who take time off for the legislature. Therefore, according to one contract lobbyist, "not many legislators nowadays know what it means to meet a payroll."

Fewer members in Colorado are between the ages of thirty-five to fifty. Instead young men and women, recently out of school and with no steady occupational experience intervening, and retired people are finding their way to legislative office. The increasing number of women have included many who have been housewives and now are earning a second income in their families. One lobbyist characterized the membership of the Colorado General Assembly as follows: "Half of them don't have work. If they lost their seats, they wouldn't know what to do." This new generation of legislators provides a very different challenge for Colorado's lobbyists.

The nature of the legislative staff also makes a difference in how lobbying is conducted. Certainly staff members offer legislators a source of information, although they have hardly eliminated legislators' dependence on lobbyists in this regard. Legislators still rely on lobbyists for both technical and political information, but at least nowadays their staff serves as an alternative source. Staff has independent input, particularly on bills where substantial policy questions are involved. Its input diminishes, however, on questions that are less grand and where special interests competing for advantage dominate the scene.

In any case, where legislative staff does play a central role, lobbyists may have to lobby them as well as their legislator masters. Although the California legislature does not approach the congressional system, where everything has to go through staff, it comes closer than any other state. Lobbyists must reckon with committee consultants, individual aides, and leadership staff. In Florida, staff in the offices of the speaker of the house and president of the senate are key players. It is difficult for a lobbyist to reach the leaders without having to first deal with their staff. While committee staff also counts in Florida, its role is secondary to that of the chiefs of staff for the speaker and president. New Jersey's key staff personnel are in the majority-party offices of the two houses. Any Trenton lobbyist would be fortunate to have preferred access to the executive directors of the assembly and senate majority parties. In Texas the staff of the members themselves might serve as a barrier, particularly in the senate.

Of the six states, only in Colorado is staffing no problem for lobbyists. The Colorado legislature has a centralized, nonpartisan agency that provides basic service to committees and members. But the staff of the Office of Legislative Council keeps its distance from political and partisan matters and can devote little attention to many of the special-interest issues that lobbyists care about. In Colorado legislators have no alternative; they must rely on lobbyists for both sides of many issues. Despite variations in the size and patterns of staffing among the states, however, the similarities in lobbyist-legislator interaction outweigh the differences. Not only in Colorado, but in California, Florida, Minnesota, New Jersey, and Texas too, lobbyists enjoy access to legislators, leaders, and rank-and-file alike. They may have to work a little harder in some places, lobbying key staff as well as members, but their positions and their messages manage to get through.

Elements of the Process

Lobbyists have to know the legislative process in a particular state inside and out. When it comes to the interstices of process, no two places are alike. Each has its own procedures and routines, and lobbyists learn and adapt to them.

For one thing, the house and senate are very different institutions just about everywhere. Often, as had been the case in Florida, the rivalry between the two chambers is even greater than that between the two parties. Senates are smaller, more individualistic, and usually the leadership is weaker. Senators are generally more experienced than their colleagues in the house, the pattern being that a number of senators have served previously in the house. Thus, it makes sense for a lobbyist to work especially hard building relationships with house members, some of whom will move on to the senate. Lobbyists may find that they have to touch more bases in senates than in houses, because power is more broadly distributed. They may also find, as in the case of Texas, that the way the senate conducts business encourages compromise. If their tasks are primarily defensive, they need to win over just one house. Yet lobbyists cannot afford to neglect either chamber. There is no telling when they will have to get a bill passed, and no assurance that a particular house will acquiesce in killing a measure they oppose.

For another thing, the work schedules of legislatures vary markedly. California meets in regular session almost the entire year, breaking during the summer months and during the fall of even-numbered years when members are up for reelection. Colorado used to meet in an unlimited first-year session, with a 140-day constitutional limit on the second year. In 1988 voters approved a constitutional amendment limiting sessions to 120 calendar days.[7] Texas is one of only seven states in the nation that still meets biennially, for 140 calendar days. But in Texas special sessions are not at all unusual. New Jersey meets year round, but sessions are held on Mondays, and normally on Thursdays too, each week except for the summer months and the fall of odd-numbered years when legislative elections are held. Whatever the schedule, one thing is dead certain. As the session nears the date for adjournment sine die, the pace quickens. The last week, and especially the final days of the session, is usually frenzied. This is the make-or-break period for legislators and lobbyists alike. The schedule and metabolism of lobbyists must keep pace with that of the legislature.

Even when the session ends, legislative activity continues. Special sessions are becoming common occurrences, especially in Texas. Committee work during the interim period is the practice in Colorado, Florida, Minnesota, and Texas. For the lobbyist, the legislature is rarely dormant. Something is always going on, and a client's interests may well be at stake.

The process by which bills are considered and voted on also varies from place to place. This naturally affects how lobbyists do their jobs. Well-connected lobbyists can usually find a legislator willing to sponsor a bill that they are pushing. For many legislators in most places, introducing a bill on behalf of a constituent or group is not considered heavy-duty work. For them, sponsorship does not necessarily imply ardent support. The bill may not get far, but at least a lobbyist has a bill introduction to show for his or her efforts. Legislators in some states are limited, however, by rule or custom as to the number of bills they may introduce at a session. Such restrictions force them to be far more discriminating. The contemporary practice in Colorado limits a member to five bill introductions. This means that legislators have to be selective in what they choose to introduce, thus making it difficult for lobbyists who are on the offensive and seeking a sponsor. It is not unusual to have a legislator beg off when asked by a lobbyist to sponsor a bill. "I've already used up all my titles" is a frequent reply. The lobbyist then has to scramble and look elsewhere.

A bill limitation, as practiced in Colorado and also in the Florida house, helps interests on the defense. So does the process generally. In some places, however, the offense gets a break. Colorado's GAVEL ("Give a Vote to Every Legislator"), which passed by the initiative process in 1988, requires that every bill be given a hearing and voted on in committee. This makes it difficult for committee chairs to bottle up legislation, as is done in most other states. But there are still hurdles in Colorado, such as the calendar for floor consideration, to be overcome.

In some places, by contrast, defensive interests get an even greater break. In Texas, according to several lobbyists, the process is designed to protect the establishment. On the house side of the capitol, the speaker has the power to refer a bill to whatever committee he chooses. And the State Affairs Committee in each chamber has traditionally been known as the graveyard for legislation. Nor are standing committees in Texas required to take up or report out bills. Furthermore, if legislation is reported out, the House Calendar Committee serves to kill bills opposed by leadership. On the senate side, an extraordinary two-thirds' majority of the members present is required to put a bill on the calendar. Therefore, only eleven out of thirty-one members of the Texas senate are needed to kill anything. That is one reason why certain groups, such as the trial lawyers, have contributed generously to senate races and why their cause has achieved strength within that body. In Texas, to be on the defense is to have a head start. Nonetheless, a head start is not everything. The system also works to get legislation through, but only after both sides have had their say. The very size of the senate and the way the body does its business work to encourage compromise. To a large extent, much of the process in Texas as elsewhere is one of devising language in legislation with which both sides can live.

New Jersey's process balances defensive and offensive considerations. On the one hand, a constitutional majority is necessary to pass a bill, so members who abstain or take a walk are essentially voting "no." In the eighty-member assembly, for instance, a bill needs forty-one votes to pass. It does not matter how many red lights appear on the tally board, but only whether forty-one green lights come on. On the other hand, during a two-year legislature, a bill is never dead, even if it seems to have been dispatched on several occasions. "A bill never loses in New Jersey," commented a contract lobbyist, "it just does not win." Once on third reading, the bill remains on third reading and in a position for a vote. So the defensive lobbyist always has to be on guard with respect to bills he or she thinks are dead, but may still breathe some life. The safest tactic is to have a bill that does not pass referred back to committee, where it can at least be bottled up if not killed.

Just about everywhere, the moment of truth for lobbyists comes during the final days or hours of the session. That is their last chance to score, or be scored against. The hope, and the fear, then is an amendment. Colorado lobbyists, who are up against a stringent limit on bill introductions, can get a legislator to introduce a measure as an amendment to another bill on the floor. The Colorado requirement is that an amendment to a bill be germane, but germaneness may usually cover a wide swath. And if the bill's sponsor agrees to an amendment, the measure favored by a lobbyist has a better chance of adoption. In Florida, probably more than anywhere else, the process of amendment dominates the close of the session. Legislators and lobbyists here are constantly on the lookout for "vehicles," that is, bills to which they can attach amendments when the time is appropriate. Thus during the final days, a number of bills become "trains," going from one house to another, with the original bill functioning as the engine that picks up car after car of amendments. These trains may include bills that passed one house but not the other or that never had a hearing in either house. Each lobbyist is intent on ensuring that the train on which his or her measure is riding does not get derailed. At the same time, each lobbyist is working assiduously to wreck the train that runs against his or her client's interests. The action is fast and furious.

Politics and Power

Any lobbyist who ignores the politics of the state and of the legislature cannot possibly succeed at the job. Politics drives the process, although in some states more than others partisanship is more acute, and in some competition is harder. Among the six states under special observation here, partisanship still is not a dominant factor in Texas. Conservative Democrats continue to control, although the number of Republicans has been increasing. Partisanship is more of a factor in

Colorado, even though Democrats have long been a minority in the house and senate. It is on the rise in Florida, however, where party affiliations have been changing and Republicans are threatening Democratic control of the senate. In contrast, partisanship clearly dominates in California, Minnesota, and New Jersey, where the contest between Democrats and Republicans is intense, continuous, and often bitter.

Naturally, partisanship is exacerbated in an election year. But the campaign in states like California and New Jersey never ends, and so there is no such thing as an "election year." Fund-raising goes on year-in and year-out, and lobbyists above all others feel the pinch. The incentives for individuals to win reelection and of parties to maintain or gain control are so powerful that lobbyists cannot help but be squeezed. When electoral politics takes over in the legislature, as in New Jersey in 1989 with the assembly speaker and senate president both running for governor, the lobbyist's agenda must adjust accordingly. The legislature's course becomes even more overwhelmed by political considerations.

As far as lobbyists are concerned, the office of governor is critical. As governor of Minnesota, for instance, Democrat Rudy Perpich vetoed business-sponsored bills on workers' compensation. His Republican successor, Arne Carlson, however, is more sympathetic to business's position. In California, the National Organization for Women went through eight years without access to the office of Governor George Deukmejian. It was not even possible for the group to work out compromises on issues like family leave. The change in governors from Thomas Kean, a Republican, to Jim Florio, a Democrat, had a clear impact on the New Jersey Business and Industry Association. With Kean, the association made headway on product liability, tort reform, and antitakeover legislation. With Florio (and a Democratic legislature) the association had to adopt a more defensive posture, especially in the environmental area.

Who controls the senate and the house is even more critical for most lobbyists than who controls the office of governor. Tort reform and product liability, for example, tend to find Republicans siding with business interests and Democrats siding with trial lawyers and consumer groups. On these issues, the lawyers have a better chance when Democrats are in the majority and business has the edge when Republicans are on top. This is the situation in Minnesota, where the trial lawyers are able to hold the line with Democratic majorities in the legislature, but would be in trouble if Republicans won the two houses. There may be little danger of that, since the Democratic Farm Labor party has controlled the legislature for eighteen of the past twenty years. In New Jersey, when the Republicans controlled the assembly, environmentalists failed to pass the Clean Water Enforcement Act. Soon after the Democrats took control (and Florio assumed the governorship), the act was passed and signed into law. In 1992 the Republicans took firm control of both houses, and the lobbying situation changed once more. By contrast, in Colorado, where Republicans hold both houses, environmentalists have had to settle for very modest gains. Similarly, where prochoice forces, mainly Democrats, are in charge, as in Florida, their opponents have little hope.

Partisan control is not the only element in the process, however. The two houses have quite dissimilar structures, processes, and makeups. In Florida, for example, the house has traditionally been more progressive than the senate. Thus, conservative interests typically defend their positions most forcefully in the upper house. By contrast, in Texas the conservatives have an advantage in the house.

Who controls the executive branch and each of the houses matters considerably to lobbyists. So does the distribution of positions of power. The influence of different interests and lobbyists depends on who is in the top leadership positions. A study of the Pennsylvania legislature observed that, some twenty years ago, the lobbyists for the Penn Central Railroad and the Sun Company were so close to the senate leadership that the press dubbed them the fifty-first and fifty-second members of that body.[8]

Whenever a new administration comes into power in a state capital, certain lobbyists are likely to rise in prominence. In Texas, those lobbyists who used to work on the staff of the speaker, Gib Lewis, entered the ranks of power-broker lobbyists. Recently, those lobbyists who had supported Ann Richards in her race for governor took on added luster when she assumed office. Florida's senate president and house speaker turn over every two years, as do most of the committee chairmanships. Different lobbyists rise with each new group of leaders. The inner circle of lobbyists therefore changes as the top political establishment does. A Florida lobbyist explained it tersely: "Had Martinez won [the governorship] and beaten Gwen Margolis [for the presidency of the senate], we'd be closed." As it was, however, this particular lobbyist was very much open for business because of his earlier career and relationships.

A connection with leadership certainly helps, but it is not sufficient. In state legislatures, as in the Congress, it is no longer possible to make one's case with a powerful few. Instead, the lobbyist now has to contact a wider group of members and touch more bases.[9] One lobbyist said it was a "different ballgame compared to when I first came on the scene." Apparently, things used to be a lot simpler—only the speaker, the committee chairman, and one or two others counted. "Today, you get your votes one at a time," this lobbyist explained, "no power brokers. It's a much more fluid situation.... Even when you think you've got a situation well in hand, you're never quite sure until the vote is over." [10]

Power is more dispersed just about everywhere today. In the New York legislature, the new senate Republican majority leader, Ralph Marino, has had to cede some of the power once held by his predecessor,

Warren Anderson, to members of his caucus. Once the rank-and-file tastes power, it is not apt to give it up. The same is true in Minnesota, where in earlier days members could not get a copy of the bills they were considering on the floor. In contrast, today information is available to everyone and each member has a copy of every bill and every amendment. For this and other reasons, power in the Minnesota legislature is widely diffused, and both leaders and committee chairs have a tougher time controlling legislation. Lobbyists have to deal with every legislator, and not just the powerful few. Texas has moved in a similar direction. In the 1970s everything was decided by the leadership. One lobbyist recalls: "If you played ball with Gus Mutscher [the speaker] and Lieutenant Governor Ben Barnes, their lieutenants would carry a lobbyist's bill, work the floor, and get it through unscathed." [11] Since then, however, the power of leaders has diminished and lobbyists now have to work the members as well.

California and Florida are not terribly different, despite the fact that leaders in each place still retain considerable power. In California no one person can make things happen. Power is spread around. As one lobbyist explains: "Today, doing business at the capitol means talking to a laundry list of barons: committee chairmen, subcommittee chairmen, majority leaders, fiscal committee members, etc. And that's only after you've talked to their staffs." [12] Florida's legislature has also suffered from fragmentation. For some time, the senate has been an individualistic body. More recently, the rise of Republicans and the emergence of African American and Hispanic caucuses divided the house. And single-member districts tended to produce parochial representatives. "There is no longer a feeling of collective will," declares one Tallahassee lobbyist.

A book detailing the dos and don'ts of lobbying in Washington, D.C., notes that, "Lobbyists must adapt to the prevailing rigors and mores of the institution." [13] As in Congress, so too in state legislatures. In the states, as well as in the nation, political and institutional change has been accompanied by change in legislative norms. Many lobbyists believe the norms are eroding, indeed that the institutional fabric of the legislature has deteriorated. They attribute this, in part, to the individualism of members preoccupied with their careers, reelections, constituencies, and pet policies. The intense struggle among single-issue groups and between the political parties is also believed to be at blame.

One historically paramount norm, keeping one's word, also appears to have weakened considerably. Lobbyists, as has been stressed, must keep their word; but legislators are freer agents. Today, they are less likely to commit. And if they do, it is not unusual for them to renege. "If someone gives you his word, it's a definite maybe," observes one Florida contract lobbyist and former legislator. Another Florida lobbyist, employed by an association, explains: "You can't depend on what they tell you. In terms of commitment, it depends on who was there last." He therefore advises that, when counting votes, lobbyists should have substantial margins to allow for switches. Otherwise, they will be in serious trouble. In earlier days people in Minnesota made a deal on a handshake. Nowadays, according to a lobbyist for an association, "You can go into a legislative office and you think you have a deal, and then you're surprised in committee." This lobbyist believes the integrity of the process has declined.

Legislators themselves recognize what is taking place and blame it on the pressures of contemporary politics. In remarks to a number of lobbyists assembled at a summer institute, Rep. John Martin, speaker of the Maine house and 1991 president of the National Conference of State Legislatures, acknowledged that "legislators make a deal during the week, and then they go home. When they come back on Monday, their minds have changed." [14] Almost as soon as they are on, all bets are off; and parties to the deal have to start again from scratch.

Recent political and institutional developments have not made life happier for veteran lobbyists. Newcomers may welcome change that breaks up the closed circles of established insiders. But the old-timers, who look back to the 1960s and even 1970s, are of a very different mind. For them, lobbying is less fulfilling now. Alan Marcus, a veteran contract lobbyist in New Jersey, spoke for many of his colleagues when he said "it's getting harder and harder to work in the political process. . . . It's become too partisan, too mean-spirited." [15]

Partisanship, ideological warfare, polarization, fragmentation all are taking their toll on the community of lobbyists. Take Colorado and Minnesota, two states with progressive traditions and strong and effective legislatures. A Colorado lobbyist related how he started in politics almost thirty years ago at a time when legislators and lobbyists together were truly trying to solve problems and made the compromises necessary in order to do so. That system, in his opinion, does not operate anymore. Now so many interests are affected by a problem that there is no real incentive to solve it. Furthermore, legislators are more preoccupied with reelection and fund-raisers and lobbyists are concerned about their clients and businesses. The environment has deteriorated because of more interests and more players and less leadership.

Minnesota's increasingly careerist legislature has also dismayed veteran lobbyists. What used to be a very compromising legislature is now much more rigid. Single-issue politics and ideological convictions are causing greater polarization—business versus labor, conservatives versus liberals, both sides of the abortion-rights issue, Democratic Farm Laborites versus Independent Republicans, and even one wing of the Chamber of Commerce versus the other. According to one lobbyist, people are so uptight that "you can't go over there and not get engaged in conversation over abortion." For that and other reasons, old-school lobbyists do not regard it as fun anymore.

The Capitol Community

Every day the Florida legislature is in session, lobbyists will gather between the two chambers on the capitol's fourth floor. This area, known as Ulcer Alley, is where lobbyists can send a note into the chamber asking a senator or representative to leave the floor and confer with them for a moment. This is where lobbyists can watch deliberations on television monitors, discuss amendments and bills with allies, and use their cellular telephones to contact their offices and their clients.[16]

A large part of lobbying is being able to reach people. Portable phones have made a big difference in this respect. Lobbyists move faster and feel more secure scurrying about with a phone at their beck and call. Neal T. "Buddy" Jones, a power lobbyist in Texas, carries a cellular phone in his briefcase. As he stood outside the house chamber, Jones pulled out the phone to make a call. Behind him, a few feet away, was a row of public phones. When asked why he didn't save money by using public phones, Jones answered with a smile: "I don't carry quarters." [17] Some lobbyists do carry quarters; not everyone can afford a cellular telephone. Those who lobby for causes cannot; some of them are said to use a can and a string in place of a portable phone.

Given modern technology—bill tracking by computer, cellular phones, and pagers—contemporary lobbyists are far better informed and more immediately in touch than their predecessors. With respect to the place and role of lobbyists in the capitol community, change is also taking place, but it is more gradual than the change in technology.

Within each capital city, legislators, staff, lobbyists, and journalists can be thought of as members of the capitol community. This community, according to the director of state government relations for the Sun Company, is a "loose-knit fraternity of independent individuals who share common interests." [18] Like the legislative arena itself, the capitol community shapes the interactions between lobbyists and legislators.

Traditional Social Life

During the sixty days when the legislature is in session, the city of Tallahassee is transformed from a quiet place, albeit the site of state government and a major state university, to a buzzing, swirling swarm of legislators and lobbyists. The city's very size and design facilitate the social lives of members of the political community. People hang around the capitol, they socialize, and they enjoy one another's company. The culture is such that legislators find themselves in the closest proximity to lobbyists. Austin is much larger than Tallahassee, but it exerts similar charm for members of the political community. Thought to be a more delightful spot than any other place in Texas, neither legislators nor lobbyists (with the possible exception of those from Dallas and Houston) are eager to return home when the session ends. The culture in Austin also encourages legislators and lobbyists to get together.

Even in Florida and Texas, socializing is interrupted on weekends when legislators go home to their districts. Florida's legislators arrive in Tallahassee Sunday evening and leave Thursday evening, unless they are on the Appropriations Committee, which meets Friday morning. Although they stay in the capital the last two weeks of the session, the socializing diminishes. In New Jersey, socializing is limited by the fact that every legislator commutes to Trenton one or two (or possibly three) days a week. In a commuter legislature, social life is necessarily limited; only those members who live relatively close to Trenton are likely to stick around after hours. Although Colorado and Minnesota do not have commuter legislatures, many members come from the metropolitan areas of Denver and Minneapolis-St. Paul. They drive between their houses and the capitol on a daily basis. About three out of five of Colorado's legislators live in Denver or its suburbs. They seldom remain for any but obligatory political and social activities. Over half of Minnesota's legislators live within commuting distance. They, too, prefer going home to staying late in St. Paul to mingle with lobbyists.

Nonetheless, the opportunities exist for lobbyists to come together with legislators in social rather than business settings. Many, but by no means all, lobbyists take advantage of such opportunities, seeking to get as much informal time with legislators as possible. This is their way of building and sustaining relationships, and of getting in some business besides. For example, during the 1983 session members of the Colorado house were invited to forty-eight cocktail parties, forty-four lunches, forty breakfasts, nineteen dinners, and twenty-three other functions during their six-month session.[19]

Many receptions are held for legislators at a hotel or restaurant or sometimes in the capitol building itself. These are sponsored and hosted by groups that range from tavern owners to cable television to health care to the education association. Almost every major association uses the reception as an occasion to bring in group members, as well as their lobbyists, and chat casually with as many legislators as possible. During the 1991 sixty-day session of the Florida legislature, for instance, about eighty receptions or similar functions were held during the day or night—on Tuesdays, Wednesdays, and Thursdays, but not during the final week.

When receptions were hosted by only a few groups, they served to get the legislature's attention. But nowadays, with everyone doing it, receptions may be losing their impact. Moreover, the large galas are now a little outmoded. For instance, Associated Industries of Florida, which represents about four thousand businesses, held its last big party years ago when nearly 100 of 160 legislators attended.[20] Nonetheless, legislators feel obliged to attend, especially if any of their constituents are present. They often do so mechanically or grudgingly, because they are obliged to show up at three or four events in the same evening. Sometimes legislators send their aides, whose main mission is to simply pick up their boss's nametag from the registration table and make it appear that the legislator has put in an appearance. Legislators try to attend as a courtesy and perhaps to show support for the lobbyist who is responsible for the function. At the start of the General Assembly's 1991 session, for instance, the Colorado Education Association held a reception from 5 to 7 p.m. About half the legislators, and mainly those from out-state, showed up. One from the Denver area, who also stopped by, said, "I came because it was right downtown, and I could do it on my way home."

Lobbyists have scant chance to mingle with legislators who are on the run at some group's receptions. Sometimes they have to settle for "pigs in a blanket" and white wine, some networking and schmoozing. They may not do much better at fund-raisers; but these too are practically obligatory. In California, where entertaining lobbyists is severely limited by law, fund-raisers have become the major social (as well as political) events. They have taken the place of entertaining in Sacramento, where during some periods there may be six different fund-raisers on the same night. "Afterwards, if you want to go to dinner," said a contract lobbyist, "you go dutch." The crowds at fund-raisers are large and legislators have little time to talk with any single individual. Still, lobbyists feel they ought to attend, to be seen and to shake hands. It is their way of showing support for the particular legislator and for the process.

A variation on the customary reception is the annual New Jersey State Chamber of Commerce train trip from Newark to Washington, D.C. Dating to the 1930s, the event brings together more than a thousand of New Jersey's politicians, lobbyists, business leaders, and lawyers, who all work the train and make and renew contacts. The trip is not the occasion it used to be, but it nevertheless permits lobbyists to ply their trade.

Lobbyists do far better, as far as "quality time" is concerned, in the watering holes, clubs, restaurants, and even their homes. They pick up the tab for drinks and dinner and, in return, have the company of one or several legislators for an hour or two. The watering hole, however, is a shadow of its former self. There is still Bones, a tavern in Jefferson City, Bull Ring in Santa Fe, Galleria in Columbus,[21] and, of course, Clyde's, an old fashioned gin mill, only a few steps from the capitol building in Tallahassee. "I can talk to ten people there," says one lobbyist, "and know what's going on." However, many more lobbyists than legislators do their fraternizing at Clyde's.

Then there are the restaurants where lobbyists treat legislators to lunch or dinner. Lorenzo's in Trenton gets a legislator-lobbyist clientele on session days, but fifteen years ago the Marroe Inn was an even more popular spot for drinks and dinner. Frank Fats is still the place in Sacramento, although California legislators cannot accept gifts such as meals from lobbyists and therefore have to pay their own way. In Denver, lobbyists take legislators to breakfast at Racine's or to lunch at the Profile, but evenings are ordinarily a time for receptions. A number of Colorado's lobbyists, particularly those representing localities, nonprofits, and cause groups, do their entertaining in the capitol cafeteria. In Austin, where the Petroleum Club is popular with high flyers, the capitol's basement cafeteria—known as the Linoleum Club—is for those with limited expense accounts. Both the basement and fifth-floor cafeterias at the capitol in Tallahassee and the basement cafeteria at the capitol in Denver also do a thriving business. Legislators and lobbyists and lobbyists and lobbyists deal with one another over a quick breakfast or lunch in fast, if not furious, fashion.

More leisurely interactions are afforded by the clubs, which are a feature of most capital cities. Virtually every important lobbyist in Austin belongs to the Austin Club.[22] Several lobbyists hold an informal gathering called the "Breakfast Club" three days a week during the session at the Governor's Club, a block from the Florida capitol. A few legislators attend. The place for lunch in Tallahassee is at the same Governor's Club, to which many of the lobbyists belong. Sacramento has the Derby Club, which has a weekly lunch attended by legislators and lobbyists—considerably more of the latter than the former. The most leisurely interaction takes place when lobbyists invite a few legislators to their homes for dinner. Home entertainment has become a practice preferred by a number of the most influential lobbyists in Florida, particularly former legislators. A lobbyist's home would appear to be one of the best settings for conversation and the development of relationships.

To some extent, too, lobbyists convene with legislators at sporting events. In New Jersey, some watch professional football from a field box at Giants Stadium. In St. Paul some get together for a home game of the Minnesota Twins. In Florida it may be a football or basketball game hosted by the University of Florida or by Florida State. There are few poker games anymore, but lobbyists will find a way to jog or play tennis with a legislator or take lawmakers for golf. For a number of them, the best form of entertainment is golf. In Austin, "the biggest deal is golf and Barton Creek is the best golf club—so you take members to play golf."

Last—and probably least in terms of their incidence—are the trips that lobbyists arrange for legislators. They may go on a hunting or fishing trip or travel to a resort or an otherwise desirable locale. There are other kinds of trips, too, such as the evening canoe trip on which two of Florida's environmental lobbyists take up to eight legislators. The cost of the entire trip runs—for the canoes, chicken, wine, and beer—under $300. For legislators, a trip may be tantamount to a free minivacation. For lobbyists, it is the most time with legislators that they are likely to ever get. For both groups, the excursions tend to be pleasurable affairs. In most states, it should be pointed out, expense-paid vacations for legislators are very much the exception to the rule. A few lobbyists do take a few legislators traveling. But most legislators are not offered, or do not accept, such blandishments.

In some states, however, trips have become a routine feature of the social environment. Texas is one such place. In 1987, for example, two lobbyists took a dozen legislators to a Florida golf resort. A month earlier, one of the two had taken a few members to the Masters Tournament in Augusta, Georgia. That same year, three legislators were treated to Super Bowl weekend. Hunting and fishing trips were really the staple of lobbyists. But reportedly the best of many trips for legislators was a visit to the King Ranch as guests of the cattle lobby.[23]

Florida is another place where lobbyist-funded trips had become rather common, as was demonstrated by the 1990 investigation by the Leon County state attorney into the travel of state legislators. He found that more than thirty legislators had failed to disclose trips (and other gifts), a second-degree misdemeanor in the state. Twenty-four of them were charged; all but one pleaded nolo contendere and paid small fines. Funded mainly by the major utilities, auto dealers, hotel industry, insurance, and big agriculture,[24] trips over the past few years extended across the continent and overseas.

A number of Florida legislators ranged far and wide in order to fish and hunt: deer and geese in Texas; turkeys in Alabama; quail in Georgia; deer and elk in Wyoming; doves in Mexico; and fish in Alaska. Pleasure trips took certain legislators to Paris, Zurich, Monte Carlo, St. Tropez, San Francisco, Lake Tahoe, New Orleans, Vail, Breckenridge, and on a Caribbean cruise.[25] Late in 1989 one out of five members of the Florida legislature attended the Breeder's Cup horse races at Gulfstream Park in south Florida, and had complimentary hotel accommodations, meals, airfare, and tickets to the track. That same year, one out of four attended the University of Florida-Florida State football game as the guest of the universities and their lobbyists. The biggest annual event for legislators has been the annual Walt Disneyworld weekend. One out of three members was there, many with their families, who were also invited.[26]

Florida lobbyists benefit from the goodwill these trips buy and the access it affords them. But in more than a few instances, the idea for an excursion is not theirs but that of legislators. Lobbyists contend that they often furnished the trips at the request of legislators. For example, a few years ago an insurance lobbyist arranged a trip to the Bahamas for supporters of the new speaker. This has since become a spring ritual. But the first trip was put together at the request of one of the speaker's legislative allies who wanted to bring his supporters together before the session. Along similar lines, Rep. Sam Mitchell has sponsored an annual hunting weekend in the Florida panhandle for legislative and lobbyist friends. Lobbyists donate the food and liquor and pay $500 each to attend what has become known as "Big Sam's Hunt," [27] defraying whatever costs legislators may incur.

Changing Times

The capitol community is not what it used to be, and it keeps changing. The old days are dimly remembered now. Lobbyists no longer preside at bars and brothels, dispensing patronage to supplicant legislators.[28] Nor are the clubs in Sacramento still the centers of life they once were. "Moose Milk," the Derby Club, "Clam and Corral," all paid for by a number of lobbyists and attended by legislators, are either history or irrelevant. In Denver the poker table in the press room and the refrigerator stacked with beer have vanished. No longer does the clerk of the house in Florida maintain a secret lounge under a stairway in the capitol where legislators can take a few snorts from a stash of liquor donated by the liquor lobby.[29] In St. Paul, the high jinks and antics of members of the house (and to a lesser extent the senate) are remembrances from a distant past.

Today legislative life is "less like fraternity life," observes Jonathan Walters. [30] Just about everywhere parties are fewer, wining and dining has diminished, and spending is down. Not too long ago a $1,000 dinner bill at the end of a legislative day in Trenton was not unusual. A large contingent of members would go out, eat, and get drunk on some lobbyist's tab. Not anymore. Entertaining goes on, but nowadays it is more of a hit-or-miss affair. "Sometimes," reported one Trenton lobbyist, "I don't even pick up the check." The Profile in Denver used to be packed with legislators, but no longer. In St. Paul the hangouts like the Gopher Grill of the St. Paul Hotel, the Criterion, or Galvin's are gone. There is no single place where one can find a group of legislators after hours. Watering holes are going out of style, and entertaining is an industry in decline for a number of reasons.

The culture is very different today; many more people are involved, including women. The back room has become crowded and the doors are no longer closed. Moreover, the process has been opened up and legislators are always under the scrutiny of the media and public. The media can be relentless in its condemnation of legislator-lobbyist socializing. The Florida press corps, for instance, has been extremely critical, as is illustrated by the following account that appeared in the *Pensacola Journal:*

> The Florida Legislature is a wide-open playland for lobbyists armed with unlimited expense accounts. And so many of their playmates— who in their spare time make this state's laws—have become so openly greedy that it's not clear that they even recognize it as greed anymore.[31]

The drumbeat of criticism can become inhibiting. A Texas lobbyist explained the dilemma of the members: "They want to have fun; and yet they work their asses off. But they can't win. They're cut to pieces whichever way they go."

Life-styles are different today. Legislators, like most other people in this society, are conscious of their health. They eat less and drink less. A lobbyist who wants to take a legislator to lunch may find that he or she spends lunchtime at an athletic club. At night, members who live nearby want to go home; the rest will take work back to their hotel rooms, apartments, or condominiums where they live when in the capital. Oftentimes, a committee will be meeting in the evening or some other work session is taking place. Most legislators are too busy for dinners and lunch. One Texas lobbyist noted that, almost five months into the 1991 session, he had had fewer than ten meals with members. Moreover, when legislators have time free they often reserve it for their colleagues. Florida senators gave up heavy-duty partying a while ago; nowadays they are more likely to have quiet evenings out together. Texas legislators, it is reported, rise early and hold private sessions along the jogging paths of Austin's Lake Travis or while rowing in a shell captained by the speaker.[32]

Families and work dominate not only for legislators, but for lobbyists too. Nearly everyone is turning away from lavish entertaining. A lobbyist in Texas loves the game of golf, but had not played once with a member during the session. He was simply too busy. A Minnesota contract lobbyist indicated that he would take lawmakers to lunch or dinner if they were old friends or if it was the only time they could meet. But he did not hang around in the evenings to take legislators out. In any case, the pickings would be too slim; no one would be around. A veteran association lobbyist in New Jersey believes his age and experience preclude the need for socializing. He wants to see his family in the evenings. "By the end of the day, I'm ready to go home," said a Florida contract lobbyist, "and I take a pile of paper with me."

Wining and dining, furthermore, is not the preferred style of many contemporary lobbyists. "If I get to the capitol early, spend my time wisely, and leave when I'm ready, that's what it takes," commented a lobbyist in Tallahassee. "A lot of the other stuff is folderol," she continued, "they stand around the same cheeseball, but nothing happens."

Newly enacted legislation has also had an impact on the community life of legislators and lobbyists. Probably nowhere has the law had a more marked effect than in California. The Political Reform Act of 1974, Proposition 9 on the ballot, effectively ended the entertainment era in Sacramento, prohibiting gifts larger than $10 to any public official in a single month and requiring detailed disclosures. The ethics law in California was tightened further in 1990 with the passage of Proposition 112 and a law enacted by the legislature. The new law barred honoraria, limited gifts, applied gift limitations to principals as well as lobbyists, virtually eliminated free trips, curtailed the postemployment of legislators as lobbyists for one year, and required ethical-conduct courses for legislators and lobbyists. It should be noted, however, that the ballot measure also created a salary commission that will facilitate the raising of legislator salaries.

But Wisconsin probably has the most restrictive laws today, at least as far as gifts and entertainment are concerned. Except in limited instances, a Wisconsin legislator may not accept anything of pecuniary value—travel, a meal, a cup of coffee—from a lobbyist or a principal. (This means that if an interest group holds a reception in Madison, any legislators who stop by must pay for whatever they eat or drink, while everyone else is treated as a guest.) A staff document suggests that to protect themselves from violating this prohibition, legislators "should ask any person who offers something of value whether or not that person is listed as a lobbyist or principal in the registry maintained by the Office of the Secretary of State." It also counsels legislators to review the list of lobbyists and principals, which is filed every week in each house.[33] It should be noted, however, that even with such restrictive laws twelve legislators and six lobbyists were charged with giving or taking meals and trips. One senator resigned and served time in jail as a consequence.

The trend nationwide is toward the limitation, if not prohibition, of gifts and the disclosure of expenditures by lobbyists on individual members. Laws are being written "to isolate legislators from the generous expense accounts of people who want to influence them."[34] Georgia and South Carolina now have stiff laws. Florida's new ethics law bans honoraria and speaking fees. It also prohibits public officials from accepting gifts worth more than $100 from lobbyists, their principals, or PACs, and requires disclosure of gifts worth more than $25. Florida legislators can still accept all the food and drink they can consume in a single sitting. Texas's new ethics law bans pleasure trips and limits the amount that can be spent on entertainment to $500 and gifts to $500 per member each year. Food and drink do not count under the limit. It also requires legislators to report any business associations they have with lobbyists. In 1991 New Jersey closed a loophole in a law that previously allowed lobbyists not to disclose how much they spent on whom if legislation were not being "expressly" considered when lobbyists were entertaining legislators.

The electric company lobbyist who spent $175,000 on Florida legislators during a two-year period is fast becoming a relic. There is already some evidence that these new laws are curtailing lavish expenditures, inhibiting wining and dining, and further changing the cultures in which legislators and lobbyists do their business. Hunting trips have dwindled. Legislators do not want to declare publicly that a lobbyist took them quail hunting in Georgia. So, if someone invites a Florida legislator on a trip, chances are that he (or possibly she) will decline. Disneyworld canceled its legislative weekend in 1991 because its value exceeded the $100 permitted for gifts.[35] Florida's lobbyists reported spending 35 percent less money during the first half of 1991 than they did during the same period in 1990.

"I didn't give anything worth more than $25 this year," said one of Tallahassee's foremost lobbyists. "Legislators don't want their names attached to any gifts," he explained. Indeed, in the last three months of 1991 only twenty-seven lobbyists reported gifts of more than $25. The biggest giver was Florida State University, with a total of 246 football tickets, followed by the University of Florida with 198 tickets and the University of Miami with 24.[36]

Today relationships between lobbyists and legislators are more antiseptic and less frequent. Walters writes that the contemporary legislator, unlike his predecessor of twenty years ago "spends most of his time in his Capitol office, confers with aides after the floor session, and then heads home in the evening relatively safe from the temptations of free-spending lobbyists." [37] Legislators and lobbyists still manage to get together, but they now do so in less costly and less exotic ways than was customary in earlier days.

Life is tougher for lobbyists, particularly for those who are trying to establish themselves and need to develop relationships with legislators. One California lobbyist who was getting started just prior to the enactment of Proposition 9 feels the restraints: "Politics has a social side to it, which requires social interchange." But after Proposition 9, getting acquainted and starting a relationship with a legislator became more difficult. Despite restrictions, however, California lobbyists continue to do their jobs and maintain their effectiveness. At least that's what a survey of 250 lobbyists reveals. Several years after the $10-per-month gift limit became law, this survey found that the balance of lobbying influence was largely the same as earlier, with no major shifts perceived in response to the virtual elimination of wining and dining. Only one out of twenty lobbyists felt that Proposition 9 had either greatly enhanced or reduced his or her effectiveness.[38] Sacramento lobbyists simply adapted to a new environment, one in which collegiality and community were diminished but lobbying went on apace.

Lobbyists today are of two minds about the prohibitions and restrictions. They appreciate that limits will allow them to draw the line with legislators who want too much. Limits will also save them money. But they also fear that disclosure or prohibition of gifts will inhibit the building of relationships. Entertainment builds relationships, and relationships build trust. As a Texas lobbyist commented, "If I can't take a guy hunting, it will be harder to get to know him." This will hurt some lobbyists (new ones, in particular) and help others (such as former legislators who already have relationships and cause lobbyists who rely less on relationships).

Ethical Climates

Recently, there has been a rash of scandals involving legislators. An FBI sting in California led to the conviction of a member of the senate, and another one in South Carolina resulted in the conviction of seven legislators. A sting in Arizona produced indictments for eight lawmakers, charged with receiving bribes. In these operations, lobbyists working undercover were used to bait the traps.

People will generalize from these worst possible cases to legislators in other states. Such broad conclusions, however, are quite inappropriate. The ethical climates vary substantially from state to state. Despite the recent indictments and convictions of legislators and lobbyists in a number of states, legislators are probably more ethical today than they were years ago. Expectations have risen, standards are higher, the press is more vigilant, and enforcement is increasingly vigorous. Years ago, members of the capitol community would not have forsaken "Diamond Tooth" Miller of New Mexico. Miller would belly up to the bar at the Bull Ring in Santa Fe wearing a button that read, "Diamond Tooth Miller, the Best Goddamn Senator Money Can Buy." Lobbyists were there to make the purchase.[39] Some of that still goes on. Money changes hands, as is evidenced by the videotapes of Arizona legislators joking cynically about government and taking money. Corruption will never be eliminated entirely. But it is no longer condoned by either legislators or lobbyists.

While the ethical climate has generally improved over the past twenty years, there have been, and continue to be, significant differences among the states. On the one hand, some have been squeaky clean over the years. Minnesota is one of them, so clean that one lobbyist declared that "You almost wish that some people would be a little more human." Colorado is another. No one here could think of a real scandal in the last twenty years. Nor could they recall unethical behavior on the parts of legislators or lobbyists (although during the spring when tickets are being sold to fund-raisers, a few lobbyists do complain). From time to time there are infractions in Colorado. A lobbyist missed a reporting deadline; and U.S. West (formerly Mountain Bell) spent $2,000 each for several legislators to enter a golf tournament but failed to disclose it as a gift. The press rode U.S. West hard.

On the other hand, in some states life is lived more loosely and it has almost been taken for granted that lobbyists were invented to pay the bill for legislators. On every possible occasion, legislators would seek out a lobbyist so that they could enjoy a free lunch or more. There is the story about a few New Jersey legislators who entered a restaurant, spotted a lobbyist for one of the major associations, and invited him to their table for dinner. Midway through the meal, the lobbyist, reacting to a bad clam, choked, turned pale, and passed out. Three waiters worked over him while the legislators continued their conversation. They did not notice that the lobbyist had left the table and the restaurant until they themselves were ready to leave. "Where did ____ go?" one legislator asked, "he's supposed to pick up the check." The day was saved, however. On his way to seek medical attention, the lobbyist had made arrangements to pay for the meal.

Florida is one place where social life had gotten out of hand, before it was recently reined in. Few legislators here were outright greedy, but practically all had become accustomed to the perquisites of legislative life in Tallahassee. They felt entitled to them. Their attitude was: "We're here to be served." Indeed, one lobbyist agreed: "We're geishas for two months." And one legislator is reported to have stated it even more bluntly: "I like people to kiss my ass."

Lobbyists did the serving. Flowers and candy were delivered to legislators' capitol offices. One senator received two oak toilet seats from a developer. Others received car alarms, auto repairs, eye exams, cuff links, and jackets, not to mention food, drink, and travel.[40] The Greater Miami Opera Company provided free opera tickets but had few takers. Some legislators went further, abusing the system. They not only expected largesse, they asked for it.

The Florida Grand Jury presentment found that lobbyists had not precipitated the abuses. Rather they were "brought about by a *distinct minority of legislators* [italics in original] who have utilized the expenditures of lobbyists to supplement and enhance their lifestyles." Several legislators routinely solicited free plane charters from lobbyists for their personal use. One legislator solicited a white-winged-dove hunting trip to

Mexico and another solicited several exotic fruit trees, which were planted at the legislator's residence at the lobbyist's expense.[41]

Nor was it unheard of for legislators dining together to send the check to a lobbyist at another table to pay. A few would dine at the Governor's Club and charge it to a lobbyist member's account. A few also had the numbers of lobbyists' credit cards and charged meals at restaurants or even gifts while they were on vacation.[42] Whenever legislators in Florida gathered for a party, like the fifty who gathered at the home of Speaker Tom Gustafson in 1989, lobbyists would be recruited to bear the costs of food and drink. Beer, wine, and spirit lobbyists were expected to provide "product," and they did. One Tallahassee lobbyist reported that he was asked to host a cocktail party for twenty constituents. Many members of the lobbying community resented what they considered to be a shakedown and the otherwise arrogant behavior of the legislative community.

Nothing in Florida, however, has matched the service rendered by a lobbyist in 1986. After a hit-and-run accident, a liquor lobbyist told the Tallahassee police that it was he, and not the legislator, who was driving the legislator's car. After the legislator came forward and admitted he was the driver, the lobbyist was asked why he lied. He replied: "You know, I am a lobbyist, and you have to take the fall when you work for a legislator."[43]

Texas is another place where some legislators have gotten used to cutting ethical corners. As in Florida, the system has been abused by members who sign the tabs of lobbyists and entertain on lobbyists' accounts. The old practice of poker games, where legislators never lost and lobbyists had to pay up, has vanished from the scene. But money is still important and the environment is still rather loose. Legislators can use their office accounts for living expenses and a number of members, particularly attorneys, are said to have conflicts of interest.

One of the reasons for this is that Texas legislators are paid only $7,200 a year. And their pay can be raised only if the electorate amends the constitution. Unlike legislators in California, who are paid more than $40,000, or those in New Jersey, who receive $35,000, or those in Minnesota, who are paid more than $26,000, legislators in Texas cannot afford to serve unless they have independent means or can benefit professionally from holding legislative office. For the past five years, they have been in session a good part of the time and have had to pay their living expenses in Austin. This is where their office accounts come into play, serving as slush funds. Lobbyists contribute and legislators (with funds that may range in the neighborhood of $100,000) are thus able to pay for the things they need in Austin—paying for rent or interest on a house, a car, meals, or supplementing their staffs. Given the disinclination of the people of Texas to raise legislator salaries, even one of the drafters of the stringent ethics reform legislation of 1991 admitted that "you can't expect them not to need a helping hand from lobbyists." In Texas, as elsewhere, lobbyists are expected to ante up more than their fair share of the maintenance costs of the political system. But standards, along with the law, are changing rapidly, and practice will have to catch up.

Lobbyist Ethics

Lobbying is closely regulated in the states. Each of the fifty states requires that lobbyists register. Forty-five require some type of reporting of lobbying expenses. Many state requirements go further. The rate of compliance is probably high, but it is impossible to be certain because enforcement is generally lax. That is because state governments spend little to monitor lobbying, ranging from about $750,000 in California to about $400 in Oklahoma. Half the states have only one or a part-time staffer to oversee the effort.[44]

The reform of lobbying has been proceeding apace in recent years. The changes in what lobbyists are permitted to spend on legislators and what must be disclosed have already been mentioned. Amendments to campaign-finance laws limiting contributions are also being adopted. They are intended to curb the influence of money, particularly that controlled by lobbyists and special interests. Revolving-door statutes have made it illegal for legislators in a number of states (including Florida and Texas) to lobby until one or two years after having left office. Some states already ban contingency fees for lobbyists, and others are seeking to do so.

Lobbying is a far different profession today. Two political scientists, both experienced students of interest-group politics in the states, observed recently that the lobbying communities have become much more professional during the last twenty years.[45] They are correct. Moreover, part of the professional character of the community is attributable to higher ethical standards and more ethical behavior.

Still, some deterioration may be occurring in the lobbying profession. In Colorado, legislative leaders became concerned a few years ago about the possibility of abuse. They appointed a ten-member committee of lobbyists to explore the problem. The committee made recommendations and legislative leaders sponsored a bill to implement them. But the lobbying community's attitude was that no rules were needed and there was no reason to interfere with their freedom. The bill failed to be enacted.

With a much larger lobbying community and increasing competition in each state capital, it has become harder to agree on norms, and the profession is attracting marginal members. Some of these members make mischief, it is said, in order to stay employed. A few hold to the belief, in the words of one lobbyist, that "You should never kill a bill so bad that [the opposition] can't come back next year, or you'll be out of business." There are backbiters and some who try to discredit their competitors.

A thorny ethical problem for contract lobbyists is conflict of interests. A conflict occurs when two or more of a lobbyist's clients have competing interests. Even though two clients may appear to have much in common, such as the Thoroughbred Horse Association and the Standardbred Horse Association, they may have differences as well. The possibility of conflicting interests can arise in any state. The more clients a lobbyist or a lobbying firm has, the greater the likelihood of conflicts. If a lobbyist has fifty or sixty clients, as some do, and is involved in a hundred or more different pieces of legislation, as some are, it is difficult to avoid such conflict. Or if a law firm, with both legal and lobbying clients, has a large portfolio, a conflict is almost sure to crop up.

Lobbyists with fewer clients—say, ten or so—are less likely to encounter conflicts, particularly if they screen potential clients. Screening is necessary. A Colorado lobbyist will not take on a client whose interest might conflict with that of a current client. He will refer such an account to a colleague. A Texas law firm with a lobbying practice does a computer check of all clients to identify situations of possible conflict. Many lobbyists leave the decision up to the clients. They inform clients of a possible conflict, and, if the clients have no objection, the lobbyist represents them both.

Sometimes, of course, a conflict may come up unexpectedly during the course of the legislative session. An ethical lobbyist will notify both clients and then choose one or the other to continue representing on the issue. It may be the first client or it the one who provides better business. The real issue, however, is the lobbyist's perception of a conflict, which is not always evident, or always clear cut, or always very important. But these are difficult judgments, as a Colorado lobbyist says, "Where you draw the line is not an easy thing to do."

Lobbyists are facing the challenges of rapidly changing rules and ethics laws and a highly critical press. The question is, can the profession respond? Even in the 1960s lobbyists had a sense of belonging to a distinct profession, according to the study of lobbyists in Oregon, Massachusetts, North Carolina, and Utah.[46] Over the past twenty years that sense has grown along with the professionalization of state legislatures. Today, most lobbyists take pride in what they do and believe they serve the cause of good government.

The professionalization of lobbying has been facilitated by the organization at the national level of state government relations personnel and, in a number of states, the organization of lobbyists. The Public

Affairs Council, an association of professionals who are responsible for government relations at the federal level, held an initial clinic on lobbying state government in 1969. Four years later it held a national conference of state government relations executives. Then, in 1975, the State Governmental Affairs Council was formed as an independent organization. It presently has as members more than one hundred large companies and associations, each with interests in multiple states. In 1989 SGAC held its first of an annual series of five-day institutes, designed to bring lobbyists together for advanced training.

Organizations have also sprung up on the state level. The Minnesota Governmental Relations Council was founded in 1978. Its purpose was to raise ethical standards and enhance the professionalism of its approximately 250 members. The Arkansas Society of Professional Lobbyists was formed in 1990, in large part to offset intense media criticism, notably by opinion columnists in two statewide newspapers who "pretty much bash lobbyists and legislators and everyone else." The society set about to tackle the problem of image through educating its members and the public.[47] The Florida League of Professional Lobbyists formed in 1989 to upgrade the ethics of lobbyists. One of its first tasks was to adopt a voluntary code, which encouraged members to avoid conflicts of interest, not tell lies, and comply with all state laws governing lobbying.[48]

Organization does not work everywhere. There is none in New Jersey, although a lobbyists's club used to exist in Trenton. A similar group, called "the Third House," existed in Denver. But as the ranks of lobbyists grew, the Denver group turned into an exclusive club and soon dissolved. According to one Colorado lobbyist, the group was very effective in straightening out the occasional errant lobbyist. For the past ten years, however, Colorado lobbyists have shown little interest in forming an organization.

In Texas organization appears to meet the needs of one part of the lobbying community but not the other. More than two hundred associations in the Austin area belong to the American Society of Association Executives. Many in-house lobbyists are active in this association. But Texas contract lobbyists have no group of their own, perhaps because of their varied interests and keen rivalries.

It would appear that in the years ahead lobbyists in the states will face the choice of either self-regulation or greater regulation by government, possibly both. The public is not kindly disposed at present toward lobbyists and their practices. A 1989 national survey conducted by Associated Press/Media General showed that 75 percent thought it should be illegal for lobbyists to contribute to legislators' campaigns, 87 percent thought it should be illegal for them to give gifts to legislators, and 67 percent thought it should be illegal for them to buy meals for legislators. Practically any scandal will lead to cries from the press and public interest groups for stricter control of lobbying. Legislators will find themselves pressured to comply with demands for reform.

It is likely, then, that regulation will increase. The results will serve to further restrict those who rely on the inside game and thereby will abet those who depend more on the outside one. If lobbyists expect to have much hope of escaping a more rigid regulatory system, they will have to regulate themselves. That will require putting individual differences aside, organizing into a state association or society, undertaking the development of an ethics code, and providing opportunities for members to grow professionally. Then, and most difficult of all, they will have to police their members and impose some form of sanctions on those who stray too often or too far. Given the nature of the capitol communities today, this is a mighty tall order to fill.

Notes

1. Seymour Lusterman, *Managing Business-State Government Relations* (New York: The Conference Board, 1983), 51.
2. John C. Wahlke et al., *The Legislative System* (New York: Wiley, 1962), 331. Daniel J. Elazar, *American Federalism: A View from the States,* 2d ed. (New York: Crowell, 1972), and Alan Rosenthal and Maureen Moakley, eds., *The Political Life of the American States* (New York: Praeger, 1984).
3. Keith E. Hamm and Charles W. Wiggins, "Texas: The Transformation from Personal to Informational Lobbying," in *Interest Group Politics in the Southern States,* ed. Ronald J. Hrebenar and Clive S. Thomas (Tuscaloosa: University of Alabama Press, forthcoming).
4. Clive S. Thomas and Ronald J. Hrebenar, "Interest Groups in the States," in *Politics in the American States,* ed. Virginia Gray, Herbert Jacob, and Robert B. Albritton, 5th ed. (Glenview, Ill.: Scott, Foresman/Little, Brown Higher Education, 1990), 147. An earlier classification of the strength of pressure groups ran along the same lines, with Florida and Texas "strong," California "moderately strong," and Colorado, Minnesota, and New Jersey "weak." Sarah McCally Morehouse, *State Politics, Parties and Policy* (New York: Holt, Rinehart, and Winston, 1981).
5. Alan Rosenthal, "The Legislative Institution: Transformed and at Risk," in *State of the States,* ed. Carl E. Van Horn (Washington, D.C.: CQ Press, 1989), 71-78.
6. See Rob Gurwitz, "California, Here We Come: The Professional Legislature and Its Discontents," *Governing,* August 1991, 64-69.
7. "Calendar" days run consecutively, while "legislative" days may exclude Saturdays and Sundays and those days during periods when the legislature is in recess.
8. Sidney Wise, *The Legislative Process in Pennsylvania,* 2d ed., Bipartisan Management Committee, House of Representatives, Harrisburg, Pennsylva-

nia, 1984, 72.
9. Kay Lehman Schlozman and John T. Tierney, *Organized Interests in American Democracy* (New York: Harper and Row, 1986), 302-303.
10. Richard A. Armstrong, "Corporations and State Government Relations: An Overview," in *Leveraging State Government Relations,* ed. Wesley Pedersen (Washington, D.C.: Public Affairs Council, 1990), 8.
11. *Dallas Morning News,* March 29, 1987.
12. John Jervis and Robert Fairbanks, "Lobbyists: A New Symphony of Service," *California Journal,* February 1985, 44.
13. Bruce C. Wolpe, *Lobbying Congress: How the System Works* (Washington, D.C.: Congressional Quarterly, Inc., 1990), 7.
14. State Government Relations Institute, New Brunswick, New Jersey, July 9, 1990.
15. Joseph Vitale, "Confessions of a Lobbyist," *New Jersey Monthly* (October 1990), 95.
16. Rowland Stiteler, "Influence Peddling," *Florida Magazine, Orlando Sentinel,* May 29, 1988.
17. *Dallas Morning News,* March 29, 1987.
18. Paul Hollrah, "Lobbying State Capitols: Rules for a New Game," *State Policy,* January 1984, 4.
19. John A. Straayer, *The Colorado General Assembly* (Niwot, Colo.: University Press of Colorado, 1990), 67-68.
20. *Tampa Tribune,* March 1, 1990.
21. See Jonathan Walters, "A Night on the Town Isn't What It Used to Be in Jefferson City," *Governing,* July 1989, 26-31.
22. Ibid., 30.
23. *Dallas Morning News,* March 29, 1987.
24. *Miami Herald,* May 1, 1991.
25. Florida Grand Jury Presentment, 1990, photocopy.
26. *St. Petersburg Times,* September 30, 1990.
27. *Tallahassee Democrat,* July 14, 1991, and March 31, 1992.
28. See *Dallas Morning News,* March 29, 1987.
29. *Rocky Mountain News,* October 23, 1991; and *St. Petersburg Times,* June 2, 1991.
30. Walters, "Night on the Town," 30.
31. *Pensacola Journal,* July 1, 1990.
32. Walters, "Night on the Town," 29.
33. Wisconsin Legislative Council staff, "Information Bulletin 91-4: Lobbying Law Requirements," January 14, 1991, 3.
34. Jeffrey L. Katz, "Sipping from the Cup of Corruption," *Governing,* November 1991, 27-28.
35. *Orlando Sentinel Star,* March 12, 1991.
36. *Tampa Tribune,* July 19, 1991, and *Tallahassee Democrat,* April 1, 1992.
37. Walters, "Night on the Town," 31.
38. The survey was conducted in 1977 and 1988 by Ken DeBow, and is cited in Ronald J. Hrebenar and Ruth K. Scott, *Interest Group Politics in America,* 2d ed. (Englewood Cliffs, N.J.: Prentice Hall, 1990), 255.
39. Walters, "Night on the Town," 26.

40. *Orlando Sentinel Star,* April 28, 1991.
41. Florida Grand Jury, "Contributions to Public Officials." Presentment, Second Judicial Circuit, Leon County, Florida.
42. *Florida Times Union,* March 19, 1990.
43. Stiteler, "Influence Peddling."
44. Associated Press survey, reported in the *Salt Lake Tribune,* July 1, 1990.
45. Thomas and Hrebenar, "Interest Groups in the States," 152.
46. Harmon Zeigler and Michael A. Baer, *Lobbying: Interaction and Influence in American State Legislatures* (Belmont, Calif.: Wadsworth, 1969), 67.
47. *Arkansas Democrat,* June 26, 1990.
48. *St. Petersburg Times,* March 1, 1990; *Tallahassee Democrat,* October 5, 1990.

CHAPTER 5

Building Relationships

Much of what happens in the state capitals comes down to basic human relationships. If, as Tip O'Neill says, "All politics are local," it is also true that all legislative politics are, at least in good part, personal. Whatever the political system or culture, the lobbyist's goal is to make connections and develop close relationships with as many legislators (and, in some states, as many of their legislative staff) as possible. One of Florida's contract lobbyists put it baldly: "Everything must be seen in terms of relationships." Not all lobbyists subscribe to this goal, and of those who do, not all subscribe equally. Contract lobbyists are the truest believers. Cause lobbyists are less concerned with the "inside" work of developing relationships. They have their issues, their members, and a sympathetic press; they therefore play mainly an outside game. That probably suits their personalities, budgets, and philosophies as well.[1] Occasionally, as in the case of the public interest groups in Colorado, cause lobbyists find the inside game clean and appealing. So one can often find them building personal relationships like most of their colleagues.

Some lobbyists believe they spend more time developing relationships than they do on direct lobbying. In the words of a Florida lobbyist and former speaker of the house, "Lobbying really is friendship more than anything else." "If you've got the wrong chemistry," according to a Colorado association lobbyist, "it's hard to do business." A New Jersey lobbyist for a university explains, "Before I ask for anything from them, I try to make friends."

The significance of personal relationships should be obvious to anyone familiar with the legislative process. Without trust, credibility, and veracity in the dealings among individuals, the process could hardly work at all. So, lobbyists try to develop relationships that allow them to demonstrate the worthy attributes they themselves possess, which is prerequisite for promoting their client's wares. Personal ties make it easier for legislators to develop trust and confidence in and a liking for those who are trying to influence them. Legislators, like the rest of us, are more apt to do things for individuals they like and trust. But it takes time for people to develop trust in one another. If, through a relationship, a lobbyist proves to be a credible, reliable, loyal, empathetic, and likable person, he or she will have made the grade; the path of direct lobbying will have been made smooth.

Natural Development

Relationships are not difficult to forge in a legislative setting. Indeed, as one Florida lobbyist and former legislator said: "It's hard up here not to develop friendships." Legislators and lobbyists naturally gravitate toward one another. Because they share a stake in the legislative system, they can commiserate and celebrate with each other.[2]

But some lobbyists have a head start, especially when they have relationships with legislators that go back a long way. Friendships that predate life in and around the legislature tend to be the closest. Friends from prepolitical days are often deemed the truest—they will be around, it is presumed, after the legislator leaves office and loses power. Kinship does not hurt either. For example, Joe Bell, an Arkansas lobbyist, is the son of Clarence Bell, an Arkansas senator. (It is reported that sometimes the father goes along with his son and sometimes he doesn't, but there is no doubt as to their relationship.) A friendship that starts out when the legislator first arrives in Tallahassee can also bear fruit. When he began a career as a lobbyist-lawyer in 1972, Jack Skelding also managed an apartment complex in Tallahassee. One tenant was Ralph Haben, then a freshman legislator. Landlord and tenant each had an interest in flying and became friends, eventually sharing apartments and airplanes. When Haben became speaker nine years later, Skelding had a built-in advantage—a long-standing friendship.[3]

Many legislator-lobbyist relationships originated in the legislature itself. In a few states, a number of lobbyists had first served on the legislative staff. About one out of five lobbyists in Sacramento came from the ranks of senate, assembly, or central staffs, which in the 1980s numbered almost eighteen hundred professionals. Several of the contract lobbyists in Trenton have also had experience on legislative partisan staffs. At least a few Florida committee staff directors or leadership aides followed their legislator bosses who opened up lobbying shops near the capitol. All of them had connections from their previous lives.

Among the closest relationships are those between lobbyists who had once served as legislators and their colleagues who continue in office. The bonding that takes place in the legislature has no substitute: the experiences shared, the favors exchanged, and the debts incurred are without parallel. A Colorado lobbyist reflected on how much of an advantage it was to be a former member of both the house and the senate. "Any way you cut it," he stated, "there is a collegial feeling among members and former members." Even a lobbyist who is related to a former member—a son or daughter, for instance—possesses a bit of an advantage.

A lobbyist who had served in a leadership position is even better off. As Florida speaker, Ralph Haben had appointed Jon Mills, then in his second term, to an important subcommittee chairmanship, he had also served with T. K. Wetherell and Bolley "Bo" Johnson. After Haben left the legislature and went into lobbying, Mills became speaker, followed a few years later by Wetherell, with Johnson slated to become speaker thereafter. They had all gone through legislative wars together and naturally felt a kinship. Having served as a leader, however, may be a doubled-edged sword. As a lobbyist today, Haben feels he cannot ask speakers to do things another lobbyist might not hesitate to request. He is especially sensitive to anything that might jeopardize the office of speaker.

As turnover occurs and new members replace older ones, these ties obviously loosen.[4] New members do not know the veterans now lobbying. But reputations endure, the respect for former speakers lasts, and someone is invariably around and ready to introduce a former legislator to a current one. In any case, a lobbyist who belongs to a "former members club" is always in a position to call on newer, as well as older, legislators for help. The mystique lingers. For the lobbyist, therefore, it is better to have been a legislator, even in a distant past, than never to have been one at all.

A lobbyist, of course, cannot establish a relationship with every member. A sorting-out process therefore takes place. Certainly likes tend to attract. Female lobbyists are more likely to develop close relationships with female legislators, African American lobbyists with African American legislators, Hispanics with Hispanics. Public-interest lobbyists appear to have especially good relationships with legislative staff. They tend to have similar values. Most lobbyists manage to develop connections on both sides of the aisle because Democrats and Republicans could go either way on many issues of interest.

Not all interactions between lobbyists and legislators are positive. Occasionally, lobbyists make enemies. Sometimes this happens because legislators don't like a lobbyist's client; sometimes it's because they don't like the lobbyist. Whatever the cause, lobbyists still have to try to reach the unfriendly lawmaker. "I cannot get along with _____," notes a Colorado lobbyist, "but I do know someone who can get to him." Although a personal relationship may be difficult to forge, one's work can still go on.

Forging Bonds

Many relationships between lobbyists and legislators just happen. More often, however, they are cultivated by lobbyists who do not wait for nature to take its course. It is a delicate process—"like courting a woman," said a member of the New Jersey lobby. It takes time. Joe Bell of Little Rock counsels patience: "I wait for the relationship to develop naturally or without trying to make it occur prematurely. Like wine, don't uncork it before its time." [5] Socializing, as much as anything else, establishes familiarity and allows for trust. It is not a dinner, or a hunting trip, or a campaign contribution but, rather, a whole string of contacts that forges the link between legislator and lobbyist.

Establishing a connection usually requires effort and money. There are many tried and true techniques, ten of which deserve mention.

1. *Entertaining.* By entertaining legislators, lobbyists get the opportunity to spend time in relaxed settings. The idea is for the two parties to get to know one another. Accordingly, they seldom discuss business—that is, legislation per se. A New Jersey lobbyist explains:

> One thing that a lot of lobbyists do is . . . discuss business. They don't want it to be a quid pro quo. *I* don't. If I were to take a senator to the Giants game, I wouldn't be inviting him because I want him to vote for my bill. I'd be inviting him because I had an extra ticket, he's a friend of mine, I know him.

Conversation, instead, revolves around sports, families, politics—wherever the lobbyist can gain common ground with the legislator. Entertaining is the means to identifying commonalities. According to one observer, "Entertainment is to a lobbyist as a wrench is to a plumber."

There are more ways to entertain legislators than one can imagine, as has been noted in chapter 4. One Louisiana lobbyist, who loves to cook, prepared a crawfish etouffé dinner for the president of the senate and a bunch of his official guests. Lobbyists take legislators to football and basketball games and to golf tournaments. They also work close to home. They invite legislators, along with their spouses, to their houses, in the belief that, "If you can get a legislator in your home with his wife, he'll get to trust you." The spouse helps considerably.

Lobbyists also work further afield. They entertain legislators at the many meetings held around the country by organizations such as the National Conference of State Legislatures, the Council of State Governments, the Legislative Leaders Foundation, and the American Legislative Exchange Council. Business groups underwrite part of the costs of these meetings and also host receptions and other social events in the evenings. Lobbyists find these to be excellent occasions for entertaining legislators one on one or in small groups.

2. *Trips.* Even further afield are the trips, which have been discussed in chapter 4. Hunting—with deer, quail, and dove as prey—or fishing are favorites for lobbyists and some legislators, particularly in the South. Off in the wilderness lobbyists and legislators can shoot, sit around, spit, and bond. No legislative business is discussed because, as a Florida lobbyist observes:

> Nobody would ever go with you again. I think you would defeat the real reason for having the trip—to get to know these guys and have them get to know you. If you started talking about legislation, they would be so on guard and everything, nobody would have a good time, and it wouldn't be worthwhile.[6]

Some lobbyists are of the opinion that a good fishing or hunting trip is remembered long after a political campaign contribution is forgotten.

Not all of the trips are strictly social. Some have as their objective, in addition to relationship building, education about an industry and its products. The Pharmaceutical Manufacturers Association makes special use of conferences and field trips on health policy and health care. It also likes to bring legislators to pharmaceutical plants in various states to observe research and development in operation. At a conference of the Western Region of the Council of State Governments in Anchorage, PMA arranged a trip for about thirty-five legislators to observe the provisions of health services in the bush country. Pharmaceutical representatives of the member companies that financed the project naturally went along. PMA believes in combining the substantive and the educational. "Once people know what this industry is doing," explained the association's director of state government relations, "it's pretty impressive."

3. *Gifts.* For lobbyists, it is better to give than to receive, at least in the process of building relationships. The gifts are small, but they do not go unappreciated. Bruce Bereano, the legendary contract lobbyist in Annapolis, showers legislators with flowers, candy, and cigars. For years he has sent flowers on Valentine's Day to secretaries of each legislative committee and birthday cards to key staffers.[7] Lobbyists range through the legislative office buildings in Tallahassee, leaving in their wake gumdrops, popcorn, peanuts, and other tidbits—all of which are largely consumed by legislators' secretaries. One lobbyist for a national food

company would typically leave a can of his company's cashews behind when he visited legislators' offices. One day, a staff member in one of the offices inquired, in jest, whether he was trying to buy votes this way. The lobbyist replied, "If I can buy a vote for a three-dollar can of nuts, it's not worth buying."

Some lobbyists offer special services instead of gifts per se. One baby-sits the small children of legislators. Another, who lives in Austin, has even invested in a Chevrolet Suburban (which seats nine; more if passengers are small) so he can haul around legislators. Services extend further. A lobbyist for cable television makes sure that legislators get a quick hook-up from the local company at their summer homes or get invited to appear on a cable interview program. A lobbyist for a telephone company helps legislators when they have trouble with their equipment or when they want a special number for a new phone. The physical therapy association will give legislators massages, the chiropractors will pop their backs, the podiatrists will look after their feet, a pharmaceutical company will screen their eyes—all gratis. In this way, legislators will get to know a lobbyist's clients in a most favorable light. A lobbyist for the acupuncturists has not yet succeeded in interesting many legislators in his client's complimentary services. But he is sticking with it. The Florida Medical Association delivers a doctor-of-the-day at the capitol during the sixty days when the legislature is in session. And when the wife of a Florida speaker of the house had a premature baby on a trip to Israel, the lobbyist for the medical school of one of the state's universities made arrangements with Israeli medical authorities for her care.

Another category of gifts are honoraria, or fees paid to legislators who address members of a company or association at one of their meetings. Some of these honoraria are truly for the service performed. Others would appear to be more in the nature of generous grants. The trend today is for states to bar legislators from accepting honoraria for duties they perform in connection with their official positions.

4. *Athletics.* There are probably few better ways for lobbyists to connect to legislators than on a playing field. Jogging, golf, crew, basketball—they all serve well. A Maryland lobbyist made it a practice of going to the Naval Academy gym early in the morning to play basketball with legislators. A Texas lobbyist made it a practice of getting into a basketball game with legislators at Austin's Metropolitan Club. Several California lobbyists play racquetball with legislators at the Capital Athletic Club. Golf is probably the optimum diversion, as far as lobbyists are concerned, in that it permits leisurely and personal conversation as legislator and lobbyist tramp from tee to tee. There has been a shift from gin mill to athletic field; as was noted by the *New York Times:* "Physical fitness is now an asset for the lobbyist the way tolerance of strong drink once was." [8]

5. *Constituent service.* Lobbyists can be enormously helpful to

legislators when it comes to service for their constituents. A contract lobbyist, who represents Blue Cross-Blue Shield, will help a constituent cut through company red tape. A telephone company lobbyist has a note pad at the ready for legislator requests on behalf of constituents who have problems with service or billing. He can take care of a problem almost immediately. The telephone company, with its emphasis on community relations, is unequaled when it comes to service. In Arkansas one legislator had a constituent who wanted compensation for five cows killed by a Union Pacific locomotive, while another had constituents who wanted an old railroad terminal made part of a local cultural center. The contract lobbyist representing the Union Pacific took care of it all.[9] An insurance lobbyist accepted the case of the relative of a receptionist working in the law firm of a legislative leader. The problem was that she was told her insurance did not cover a bone marrow transplant. A lobbyist for a state university estimated that he spent over a third of his time on service to legislators' constituents on matters of admissions, financial aid, and housing. He described the process: "Some people in my position in other schools have an admission or two in their pocket, so if a really key legislator has a constituent who wants to get admitted, he will see to it that the kid gets admitted.... I can't do that." What he does instead is to provide legislators with as much information as possible about the constituent's admissions case.

6. *Appreciation and acknowledgment.* There are a host of gestures more subtle than entertainment or gifts. Yet they, too, are effective in relationship building. Respect for members and for the institution is necessary. This comes most naturally to lobbyists who have served in the legislature. Recognition also matters. Groups such as the California Society of Certified Public Accountants honor a "legislator of the year." Just about every group gives, and most legislators receive, a plaque in appreciation of their service, support, or performance. For example, after the Florida legislature appropriated almost one million dollars to the Greater Miami Opera, one of its lobbyists proposed that key legislator supporters be sent a framed poster with a small plaque reading: "BRAVO AND THANK YOU! GREATER MIAMI OPERA 1987." He explained that, "I like members of the legislature to think about my clients all the time." And the best way for them to do that, he added, "is to put something on their walls." [10] Furthermore, after every battle or even skirmish, the lobbyist should thank and praise the legislators who were involved.

7. *Understanding.* The lobbyists who, during interim periods, travel to legislators' home districts demonstrate a real understanding of where members live. A Minnesota lobbyist makes good use of the time when the legislature is not in session. He visits members in their homes, drives out to the fields where they may be farming, takes them a cold beer, and inquires as to their concerns. "If you drive two hundred miles,

they'll remember that." Before the session begins and after the primaries, one of the leading contract lobbyists in Maryland visits each newly nominated legislator who will not be facing much opposition in the general election. He has breakfast, coffee, lunch, or dinner with almost every new member. (Getting them to go out for a meal cuts out the distractions of secretary, telephone, or office routine.) Seeing them in the context of their districts gives this lobbyist an understanding that few of his colleagues possess.

An aspect of understanding is a sympathetic ear. Lobbyists have to be good listeners, tolerating the most banal or rambling discourse. If lobbyists appear not to care about legislators' interests, legislators are sure not to give a rap about those of the lobbyists. One lobbyist, who knows from the experience of having served in the legislature, prides himself on being an "informed listener." He points out that, "Nothing is as dear to a new member as his recent election. They never tire of talking about it." Therefore, he informs himself about their campaigns and not only listens but also responds to their conversation on the subject.

8. *Advice.* In addition to sympathy, advice is also sought by legislators. "I have an idea, can you help?" Or, "How do I fight this?" To an environmental lobbyist in New Jersey: "Should I put this bill in?" To an environmental lobbyist in Florida: "I want to file an environmental bill; what would you suggest?" One firm in Tallahassee is frequently consulted by legislators and legislative staff for advice on legislative language. "They know we're proficient in certain areas," said a leading lawyer-lobbyist. On a specific subject, for example, one of the firm's attorneys is so expert that legislative staff will not move before checking with her. Her advice is mainly technical: "This is what will happen if you do this, this is what will happen if you don't." In Colorado, an association lobbyist with particular expertise answers many legislator questions regarding unemployment insurance and workers' compensation. An experienced Texas lobbyist is especially well versed in the parliamentary process. As the session draws to a close and rules and process become critical, more and more members turn to him for advice. A Minnesota lobbyist who has general knowledge but no particular expertise volunteers information from his perspective to friends in leadership—alerting them to incipient issues, who wants what, and what is likely to be going on.

9. *Assistance on legislation.* Years ago, Harmon Zeigler and Michael Baer, in their examination of lobbying in four states, pointed out that legislators used lobbyists to influence other legislators and the public.[11] That is still the case. In Colorado legislators will check with the education association lobbyist to see whether their bills are consistent with the organization's policy and whether the association will testify and lobby in their behalf. Another lobbyist for an influential Colorado

association also receives requests each session from legislators who want to broaden the backing for bills they are sponsoring. If it does not run counter to group policy, she will sign on. Legislators, in fact, may seek support from lobbyists more than might be imagined. A 1987 Gallup survey asked New Jersey legislators how frequently they looked to lobbyists for support for their bills. While 7 percent responded "frequently," as many as 44 percent responded "somewhat frequently," and only 11 percent replied that they did not rely on lobbyists "at all." In Minnesota a 1987 survey of lobbyists found that a third of them saw as one of their chief tasks that of helping legislators to build support for their bills.[12] Sometimes it is a matter of horsetrading. If lobbyists help legislators get their bills passed, legislators will help them. Sometimes it is more subtle. Lobbyists may act as intermediaries for legislators, passing the word to others.

10. *Campaign contributions and involvement.* Relationships thrive in the context of legislators' election campaigns. There is nothing closer to the heart of a politician than the current election, the one coming up, or the one before. Political contributions build relationships. This is not the occasion to enter into the debate over what campaign contributions buy, independent of other factors.[13] Suffice it to say, lobbyists are never sure of just what is expected and just how a PAC or personal contribution will be received. Their operating assumptions are that giving cannot hurt and that it helps to connect lobbyist and legislator. By the same token, they reason that *not* giving (if one has the bucks) *can* hurt and surely will do nothing to strengthen connections.

Further campaign involvement may pay greater dividends as far as relationships are concerned. Teacher associations that endorse candidates and whose members work locally in their behalf help to strengthen the ties between their agents and the preferred legislators. Many contract lobbyists themselves play a significant campaign role, helping to raise money for legislators, particularly for those who have difficulties raising money on their own. These campaigner-lobbyists are extremely helpful to legislative leaders, bundling money from their clients and delivering it to the legislative parties. A few play an even larger role—in gubernatorial campaigns and in legislative races as well. Jim Krog, a prominent Tallahassee lobbyist, worked the capitol by day and campaigned by night.[14] He is now on the staff of Governor Lawton Chiles. Maryland's Bruce Bereano is another major player in campaigns. With five PACs under his control, in the 1990 elections he contributed small amounts to the campaigns of 30 of 47 senators and 67 of 141 delegates. The dollar amounts were not large, but the thought was probably more important than the size of the gift.

Campaigns for leadership positions in the legislature also involve a few lobbyists. Bereano helped a challenger to unseat a senate president and was also involved in a speaker's race. In Florida, the campaign of Bolley "Bo" Johnson for house speaker (years in advance of his designation) was funded by lobbyists for health care, pari-mutuel, and agricultural groups. The money was used for Johnson's travel around the state to visit with legislators, and for staff salaries and promotional mailings.[15]

Trial by Fire

However a relationship between a lobbyist and legislator gets forged, it must undergo trial by fire. And the relationship is tested repeatedly as legislators and lobbyists work together in the legislative process. No matter how effectively lobbyists cultivate the social side, they must also meet the professional standards that legislators have established for them. For the most part, it is a one-way street. Lobbyists have to satisfy legislators, who depend on them for information and assistance. So a number of tests have to be met if relationships are to be maintained.

First, in order to be productive, relationships must be durable. The longer lobbyists have been around, the more likely they will have developed solid ties. There is no substitute for longevity.[16] One legislative leader advised a group of lobbyists to "act like you're around for the long haul." The worst thing is to "hit and run." [17] Beyond that, lobbyists who have put in time and dealt with legislators on many issues in a variety of circumstances will have proved themselves. A contract lobbyist in New Jersey reflected that legislators trusted him because he had been in Trenton (in various capacities) for twenty years, they had dealt with him, and he had "never let anybody down."

Second, lobbyists must be credible. "When a legislator looks at me," said a Colorado lobbyist, "I want him to see credibility." To be deemed credible, lobbyists will have had to keep their word where their word counts most—on matters of political and legislative business. They have to present "the whole truth," not just their client's truth. That means informing the legislator of the other side of the issue, the "down side" from the lobbyist's point of view. That is not difficult to do because, as a Florida lobbyist notes, "I've never seen a position without merit. I just think that I've got more merit to my position." He has met the test; legislators can count on his word and rely on his assessment. "If I go to them and ask them, they won't even question me. They trust me." It takes time and effort to reach such a position. A Colorado cause lobbyist saw the challenge as follows: "You get credibility in teaspoonsful and you lose it in gallons." Any lobbyist can deceive a legislator, but only once.

Third, lobbyists must also be effective. This goes further than credibility. "It's not just that you're an honest guy," according to a public interest group lobbyist in Colorado, "but that you're an effective guy." Legislators will distance themselves from lobbyists who are perceived as losers in the capitol community.

Fourth, there is also the test of reliability. Most important, reliability means eliminating—insofar as possible—the element of surprise. Legislators are on the receiving end of enough surprises and they do not want any more. If a lobbyist intends to work against their bill, they want to know early on. If a lobbyist is planning to introduce an amendment to their bill, they insist on advance notice. A contract lobbyist in Texas explained his modus operandi: "When I find a problem, I call the person I have a problem with. If I'm going to try to amend or kill, I'll go to him and try to work it out." A heavy-hitting contract lobbyist in Florida explains: "If they get blindsided, you're dead." Moreover, lobbyists must keep legislators informed of any changes taking place and what is happening. This will help avert surprises.

Fifth, there is the test of empathy. A lobbyist must be able to put himself or herself in a legislator's shoes. That means the lobbyist must never forget that "the foremost desire of people in power is . . . to stay in power." [18] Lobbyists appreciate this and will not embarrass a legislator nor make him or her look bad. Instead, they tend to be protective. Even if legislators have reneged on a commitment, lobbyists will understand and let them off the hook. A contract lobbyist in New Jersey, who had served on the legislature's staff, met the test of empathy:

> I don't want to hurt them. I don't want to buffalo them. I don't want them to vote for a bill they shouldn't vote for. I don't want them to lose an election because I get them to vote for some unpopular thing. . . . Then I've lost that person for good.

Any good lobbyist must know the legislator's district and position and appreciate the pressures on him or her. A Trenton lobbyist observed that "if the guy has a big organized-labor faction in his district and you are representing a bill that labor is against, you don't ask him to go with you." Instead, the lobbyist goes to others. An Arkansas legislator recounted how, during his second term, he asked a lobbyist about a specific bill. The lobbyist, who was for the bill, gave the legislator the pros and cons, but then added, "Gus, I know the district you represent and you can't vote for this bill." The legislator recalled that he would "always respect him for that." [19] Even when the lobbyist and legislator are on opposite sides of a legislative battle (which, in view of the many issues, happens frequently to people in a close relationship), the lobbyist must be careful not to let the legislator get cut up. The advice of a Texas lobbyist is: "Win gently."

Sixth, lobbyists must possess good judgment, which covers a variety of virtues. They must not offend legislators, no matter what. A Florida lobbyist for one of the cities had had words with a legislator. It took several years for their relationship to be repaired. "I'd been righteously indignant," she admits, "when I shouldn't have been." Lobbyists must also have the judgment not to be offended, and certainly not to take defeat personally. Stoicism pays dividends. "If someone is doing something to me," indicated a Texas governmental lobbyist, "I want them to feel bad." His hope is that they will feel they owe him one. If they are exercising judgment, lobbyists will also not gossip about members or put any of them down. Nor will they boast of the relationships they have or how they wield influence on issues or members.

How Relationships Pay Off

When Leon County prosecutors were probing into the undisclosed travel of Florida legislators, lobbyist Willie McCue testified that the purpose of outings such as hunting trips was to help pass bills in the best interest of one's client or to defeat bills that would hurt one's client.[20] It should come as no surprise that lobbyists are representing their clients' interests before the legislature, and that most of their activities are designed to advance those interests. It would be strange were it otherwise.

Assuming that such trips and other social activities help to build relationships between lobbyists and legislators, the question is, what are the payoffs? Lobbyists themselves deny that such relationships (or campaign contributions, for that matter) necessarily lead to votes. They do admit, however, that a relationship with a legislator affords them access. "It is not a question of influence," said a New Jersey lobbyist, "it is a question of access." According to Florida lobbyist Ralph Haben, "You are building natural access, and that is what this game is all about." [21]

What access means is not entirely clear. Nearly everyone can get, or has, access to a legislator, at least in some form and to some extent. At a minimum, access would appear to mean preferential treatment.[22] But "admission," "approach," or "entrance"—the dictionary definitions of "access"—are too weak to convey the benefit to lobbyists of relationships with legislators. A stronger word is "connection," meaning a tie or a bond—one that results from an ongoing relationship. A connection enables lobbyists to advance their positions on issues more effectively.

Such a connection is especially useful at critical times. Not everyone can get through to a legislator at will, but a good relationship means that a lobbyist has an opportunity for contact at practically any point in the legislative process. If, for example, a senator has thirty pink slips, the connected lobbyist will be one of the five telephone calls that gets returned. At the end of the session, when hundreds of bills have to be dispatched, reaching a legislator can be especially difficult. But if there is trust, understanding, and a track record of dealings, the lobbyist will get a legislator's attention. "If we get down to the clutch and I have to see the speaker," says one New Jersey lobbyist, "I'd be able to get an appointment." A lobbyist with a strong tie will get in the door at the critical moment. A strong connection is the result of a relationship that has been built over time. As a result, the lobbyist needs only a few minutes to make his appeal. There would be no need for introductions, explanations of organizational affiliation, or otherwise setting the stage.

If lobbyists have been properly attentive in building relationships, they have learned as much as possible about the legislators with whom they are dealing. One of the products of such study is that they will know what type of information will work best with a particular individual, and how and when it should be communicated. Some legislators like it written, some like it oral; some prefer words, some prefer numbers. Certain ones are partial to analysis, others need case examples. Some like it hot, others cold.

Relationships make lobbyists not only better dispensers of information but also more likely recipients. In his study of lobbying at the federal level, Robert Salisbury makes the point that lobbyists need access "not so much to apply pressure or even to advocate policy as to be told when something important to them is about to happen." [23] The same applies at the state level. Moreover, legislators who have connections to lobbyists will furnish them with valuable tidbits. A lobbyist may have a problem with a particular legislator but not realize it until a friendly legislator points it out. Only then can the problem be addressed. During the final weeks and last days of a session, when things are moving at a frenetic pace, lobbyists roam the halls of the capitol trying to anticipate events. Who is going to do what to whom is vital information. One can learn from colleagues, and also from friends who are members. They become watchdogs for the lobbyist. They see that "Old ___ is going to get screwed." They will pick up the phone and call old ___, the lobbyist, to warn him. Good relationships therefore afford significant tactical advantages.

One thing a legislator can do for a lobbyist friend is to introduce him or her to other members. Opening a door at the right moment can make a big difference. For example, one lobbyist had a problem with the Dade County (Florida) delegation. He sought the assistance of legislator friends from the Panhandle. One of them approached a legislator from Miami on the lobbyist's behalf: "You can trust ___ to shoot straight with you." That got him in, and the problem was worked out.

If lobbyists are well connected, moreover, they are more likely to gain a seat at the table. That means that they are in on critical decision making, as will be discussed further in chapter 8. Who they represent obviously counts, but who they are counts as well. Depending on their relationships, they may be invited into the back room to participate in the crucial negotiations that take place between opposing sides. And they can be included in the drafting of amendments, which have so much to do with legislation's final shape. If they do not have a chance to participate in the specific details and language of legislation, their influence will be diminished.

A relationship, moreover, makes it more difficult—but by no means impossible—for legislators to oppose lobbyists on issues that they are carrying. "It's harder to vote against someone you know than someone you don't know," concludes a Minnesota association lobbyist. It is particularly hard for legislators to vote against someone they like. "If you like them," commented a Florida senator, "it's easier to support them."

Personalization helps all lobbyists, especially those with large organizations as clients. A lobbyist in Minnesota believes that personal relationships are extremely important for him because "if they are going to cut someone's throat, they have a picture of me." It is too easy if the target is anonymous.[24] One oil lobbyist is particularly appreciative of the benefit of personal relationships. "They can't disassociate big oil from me, a person," he says. That helps his case.

Even if a legislator cannot vote with a lobbyist, there are other ways to lend a hand. A lobbyist for a Texas association acknowledges that "some of the best relationships I have are with members who never give me a vote." But they will help him in committee or give him information. If a lobbyist approaches a legislator, a friend, with "I need this," drawing on the relationship, then the legislator may vote to get a bill out of committee (although he or she will oppose it on the floor). Or legislators may pass a bill in one house (but not the other) for an old buddy. That permits the lobbyist to move things ahead.

Although a legislator friend may not vote right or even help out, he or she may not hurt the lobbyist as much as might otherwise be the case. There are various degrees of opposition, from a simple nay vote to leading the charge against a bill. Personal relationships work to soften up the opposition from legislators.

If a connection exists, not only will a legislator give a lobbyist the benefit of the doubt, but—depending on the issue—the legislator may well go along with the lobbyist. The legislator will obviously lend support, if that is his or her inclination anyway. The legislator will also be inclined to help, if other things are equal or nearly so, if no major policy issue is involved; if there are no party positions on the matter; if the legislator's constituency is unconcerned or unaffected; if one group has not contributed significantly more to the legislator's campaign than the other; and if the legislator has no real feeling on the subject. A California assemblyman noted that there was a whole range of issues that did not affect one's area of expertise or one's district. When a lobbyist asks for your vote, he says,

> You usually don't have time to weigh the policy. You're faced with a daily agenda of forty bills, and this one hasn't caught your attention, and the person asking for the vote has been nice to you in one way or another ... you're likely to go with that person.[25]

Many special-interest issues, which were discussed in chapter 3 above, qualify. Under such circumstances, when a lobbyist friend asks for support and justifies his or her position in public-policy terms, the legislator will probably go along.

Sometimes, however, lawmakers find it impossible to support either the causes or clients of lobbyists they may like. And many legislators inherently want to help and please people. So they feel that they are owing. During recent years legislators have been especially unkind to certain interests, such as tobacco and alcohol. But lately legislators appear to be making that little extra effort for lobbyist friends representing these losing causes. If at all possible, they would like to do something for such unfortunates. The tobacco industry has been hit by excise taxes and restrictions on smoking in public places, and even the most accommodating legislators have gone against the Tobacco Institute and the industry's contract lobbyists. Therefore, when faced with an industry issue that has some merit and appeal, like prohibiting discrimination by employers against employees who smoke off premises, the attitude of legislators is, "Let's give them one." And eight legislatures have passed laws designed to protect smokers from discrimination. In these states, tobacco lobbyists had something to be happy about.

To have a good relationship with legislators confers power on a lobbyist. For one to be close to power is tantamount to possessing it. In the capitol community lobbyists are constantly measured by legislators, statehouse reporters, and other lobbyists, in part, according to who they know and how well they know them. In addition, relationships with the right people impress the lobbyists' clients—the state relations manager of a company, the board of directors, or maybe the CEO.

All of this is wonderful for the lobbyist, but it is not enough. In lobbying, as in other enterprises, there is a bottom line. A Florida lobbyist, who had previously served in the legislature, had the bottom line in mind when he stated: "I don't care who you are, who you were, or who you know, you have got to win." And to win, lobbyists have to work at more than building relationships.

Notes

1. Frank Smallwood, a political scientist who served in the Vermont senate, preferred business lobbyists. He found them to be direct, pragmatic, and down-to-earth, while the cause lobbyists were diffuse and appeared to represent personal policy preferences. He trusted the former more than the latter. Smallwood, it should be noted, is a Republican. Frank Smallwood, *Free and Independent* (Brattleboro, Vt.: Stephen Greene Press, 1976), 167.
2. Larry Landry, "The Art of State Government Relations," in *Leveraging State Government Relations,* ed. Wesley Pedersen (Washington, D.C.: Public Affairs Council, 1990), 94.
3. *Pensacola Journal,* June 26, 1990.
4. This is one of the reasons for "revolving door" laws that prohibit legislators from lobbying for a specific period after departing the legislature.
5. *Arkansas Democrat,* June 24, 1990.
6. *St. Petersburg Times,* July 18, 1991.
7. Keith F. Girard, "Bruce Bereano," *Regardie's,* June 1987, 33; *The Sun* (Baltimore), March 13, 1983.
8. *New York Times,* July 23, 1989.
9. *Arkansas Democrat,* June 24, 1990.
10. *Miami Herald,* December 11, 1990.
11. Harmon Zeigler and Michael A. Baer, *Lobbying: Interaction and Influence in American State Legislatures* (Belmont, Calif.: Wadsworth, 1969), 102-103.
12. Gallup Organization, "The 1987 Gallup Survey of the New Jersey State Legislature" (Princeton, N.J.: Gallup, 1987), 17; Craig H. Grau, "Minnesota: Labor and Business in an Issue-Oriented State," in *Interest Groups in the Midwestern States,* ed. Ronald J. Hrebenar and Clive S. Thomas (Ames: Iowa State University Press, forthcoming).
13. We shall examine campaign activity and what money buys as separate issues in chapter 6, below.
14. *Miami Herald,* May 8, 1990.
15. *Tampa Tribune,* August 4, 1991.
16. Zeigler and Baer, *Lobbying,* 136.
17. Sen. Stanley Aronoff, president of the Ohio senate. (Remarks at the State Government Relations Institute, New Brunswick, N.J., July 10, 1990.)
18. Paul Hollrah, "Lobbying State Capitols: Rules for a New Game," *State Policy,* January 1984, 4.
19. *Arkansas Democrat,* June 24, 1990.
20. *St. Petersburg Times,* July 31, 1991.
21. *Pensacola Journal,* June 26, 1991.
22. John R. Wright, "Contributions, Lobbying and Committee Voting in the U.S. House of Representatives," *American Political Science Review* 84 (June 1990): 418.
23. Robert H. Salisbury, "The Paradox of Interest Groups in Washington—More Groups, Less Clout," in *The New American Political System,* ed. Anthony King, 2d version (Washington, D.C.: AEI Press, 1990), 203-229.
24. The same phenomenon appears to be involved in people's assessments of

their legislator and *the legislature*. They are positive toward their legislator, who is a live person, but are negative toward the legislature, which is an abstraction.

25. A.G. Block, "The Ethics Jungle," *California Journal,* April 1990, 177.

CHAPTER 6

Playing Politics

In addition to building relationships with legislators, lobbyists also enter into the game of politics itself in order to improve their odds in the legislative arena. One way they do this is through election campaigns, where the stakes have become increasingly high for legislators. With careers in public office becoming more appealing, legislators have a lot riding on winning. By the same token, as Republicans and Democrats become increasingly competitive, each party has a lot riding on gaining (or maintaining) control of the statehouses and senates.

Because elections are so important to legislators, the role of lobbyists and clients in campaigns has meaning apart from relationship building. In the first place, lobbyists and the groups they represent give—and give generously—to the campaign war chests of legislative parties, incumbents, candidates fighting over an open seat, and even challengers. They do so to help elect friends, create obligations, improve access, and so forth. On occasion, their purpose is to defeat enemies. In the second place, lobbyists and their clients play independent roles in the campaign, devoting substantially more in organizational effort to accomplish their purposes.

Lobbyists engage in politics in yet another way—bypassing the legislature altogether and going right to the people. This is the increasingly popular "initiative" game that enables the electorate to vote on amendments to the state constitution and/or on statutes. It is played to a fare-thee-well in California, to a lesser degree in Colorado, and from time to time in Florida and eighteen other states. Here, it falls to lobbyists and the forces they represent to persuade, not the legislators, but the people themselves.

Paying the Freight

Money is a focal point for political campaigns because the costs are so high. Media advertising, polling, direct mail, and consultants do not come cheap. They are thought to be worth the price because they are effective. In view of the incentives, it is not surprising that so many candidates are willing to pay. In California, it can cost each side one million dollars or more to win an assembly seat. Even if there is little competition, California's incumbents want to short-circuit a serious contest by amassing a huge war chest to scare off potential challengers.[1] In Florida, for example, one house incumbent, unchallenged for five years, raised $136,000 by the beginning of 1990 for his campaign later that year. When asked why, he responded that before every election he presumed he would have an opponent, even if he did not have one before. Not only in California and Florida but in New Jersey and Texas as well, fund-raising by candidates resembles an arms race. It has certainly become one of the principal activities of legislators. The average member of the California legislature, estimate has it, spends almost half his time, in one guise or another, raising money.

The costs of campaigns are far more modest in some places, like Colorado, which one lobbyist calls "a small-potatoes state." Although here, too, campaign expenses have been rising of late. By 1988 house campaigns costing $20,000 to $25,000 were normal; and ten candidates spent more than $40,000. One senate candidate spent as much as $70,000 that year, and four others spent in excess of $40,000. Even in Minnesota, which along with Wisconsin had a system of partial public funding for legislative campaigns, members had to hustle to raise the nonpublic part of their funds.

Someone has to pay. Most candidates cannot afford to, and the public, for the most part, refuses to. Individual citizens, with no business to conduct before the legislative bar, provide some of the dollars simply because they favor one candidate or one party over the other. But by far the largest share of the tab in most races is picked up by those with deep pockets, the so-called special interests. These are the business, labor, and professional groups that seek "redress of grievances" from the same legislators they endow. Lobbyists and their principals fuel what a Florida lobbyist calls "the giant engine that costs so much."

Lobbyist Giving

Legislative leaders, party caucuses, and legislative rank-and-file are constantly asking lobbyists and their principals to buy more and more, and higher- and higher-priced, tickets to the fund-raisers they sponsor.

Most fund-raisers are in the form of receptions or dinners, but more imaginative ways of separating lobbyists from their money have also been used. In some states summers are filled with golf tournaments—so much so that lobbyists might think they were on the PGA tour.

In most places these events take place year-round, but they tend to occur with greatest frequency when the legislature is in session. It is unseemly to have a committee meeting on a bill during an afternoon and the committee chairman's fund-raiser that evening. Minnesota has prohibited legislative fund-raisers while the legislature is in session. Florida followed suit in 1989, banning them during the legislature's sixty-day session. They were all moved up to the months prior to the session, when legislators were in Tallahassee for committee meetings. In California, a state that cannot be matched at the money game, more than a hundred fund-raising events were held after July and before the election of 1990, including a special end-of-the session briefing that cost $2,500 a head.[2]

Lobbyists are not averse to attending fund-raisers. As a Minnesota lobbyist said, "To be good at this job, you have to be part of the process." Showing up at legislators' fund-raisers is a way to participate in the process and to signal support. It permits lobbyists to mix and network, and occasionally to enjoy themselves besides. But the number of invitations lobbyists receive and the costs involved have been rising dramatically. One veteran lobbyist in Trenton felt the squeeze: "If I responded to every legislator and candidate . . . who tries to sell me tickets to a cocktail party for fund-raising, it would be easily $50,000 per year." He and his colleagues have to be selective. One of them buys tickets only for fund-raisers given by leaders or committee chairmen or members he knows well. Another makes it a rule never to buy tickets to party events, only to functions put on by individual members. Still another insists on contributing only to the legislators who helped him when he needed their help, and not to those who did not.

The solicitation of funds from lobbyists has become a high-pressure activity. Legislative party leaders, who now have fund-raising as one of their major functions, are particularly difficult to turn down. The house speakers and senate presidents in California, Florida, and New Jersey are especially effective in raising money for their party candidates. Sometimes they host fund-raisers for party members, which lobbyists are sure to attend. They also have their own PACs, the monies from which are usually distributed to party candidates in tough races.

"Leadership funds," according to a Florida lobbyist, "develop the idea that lobbyists have to give—or else." Such a charge was made publicly by a lobbyist for trial lawyers in New Jersey. She alleged that in 1989 four assembly leaders, all Democrats, threatened that if her group did not give $20,000 to the Democratic political action committee, its bills would not get posted by a new speaker. An investigation by the state attorney general did not substantiate the lobbyist's charges. Yet the understanding in Trenton is that lobbyists will ante up for the political system. If not them, who else!

Individual legislators pay close attention to who is giving by making use of computer printout generated by the agency with whom contributors are required to file. A Florida lobbyist and former house speaker, Don Tucker, says they are hardly bashful: "As soon as I walk into a legislator's office, some of them say, 'My campaign account is open'."[3]

No one is precisely certain of what message the legislators are sending, but lobbyists generally interpret it to mean that giving is the better part of valor. Some members, according to a California lobbyist for a professional association, are "outrageous in their behavior." Most are more restrained. Nevertheless, lobbyists have a good idea of what is expected. Every invitation to a fund-raiser, every casual remark about money, carries a "psychological implication," one lobbyist asserts, that you have to pay to play. "You almost feel like you *have* to contribute," says a New Jersey lobbyist, "There are certain expectations when one gets to be a major player in the state's political environment; expectations that one will contribute and get their clients to contribute."[4] It is hardly surprising, then, that more and more lobbyists get the feeling that they are being shaken down. Some think legislators and lobbyists are both to blame. More commonly, however, lobbyists feel victimized by a system that has gotten out of control.[5]

"We didn't make the rules, we just play by them," responds a contract lobbyist in Trenton in justifying his activities. He, along with a number of his politically active colleagues in New Jersey and elsewhere, plays the money game to the hilt. He gathers up contributions from many of his clients, "bundles" them, and presents them to the senate and assembly parties. If his clients were to contribute separately, it would tend, in his opinion, to diffuse what he was trying to put together. Moreover, it would not enhance his own standing with New Jersey legislators, as the larger contribution that he delivers does. A nonprofit group like the Greater Miami Opera cannot give to a candidate, but its lobbyists can still be helpful. They have urged board members to raise campaign contributions for legislators who had helped them to get an appropriation.

A few lobbyists not only give on their own and their clients' behalf but also work to raise money for legislators who are particular friends.[6] In Colorado lobbyists have taken on a more active role as campaign contributions have increased in importance. They are now putting together fund-raisers for legislators. In the words of one of them, it has become a case of "lobbyists shaking down lobbyists." With laws being enacted to limit contributions (as are now on the books in California,

Florida, and Minnesota), lobbyists will be assuming an even greater role—that of bundling individual contributions. It will be their responsibility to get more small contributions from individuals within firms, organizations, and families and still raise sufficient funds for a candidate to run an effective campaign.

Political Action Committees

Legislators can rely on lobbyists and other individuals as a source of funds. In some places, they can also count on corporations and labor unions. Corporate contributions are permitted in twenty-four states; they are allowed in seven others, except for certain industries (banks, insurance, utilities). Among other places, corporations are prohibited from giving in Minnesota. Ten states prohibit union contributions, including Texas. But the primary channels for campaign giving today are the political action committees sponsored by labor, business, associations, and causes. PACs are organizations that collect contributions from particular classes of individuals for the purpose of influencing elections.[7] The rationale is that, by aggregating small donations from a large number of contributors, similarly situated people can maximize the effect of their money.

PACs have grown in numbers, resources, and market share since the 1970s. At the federal level, the number of PACs grew from 1,146 in 1976 to 4,828 in 1988, with corporate PACs increasing from 433 to 2,008 and labor PACs from 224 to 401. Growth has been similar in the states. Studies have shown that in the state of Washington the number of PACs and their resources doubled from 1978 to 1980; in Wisconsin and New York they doubled from the late 1970s to the mid 1980s, in Illinois the number rose from 54 in 1974 to 372 in 1982; and increased in Oregon from 57 to 410 during the 1970s. In Minnesota PACs increased from 181 in 1976 to 397 in 1992. In New Jersey the number of PACs rose by 118 percent between 1983 and 1987, with contributions to legislative candidates up from $1.5 million to $2.8 million. Nowadays, the percentage of candidates' campaign funds that derive from PACs varies from state to state; but it is not unusual for these committees to account for half of the contributions legislators receive. A review of the campaign-finance literature shows that by the mid 1980s PACs accounted for one-third of the funds for legislative candidates in Pennsylvania and Missouri. In California and Washington PACs were the greatest sources of contributions.[8] In the words of one lobbyist, PACs have become "a welfare program" for legislative campaigns.[9]

PACs proliferate because as one group establishes a PAC, another one feels that it must match the action. "If other people do it, you have to do it," said a New Jersey lobbyist.[10] Within the past decade, practically every one of them has organized a PAC on the assumption that it is "part of the political program you have to have to be effective." Two-thirds of state chambers of commerce operate PACs.[11] In a survey of fifty-five companies, it was found that forty had PACs that made contributions to state candidates.[12] In the pharmaceutical industry, for example, twenty member companies participate in five state PACs—in California, Florida, Illinois, New York, and Texas—which are coordinated by the Pharmaceutical Manufacturers Association. Certified public accountants maintain their own PACs; societies in thirty-five states have them.

The best-endowed PACs are not usually those of the business associations. In Florida the Associated Industries PAC is relatively small, but the association's four thousand member companies give through PACs of their own.[13] Similarly, California business associations have small PACs because member companies prefer to make their campaign contributions directly.[14] The biggest bundles of money generally come from the associations of doctors, trial lawyers, realtors, developers, teachers, and sometimes labor unions.

Not everyone has a well-developed PAC, however. Minnesota law requires that corporations with PACs have individuals contribute to individual accounts and have a say as to where their contributions go. This acts as a deterrent to an effective PAC. Some companies have not gotten around to developing a contributions strategy, so their PACs limp along. Some have decided that they should not tie their influence to spending money. IBM is probably one of the largest business organizations without a PAC. While oil companies, such as ARCO and Texaco in California, make corporate contributions, the American Petroleum Institute decided that none of its state councils could have a PAC. A lobbyist for one such council bemoaned the situation: "We're Big Oil, but we can't even play with nickels and dimes." Associations of municipalities and counties are not permitted PACs and public interest groups and nonprofits either cannot or are not expected to give. Although the money game is not theirs to play, they are not penalized for not playing.

PACs raise money by a variety of means—direct mail, special events, personal contact, payroll deduction, and so forth. One survey found that corporations and labor groups often use payroll deductions.[15] Almost half of the state CPA societies use a dues-checkoff system, while the others solicit their members. Large groups who have much at stake and whose members are politically sophisticated can raise the most money for their PACs. Lawyers fit the description. In Minnesota, for instance, about half of them contribute to their association's PAC. Teachers are also excellent providers, and state education associations have devised dues check-off systems that facilitate the flow of funds.[16] The Minnesota Education Association PAC receives $10 from everyone, unless they indicate to the contrary. The New Jersey Education Association counts on $10 to $20 from its thirty-five thousand members, making the NJEA the third-largest PAC in the state in 1989, when it contributed $371,000 to campaigns. It is more difficult, in contrast, for companies to raise monies from employees. Their yield is far below that of teachers. A 10 percent contribution rate is about par.

Once money is raised, principal responsibility for decisions regarding contributions is commonly made by a board or committee.[17] A group's lobbyist usually has a role in deciding to whom the funds are to be allocated. Often the lobbyist is the individual running the PAC. Whether or not a board or committee has the final say, the lobbyist will ordinarily have the most to say. Although the process tends to be relatively closed, it can be quite open. A lobbyist for a major pharmaceutical company expounded his philosophy: "Can you explain it to your mother? That is the ultimate test of anything you do." The company will also have a contribution strategy determining which legislators affect core issues; ensuring continued support; and indexing legislators' activity. Several company committees, which include executives as members, have responsibility for deciding who would receive money, based on research and advice from staff.

Allocations by the education associations are determined by means of a democratically based endorsement process. For the California Education Association, first-level selections are made by local chapters, and the second-level endorsements are by a state council. Colorado's state education association sends each candidate a questionnaire, and the local chapters interview them. The locals make their recommendations to the association's PAC, which can accept or reject it. But the PAC cannot endorse any another person in the district. In New Jersey, an operating committee (composed of NJEA's officers, members of its government relations and executive committees, and the county association presidents) endorses candidates on the basis of their responses to a questionnaire and of screening committee reviews. In Texas, teachers make nominations locally, but the state association PAC has to be involved if an endorsement is to be made and a contribution given. If the state PAC rejects a local nomination, a process of fact finding and negotiations takes place.[18]

Contract lobbyists have a more informal approach. Some of them direct their own PACs, such as Bereano in Maryland, who ran the Bereano-PAC and served as director or advisor to about ten others. Most of them provide advice to their corporate and associational clients who have their own PACs. Their combined influence in this respect is estimable.

PACs have various motives for giving money to legislators.[19] The following motives help to determine who gets what and how much is given:

1. To show support for and to help elect friends;
2. To oppose and to help defeat those who are not friends;
3. To support those who are likely to be reelected, especially those who exercise considerable influence;
4. To gain or improve access to members, particularly influential ones; and
5. To attempt to change the odds by affecting the overall outcome of an election.

For the most part, lobbyists and the PACs they influence pursue the objectives noted in the first, third, and fourth items on the above list.

Incumbents, of course, are on the receiving end of most PAC gifts. A study of campaign giving in Minnesota documented this.[20] PACs in Colorado, Louisiana, and Minnesota have also favored incumbents over challengers. A recent survey of PACs in these three states found that about half say they favor incumbents, while another half have no preferences along these lines. In New Jersey during the 1980s, about 80 percent of the PAC money went to incumbents.[21] The rationale for favoring incumbents, according to a California lobbyist, is: "We make campaign contributions to all members of the legislature since all of them have a vote." [22] Another Californian, who lobbies for an association of professionals, explained that in 1990 his group contributed to seventy-five out of the eighty incumbent assemblymen and ten to fifteen of the forty incumbent senators. Its PAC operates on the principle that "if the individual hasn't hurt the profession, we'll support the campaign." The only ones eliminated, therefore, are out-and-out enemies.

Many groups apply a stricter test for supporting the reelection of incumbents. They must be real friends. The trial lawyers, for example, give to legislators who share their philosophy. Business associations tend to give to incumbents who are sympathetic to business. PACs directed or influenced by contract lobbyists are more apt to contribute to those who have been helpful to their clients. Sometimes, one's friends tend to be in the Democratic rather than the Republican party, as in the case of teachers' unions and organized labor. Sometimes, one's friends tend to be in the Republican party, as in the case of most business groups. But partisan friendship usually is tempered by which party is in the majority. Thus, New Jersey business has been kind to Democrats, who have had control of both houses of the legislature for most recent years. Similarly, Colorado teachers in 1990 gave one-third of their endorsements to Republicans, who appear to practically have a lock on the two houses.

One thing is certain in fund-raising. Leaders and key members pull in more contributions than rank-and-file. The amount a PAC contributes usually depends on the leadership position, chairmanship, and committee assignment of the recipient. Whether an incumbent sits on a committee overseeing the group's affairs may be as important as anything else. Thus, the members of committees with jurisdiction over economic matters usually fare well. In California, for example, the work of the Assembly Finance and Insurance Committee affects insurance companies, banks, savings and loans, thrifts, credit unions, and doctors and lawyers. Its members receive more in campaign contributions than any other legislators.[23] The state-relations director of one national association explained that his group generally gave to people in key positions, but "not to those [in key positions] who consistently screw us."

Speakers, presidents, and majority and sometimes minority leaders naturally hold the most key positions. They solicit funds from lobbyists and PACs, which they then allocate to incumbents and challengers in their parties, with preference given to those in competitive races where money can make the greatest difference to party fortunes. Lobbyists find it difficult to resist such leadership appeals, and a few actually welcome them. A New Jersey contract lobbyist, with a record of service to his party, would rather give to leadership committees than get involved in individual races. Leaders represent the membership and, in his opinion, should be entrusted with the bulk of funds lobbyists raise. They, in turn, can disburse the money themselves to whomever they feel is most deserving. Most lobbyists, however, would rather make their own choices and receive direct credit than let the leaders take matters out of their hands. Some association and company PACs, in fact, have a policy of contributing only to individual members and not to leadership committees.

Finally, some groups in some places target key races where they have friends or enemies. Money can have considerable impact in these contests and the outcome can affect the success of a group's program in the legislature. The teachers and trial lawyers and, from time to time, business interests put themselves at risk here. We shall examine such engagements below.

Whatever the allocation process or the amount contributed, the way it is presented also counts. Contract lobbyists benefit from making the presentation themselves, although their clients get less credit this way. The consensus among state government relations professionals is that a member of the group should hand the contributed checks to the legislator in his or her own district. The presentation is best made by a key contact or constituent at a special breakfast or in the legislator's office. The idea, according to an association lobbyist in Minnesota, is to "get them where they live." When a member of a group delivers a contribution to a member in his district, the conversation need not be lengthy. A typical approach, according to New Jersey senator Lee Laskin, is: "How ya doin' Lee? Good luck. We're concerned about mortgages. We hope you can do something about that."[24] The money is given and the message is received.

What Does Money Buy?

Public-interest groups and the press have no doubt that money talks and that legislators listen. Admitting that well-heeled groups have a constitutional right to lobby the legislature, the executive director of New Jersey Common Cause articulated a widely held view: "What distorts it is the volume with which the special interests speak, and the amplifier is campaign contributions." [25] Along these lines, environmental and consumer groups complain specifically about the monetary advantages of business. Many critics of the campaign-finance system in the states argue that contributions tend to buy particular votes, even if they do not buy particular legislators. There is little evidence to support such contentions, even though those groups and organizations that make the biggest contributions are also likely to wield substantial influence. The influence, however, may have preceded the money rather than derived from it.

Considerable research has been conducted on the impact of campaign contributions at the congressional level. Most of the studies have tried to relate money to roll-call votes, with very mixed results. Some have found a relationship; others have found a weak relationship, with party, ideology, and constituency more important; and still others have found little or no relationship. But studies that focus on floor votes fail to take into account many key actions, which take place elsewhere, or more subtle ones, which are difficult to discern and impossible to quantify.[26] A few congressional studies, though, have gone further. One examined contributions to members of the House Ways and Means Committee and found indirect influence. Money tended to "facilitate access and amplify lobbying messages," rather than serve as a direct exchange for favors.[27] Another study, which also looked at the politics of committee decision making, concluded that the participation of members was more important than their votes, especially in the case of representatives who were sympathetic anyway. Money mainly bought the marginal time, energy, and legislative resources that committee participation required.[28]

How congressional representatives spend their time, and the time and effort they spend for or against particular policies, may be at least marginally affected by campaign contributions. But, as has been suggested, members of Congress are usually already sympathetic to most of the groups that contribute to them.[29] The same is true at the state level, where contributions tend to be rewards for past support rather than inducements for future support.

From the point of view of lobbyists, campaign contributions are part, but only part, of what goes into the building of relationships. They also bear independent fruit, some of which is not unlike that produced by close ties between individual lobbyists and individual legislators. What does money attain?

First, money produces access, or at least the assurance that their issues will get a fair hearing. In the words of a former lobbyist in Ohio: "Campaign contributions do not buy votes ... but they do buy access to an individual and an ability to speak one's case." [30] They make it easier to get an appointment—to get into a legislator's office. Even when PAC money goes only to friends, lobbyists believe that money still smooths the way. Clay Jackson, one of California's major contract lobbyists, puts it this way: "Money gets you in the front door but doesn't guarantee a front-row seat." [31] A Texas lobbyist for an organization that has no PAC recognizes the value of contributions. "They listen to you a lot quicker," he admits. If a lobbyist brings a check, he or she will have an opportunity to discuss issues with legislators before the session starts. And the earlier the discussion, the better.

Second, in some places and with some members, a campaign contribution from those who are expected to give is regarded simply as table stakes. There is no quid pro quo as such, but simply an ante for getting dealt a hand in the game. A lawyer-lobbyist described the system in Texas as one of "pay to play." If one doesn't contribute, there is no point in visiting a senator's office. According to one expert on the subject of lobbying in Washington, D.C., political contributions ensure a role in the dialogue—"today and tomorrow, on the pending issue and the next one." They are, however, not downpayments on results.[32] An association lobbyist in New Jersey states: "A contribution is between a gift and a bribe. One is without expectations; the other is with expectations." Another lobbyist in Trenton agrees that campaign contributions do not guarantee anything, although they have become "a precondition to even discussing legislation with any member of the legislature."

Third, the absence of contributions, where they are expected, may be more harmful than their presence is helpful. A Minnesota lobbyist and former member of the legislature maintains that while a business group might not need to make a contribution, legislators may be waiting for it. Therefore, in his view, "it's better to give than explain why you didn't." A contribution, moreover, highlights a lobbyist's presence; and a lobbyist cannot be successful without one.[33] Another Minnesota lobbyist, who must do his work without benefit of PAC, observes that "what a PAC gets you is that you're not noticeable by its absence." If money talks, then no money also talks—and lobbyists cannot afford the latter. Moreover, once a lobbyist gives, it is difficult to stop—or even to cut down. A New Jersey lobbyist described what happened when he reduced the size of his contribution to a member who had not been very friendly to his issues. The member got annoyed and complained to him. The lobbyist had no way of knowing whether or how that annoyance would affect whatever case he would make in the future.

Another lobbyist, from Colorado, makes it a policy of not contributing to campaigns. The reaction of one senator was: "Why should I listen to you? You've never donated to my campaign." But, according to the lobbyist's recollection, that type of reaction occurred only four or five times in the last half-dozen years. "It wouldn't hurt anybody, if they refused to give—if they had the balls to say no." Still, Colorado's political environment is less high-pressured than that in many other places. Lobbyists in California, Florida, New Jersey, and Texas are uncertain of the consequences of saying "no" very often. Given the uncertainty, it makes sense for them to ante up. Otherwise they risk the perception that they are not players, or even worse.

Fourth, contributions serve not only to keep lobbyists and their clients in the game but also to make them competitive with other players. In an environment where interests engage in continuous and keen rivalries, no lobbyist wants today's actual opponents, or tomorrow's possible opponents, to get ahead. New Jersey lobbyist Monica Walsh sees the role of campaign money in this way: "It's just keeping even with everyone else." [34] "You can't name a lobbyist who has won with money," declared a representative of a New Jersey association. "All I want money to do is keep me even." The state governmental relations director of a national association with substantial interests in a number of places agreed as to what money buys. "It keeps us in the pack, although it doesn't give us more than anybody else."

Fifth, much like relationships, campaign contributions matter at the margins. One New Jersey legislator is said to have accepted regular contributions from the business community and then done everything the environmentalists wanted. On the major issues that were involved for this particular legislator, other factors outweighed the influence of money. Generally, money may play the deciding role only on issues that do not affect a legislator's district and do not become visible and highly controversial. There are many such minor matters, and on these money can make a difference.

It may have made some difference, for instance, in the battle between the optometrists and the ophthalmologists in New Jersey. The New Jersey Optometric Association, in a fund-raising letter to members, urged them to contribute "tons of bucks" to get their bill passed. The optometrists managed to outdo the ophthalmologists in contributions by over more than four to one, and in 1991, after a decade-long struggle, they got their bill.[35]

Often neither the lobbyist nor the legislator is aware of the effects of a contribution. John Vasconcellos, a veteran member of the California assembly, detailed one possibility:

When you know that the next day you've got to go ask for a thousand dollars or five thousand dollars for your campaign from some group, it is more and more difficult to be explicitly "anti" their position. You may speak against them, but you speak more softly rather than rant and rave.[36]

One of Vasconcellos's colleagues, Lloyd Connelly, recalled his "no" vote on a particular bill. After the assemblyman left the floor, the lobbyist against whose bill he had voted approached him and was profuse in his thanks. The lobbyist was grateful because, even though Connelly had voted against the bill, he had not spoken out. If he had spoken against the bill, he might have carried four or five more negative votes, which would have increased the likelihood of a veto by the governor.[37] The lobbyist may have had reason to have been grateful.

Campaign contributions may matter much less than many people believe. But lobbyists always want whatever edge they can get. In the case of campaign expenditures, a candidate is never entirely sure what the right amount is and whether more spending makes much of a difference at all. In the case of campaign contributions, a lobbyist is never entirely sure of the consequences of giving or of not giving. When New Jersey legislators were asked by a Gallup survey what kind of impact campaign contributions had on their relationship with contributor groups, 45 percent said "positive" and 7 percent said "negative." The rest did not venture an opinion.[38] If this pattern of responses is any indication, then political contributions certainly do not hurt. They probably help. So why not be safe rather than sorry!

Engaging in Battle

In the case of some interest groups, political involvement goes further than contributions to friendly or important legislators. Their involvement can be intense and targeted to key races. In these instances, a group's objectives are to punish enemies, reward friends, and alter the lineup of proponents and opponents in senate and house ranks.

Influential groups that experience defeat on a vital issue may respond by seeking to change the odds in the legislature. They may also want to restore their reputations as powers by taking reprisals. New Jersey's dentists, for example, went after three incumbents whom they deemed hostile to their interests. Two of them were defeated, and the dentists claimed credit.[39] The New Jersey Education Association in 1979 took on the Democratic chairman of the assembly education committee, who was considered a threat to tenure.[40] He lost his race, and the teachers took credit. Colorado's optometrists and ophthalmologists fought it out in the legislative arena and in campaigns. After failing to match the optometrists for some years, the ophthalmologists in 1990 finally helped to defeat an incumbent legislator who had favored their opponents during the session. They felt much better as a result.

Major battles between powerful groups occur in many places. In Texas, for example, the trial lawyers and business interests have fought vigorously against one another's candidates in campaigns in order to get the upper hand in the legislature. For the past fifteen years, the Texas Trial Lawyers Association appeared to have control of the Texas senate. But opposition to the group grew, as business and other groups coalesced in an association named the Texas Civil Justice League. Having suffered some setbacks in the legislature, the trial lawyers targeted five key senate districts in the 1988 elections. But in all five races their candidates lost. One consequence was that the trial lawyers changed their strategy from one of belligerence to one of making friends in the legislature.[41] Since then, they have regained some ground, and they continue to pursue the political game. Their opposition, however, has been less politically astute. One Texas lobbyist criticized the business community for pouring money into lobbyists when it should have been pouring it into campaigns in order to change the composition of the senate.

In recent years, the issue of abortion rights has galvanized group involvement in campaigns. Those on either side of the issue will endorse certain candidates, target others for defeat, contribute funds to campaigns, assist with phone banks, and provide volunteers either to the campaign itself or through independent efforts. A study of the activities of these groups in selected legislative races in the 1989 New Jersey and Virginia legislative (and gubernatorial) elections reveals somewhat mixed results. The abortion issue had impact, but the groups themselves were not always welcomed by the candidates as allies. Some legislators appreciated their support; others were wary of their endorsements, feeling that the groups were too extreme. Moreover, the prochoice groups were criticized for advancing the issue more than the candidates.[42] But the involvement of these groups was intense and promised to be more so in the campaigns of 1992.

Legislators can be intimidated by a group's threat to support a challenger. The lawmaker's attitude toward the group may undergo a subtle, or not-so-subtle, change. If a group *almost* succeeds in unseating an incumbent, that legislator is likely to make a greater effort to see eye-to-eye with it. Accommodation may not be entirely possible, but the effort will be made. And if a legislator is defeated, the message to the capitol community is heard loud and clear. One participant in the electoral struggle acknowledges that, "if your opponents defeat a legislator on your side, it has tremendous impact. . . . We [then] have to defeat one of theirs to get on track."

Groups willing to target close races, oppose incumbents, take dramatic action, and commit people as well as other resources to the fray can be formidable. As the director of one such group declared: "When we win, we win big. When we lose, we lose big." In some state campaigns environmental groups are effective. For example, New Jersey's environmentalists get into races where they can make more of a difference. Their contributions to candidates are in kind—a canvass, media work, radio ads, literature drops—and they operate according to their own campaign plan. Their "resource endorsements" have had considerable effect. One year, for instance, they campaigned for a Democratic challenger who won in a marginal district. Although he had not been an environmentalist when he declared his candidacy, he ended his campaign as one. Then, serving in the legislature, he became a leading spokesman for environmental interests.

Labor traditionally takes on a role in elections. New Jersey provides an example of its recent involvement. The Communications Workers of America (CWA), the major union for state employees, threatened to back its own independent candidates in the 1991 election in nine of forty legislative districts. This threat was announced when the Florio administration proposed layoffs and demanded salary and benefit givebacks from state government employees as a means toward reducing a huge projected deficit in the 1992 budget. CWA's independent candidates would have taken votes away from incumbents and could have cost Democrats control of both houses. (As it turned out, the Democrats did lose both houses, but mainly because of an antitax vote by the electorate.) After the budget had been settled by the Democratic governor and legislature without the deferral of raises or sacrifice of benefits, CWA dropped its threat. But organized labor in New Jersey continued to be critical of the weak Democratic support of priority labor initiatives, particularly on health care. In July 1991 AFL-CIO leaders put a moratorium on all financial contributions to candidates for the legislature. At its fall convention, to evidence its displeasure, the union decided to restrict official endorsements to only a handful of "proven friends." Finally, the New Jersey Industrial Union Council limited its endorsements to 50 of the 120 legislative races, the fewest since the labor group began operating more than twenty years before.[43]

Few groups become as involved in legislative campaigns as teachers and therefore few have comparable clout. In a 1987 survey Minnesota legislators ranked teachers as the most effective group (with labor just behind) as far as campaign assistance was concerned.[44] Teachers' groups are the ideal political organization because they are locally based and widely dispersed. There are one or more schools in every legislator's district; and where there is a school, there are teachers. Teachers are educated; and they have high voting rates and time after school hours to participate in politics. Moreover, they are politically motivated and their organizations are skillfully managed.

Teachers associations are unlike other organizations in having such an array of resources that can be devoted to politics. The Texas State Teachers Association, for example, has gotten involved in campaigns at the grass-roots level. The Colorado Education Association (CEA) has provided volunteers for two out of three candidates it endorsed. In addition to furnishing funds, CEA provided analysis, established phone banks, and even hired political consultants (for a few priority races). The association's posture is: "We want a piece of your campaign." [45]

The New Jersey Education Association (NJEA) has an integrated campaign support system. The combination of money, association effort, and volunteers makes a real impression. NJEA will not give funds directly to candidates. Instead, its PAC approves the expenses of committees of educators who are campaigning on behalf of endorsed candidates. Each committee works with a minimum of $3,000 which it spends on mailings, door-to-door canvassing, mobilizing members to vote, and get-out-the-vote activities on election day. Given the strength of its organization and its contribution to legislative elections, NJEA has been especially helpful to legislators—primarily Democratic ones—in New Jersey. But the teachers refuse to be taken for granted. In 1991, after Democratic majorities in the senate and assembly had taken away $360 million from the just-enacted Quality Education Act in order to ease property taxes (having also imposed spending caps on the schools), NJEA reversed its traditional endorsement preferences. Instead of favoring the Democratic candidates, it endorsed only three of them, espousing forty-six Republicans, with thirty-four of the total endorsements going to incumbents.[46] NJEA also targeted the Democratic senate president, John Lynch, for defeat. New Jersey's teachers were playing politics with no holds barred.

Nowhere have teachers played as large a role as they have in Alabama. In the 1970s the Alabama Education Association (AEA) started recruiting candidates for the legislature and began winning seats. Business began to organize in response to the AEA victories, recruited its own candidates, and won back a number of these seats in 1986. Unfazed, the education association redoubled its political efforts and regained its clout: 58 of the 140 members of the legislature are teachers, former teachers, or spouses of teachers.[47]

Going for Votes

Lobbyists do not necessarily confine their activities to the legislative arena. In those states where the constitutional or statutory initiative exists, they and those they represent have the option of taking a proposal directly to the voters. In California more than anywhere else, the initiative has been used increasingly in the past forty years. The number of initiatives filed has nearly doubled each decade since the 1950s, with many of them filed by single-issue groups, other interests, and even state elective officeholders. The 1980s saw initiative campaigns for no-fault insurance, handgun regulation, the regulation of insurance rates, the regulation of lawyer fees, bottle deposits, cigarette taxes, water resources, toxics, antismoking, and establishing English as the official language.[48] The California Teachers Association has made effective use of the initiative. One of its objectives was to make the education budget inviolate. But it would have been impossible to persuade the legislature to earmark a special fund for education. So CTA spent three years preparing an initiative, which it sponsored as Proposition 98 in 1988. Requiring 40 percent of state tax revenues be devoted to elementary and secondary education, the proposition passed.[49]

If lobbyists and the groups they represent lose in the California legislature, or if they think they cannot win, they will turn to the initiative. Environmentalists attribute their frequent resort to the initiative to their lack of success in the legislative process. Even if they have a chance in the legislature, groups may decide on the initiative campaign anyway. It is a good way to publicize an organization's issue (or an individual's candidacy for statewide office), and it offers the opportunity for an organization to achieve greater strength. Moreover, the initiative may serve to prod the governor and the legislature to take action. As a lobbyist for an environmental group said, "Now we have a viable threat that we'll do an initiative if the bill does not pass." The pressure on the legislature can be considerable.

The interests of business groups, in particular, have been assaulted by initiatives—mainly by those on automobile insurance and the environment. In 1988 the insurance industry spent $80 million fighting Proposition 103, which passed nonetheless. Business adopted a different strategy for the 1990 ballot, on which Big Green and a number of other initiatives were to appear. Its strategy was to load the ballot with counterinitiatives or "stealth" initiatives in an effort to confuse the political situation and confound the electorate. This strategy apparently worked, for only a few initiatives (including Proposition 140, which established term limitations for members of the legislature) passed.

Colorado has also made use of the initiative to bypass and change the legislature. For years the state chapter of Common Cause had tried unsuccessfully to weaken caucus control of legislation. The organization was perceived, particularly by majority-party Republicans, to be "nagging and ineffectual." But Common Cause had the last laugh. It used its campaign for the Give-a-Vote-to-Every-Legislator (GAVEL) initiative to change that perception. The campaign, supported by the Colorado League of Women Voters and the press, overwhelmed the opposition.

GAVEL was approved by the electorate, and the legislature had to live with new restrictions. Common Cause had demonstrated that it could play hardball politics. "While it lost the affection of legislators," observes one lobbyist, "it won their respect."

In California, and to some extent in Colorado too, it is up to the lobbyist to help determine whether the initiative is the appropriate strategy for a client. Lobbyists of all stripes, particularly those working for causes, are key decision makers in choosing between an initiative campaign or braving the legislative process. If the initiative route is chosen, lobbyists will hire consultants to run the campaign; after that their involvement will vary. In all likelihood, however, they will continue to be involved until the electorate has voted on the issue.

Notes

1. A. G. Block, "The Ethics Jungle," *California Journal*, April 1990, 177.
2. James Richardson, "Special Interests Dominate the Legislative Session," *California Journal*, November 1990, 527.
3. *St. Petersburg Times*, May 31, 1989.
4. Bill Glovin, "The Quintessential Art of Lobbying," *New Jersey Business*, July 1987, 62.
5. See Josephson Institute of Ethics, *Actual and Apparent Impropriety: A Report on Ethical Norms and Attitudes in State Legislatures* (Marina del Rey, Calif.: The Institute, January 1992), app. B.
6. See *Evening Sun* (Baltimore), December 27, 1989, on Bruce Bereano.
7. See Charles S. Mack, *Lobbying and Government Relations: A Guide for Executives* (New York: Quorum Books, 1989), 157-169.
8. See, for instance, James D. King and Helena S. Robin, "Political Action Committees in State Politics." (Paper prepared for the Annual Meeting of the American Political Science Association, Washington, D.C., August 29-September 1, 1991).
9. See Bob Narus, "Pacs Vobiscum," *New Jersey Reporter,* November 1982, 6-14.
10. Ibid., 11.
11. Charles S. Mack, *The Executive's Handbook of Trade and Business Associations* (Westport, Conn.: Quorum Books, 1991), 89.
12. Public Affairs Council, *State Government Relations: Results of a Survey of 55 Corporations* (Washington, D.C.: The Council, 1986), 26; also Seymour Lusterman, *Managing Business-State Government Relations* (New York: The Conference Board, 1983), 10.
13. Rowland Stiteler, "Influence Peddling," *Florida Magazine, Orlando Sentinel,* May 29, 1988.
14. Max Boot, "Business Associations—Big Names, Less Clout," *California*

Journal, October 1988, 455.

15. King and Robin, "Political Action Committees," 16.
16. Other groups also allow members to check off a box contributing to a PAC as part of filling out the form to pay their dues.
17. King and Robin, "Political Action Committees," 17-18.
18. The teachers association in Texas makes use of a system of record votes for legislators, each of which is assigned a numerical value related to its importance. Points are also awarded to legislators for their strategic location, and other factors are also entered into the calculation. These analyses serve as a basis for the teachers' endorsement.
19. Mack, *Lobbying and Government Relations,* 155.
20. Ruth S. Jones and Thomas J. Borris, "Strategic Contributing in Legislative Campaigns: The Case of Minnesota," *Legislative Studies Quarterly* 10 (February 1985): 102.
21. King and Robin, "Political Action Committees," 4, 18-20; New Jersey Election Law Enforcement Commission, "ELEC White Paper: Is There a PAC Plague in New Jersey?" November 1991, 48.
22. Daniel Carson, "The Cable TV Tangle: A New Industry Learns the Legislative Ropes," *California Journal,* June 1988, 252.
23. A. G. Block and Stephanie Carviello, "Putting on the Squeeze," *California Journal,* April 1987, 179.
24. Narus, "Pacs Vobiscum," 9.
25. Ed McCool, quoted in *Star-Ledger,* June 29, 1990.
26. David B. Magleby and Candice J. Nelson, *The Money Chase: Congressional Campaign Finance Reform* (Washington, D.C.: Brookings, 1990), 77-79; Kay Lehman Schlozman and John T. Tierney, *Organized Interests and American Democracy* (New York: Harper and Row, 1986), 256.
27. John R. Wright, "Contributions, Lobbying, and Committee Voting in the U.S. House of Representatives," *American Political Science Review* 84 (June 1990): 434.
28. Richard L. Hall and Frank W. Wayman, "Buying Time: Moneyed Interests and the Mobilization of Bias in Congressional Committees," *American Political Science Review* 84 (September 1990): 798, 814.
29. Jeffrey M. Berry, *The Interest Group Society* (Boston: Little, Brown, 1984), 173.
30. *Akron Beacon Journal,* October 9, 1988.
31. Sigrid Bathen, "Lawyer-Lobbyists Become Big Fish in the Capitol Pond," *California Journal,* February 1990: 114.
32. Bruce C. Wolpe, *Lobbying Congress: How the System Works* (Washington, D.C.: Congressional Quarterly Inc., 1990), 46.
33. Ibid., 47.
34. *Star-Ledger,* June 29, 1990.
35. Ibid., December 20, 1991, and January 12, 1992.
36. Quoted in Block, "Ethics Jungle," 177.
37. Block, "Ethics Jungle," 177.
38. Gallup Organization, "The 1987 Gallup Survey of the New Jersey State Legislature" (Princeton, N.J.: Gallup, 1987), 13.
39. Narus, "Pacs Vobiscum," 8.

40. Paul Feldman, "Those Who Can, Lobby," *New Jersey Reporter,* April 1983, 27.
41. Kathleen Sylvester, "The Chastening of the Trial Lawyers," *Governing,* February 1991, 30.
42. Debra L. Dodson and Lauren D. Burnbauer, *Election 1989: The Abortion Issue in New Jersey and Virginia* (New Brunswick, N.J.: Eagleton Institute of Politics, Rutgers University, 1990), 123-129.
43. *Star-Ledger,* September 17, 1991, and October 21, 1991.
44. Craig H. Grau, "Minnesota: Labor and Business in an Issue Oriented State," in *Interest Groups in the Midwestern States,* ed. Ronald J. Hrebenar and Clive S. Thomas (Ames: Iowa State University Press, forthcoming).
45. CEA has been loyal to its supporters in the Colorado General Assembly. In 1990 it did not endorse three of its own members, who were running against tried and true incumbent friends.
46. *Star-Ledger,* September 17, 1991.
47. Alan Ehrenhalt, *The United States of Ambition* (New York: Times Books, 1991), 173.
48. Charles M. Price, "Initiative Campaigns: Afloat in a Sea of Cash," *California Journal,* November 1988, 481-484.
49. CTA has also been involved in other initiative campaigns. In 1990, its PAC contributed funds to ten initiatives, and CTA put major effort into four.

CHAPTER 7

Generating Support

If direct lobbying refers to what gets done in the legislature itself, with lobbyists and members interacting with one another, indirect lobbying refers to what takes place on the outside to support the efforts inside. Support can be furnished by groups that coalesce to form a coalition. It can also come from the grass-roots level—local association members, company employees, plant managers, clients, suppliers, and so forth. Finally, support—or *perceived* support—can come from the public itself, and is generated through the media, public relations campaigns, and advertising.

Coalition Building

One of Maryland's leading contract lobbyists, Bruce Bereano, thinks that one of a lobbyist's first tasks is to identify groups with similar interests to those of his client. He illustrates such advice by his experience representing a closed panel of dentists, a group that had furnished dental services to businesses that provided employees with a dental insurance plan. The Maryland Dental Association (MDA) challenged this arrangement with legislation that would have mandated a certain mode of dental care, thus jeopardizing the arrangements for contracting practitioners. In order to repulse the MDA, Bereano put together a coalition of businesses, labor, universities, and other groups that benefited from his client's practice.

Nowadays, organizations seldom act in isolation from like-minded groups. Usually several of them will form a loose confederation on either side of an issue.[1] The word "coalition" has thus become one of the buzzwords of contemporary lobbying, and coalition building has become one of the major tasks of contemporary lobbyists. "Whenever you can put a coalition together, you do it," counsels one Colorado lobbyist. The more groups on one's side and the fewer on the other, the more effective the effort. As a Florida lobbyist put it, "The more people who hit 'em [the legislators], the better off you'll be."

Coalition building is not easy, but it is well worth the effort. From a legislative perspective, its value is clear. The greater and more broad-based the support, the more likely that legislators will see the wisdom of a particular policy direction. At the very least, they will have the rationale of widespread support to justify their position. The creation of a large coalition, according to one observer, "provides the comfort level necessary to make it easier for politicians to endorse your group's goal."[2] The downside of a coalition is that each individual member forgoes control. One view, albeit held by a small minority, argues that "you should just go out and do it, and other groups will follow you." Do not spend valuable time, this argument goes, trying to keep a diverse organization in tow.

For our purposes, a coalition is a loose collection of organizations that cooperates to accomplish common objectives. It is different from a single-industry association, such as the soft-drink manufacturers, or a multi-industry association, such as the chamber of commerce. A coalition may be ad hoc or relatively stable, made up of like-minded groups or strange bedfellows, and with or without formal organization.[3] Coalitions vary from issue to issue, time to time, and state to state depending on the groups and the lobbyists involved.

Identification and Recruitment of Members

"The first thing I do," reported a California lobbyist, "is to figure out if there's anyone else out there to help." Thus, the initial task of the lobbyist is to identify potential members of a coalition. The question is what other ox is being—or would be—gored by an issue or measure. In California a bill was being pushed to ban tax deductibility with regard to advertising tobacco and alcohol products. A lobbyist for a beer company quickly calculated all the different parties that would be harmed by this move. Newspapers were among those who would feel the effects. The lobbyist had no trouble putting a coalition together. In Colorado the issue was a bill to ban cigarettes from vending machines. The tobacco companies naturally formed the core of an opposing coalition, but vending machine and candy companies also joined.

In New Jersey dental assistants opposed the dental association's plan to create a category titled "limited registered dental assistant." The dental assistants' lobbyist recruited the Dental Hygienists, State Nurses Association, Dental Assisting Educators, and the University of Medicine and Dentistry of New Jersey into the coalition. Another New Jersey lobbyist, representing business clients on the issue of product liability, identified for his coalition—the Federation of Advocates for Insurance Reform (FAIR)—more than fifty groups that faced liability problems. These groups included the Policemen's Benevolent Association, the Hospital Association, the School Boards Association, the Society of Certified Public Accountants, Squibb, Johnson & Johnson, the Restaurant Association, and the Food Council.

Once potential members are identified, it is up to the lobbyist to recruit them to the cause.[4] That means framing an issue in appealing terms and motivating others to take certain action.[5] Success in this regard depends on a host of factors, not the least of which is the issue itself, the relationship among the groups, and the lobbyist's persuasiveness. Those groups with a history of taking part in coalitions to support others on issues that are marginal for them have a better chance of succeeding than groups that have traditionally acted alone. Coalitions generally come hard to organizations whose issues are low on other groups' agendas. Yet those that are willing to trade support on issues are in a better position. They have something tangible to offer one another. One pharmaceuticals lobbyist suggested, for instance, that: "It's a good quid pro quo to tell the docs that you'll help them in return for their help on Medicaid."

More subtle is the lobbyist's job of taking out potential opponents. Lobbyists cultivate relationships with various groups. Such relationships make it less likely that the cultivated group will join a coalition in opposition to the lobbyist's objectives. For example, bridge building is one of the principal lobbying strategies of the trial lawyers in Texas. They hold a joint retreat with doctors every year, work with senior citizens and the American Association of Retired Professionals, and have reached a modus vivendi with the automobile dealers in the state. The aim has been to deter such groups from joining the opposition.

The Nature of Coalitions

There are coalitions of natural partners and of strange bedfellows. They may include any combination. One thing is clear, however: even groups that appear to have similar interests and aims are not easy to bring together. Many associations and organizations suffer from internal disunity, as we saw in chapter 2. Yet an organization must usually develop a consensus within before it can be part of an effective coalition.

Achieving unity is no simple matter for many groups. Business is particularly fragmented, even Balkanized. "It is rare," observed one lobbyist in Austin, "to find business in this state unified against anybody." Instead, tax issues split the service and manufacturing sectors, and other issues divide businesses according to size or product. In Texas perhaps the only big issues on which business has been united in recent years are tort reform and product liability.[6] Environmentalists, even within the same organization, also encounter difficulties. Purists disagree with pragmatists, and it is not easy for them to resolve their differences. "There are more environmentalists per square foot," observes one public-interest lobbyist from Colorado, "but they are the least effective group for their numbers." Another public-interest lobbyist from New Jersey described coalition work as extremely challenging mainly because everybody has different interests. Although various environmental groups all agree in general on issues, "individual interests and individual tactics and strategies tend to vary among groups."

Still, certain groups are easier for a lobbyist to bring together than others. Some already have membership in a formal organization, such as the New Jersey Environmental Federation. This group has been in operation almost ten years as a coalition of about forty-five environmental, labor, and civic member groups. When the Clean Water Enforcement Act was at the top of the New Jersey PIRG agenda, more than one hundred environmental organizations signed on and worked in the coalition. On the regulation of smoking, the coalitions on each side are also natural ones: physicians and heart, lung, and cancer societies versus the tobacco industry, retail merchants, the restaurant association, and others with an economic interest in tobacco.

In Minnesota a group of six major utilities—two electric, two gas, and two combination—work hand in hand on three out of four issues that affect them. The Pharmaceutical Manufacturers Association's main allies are state medical associations, which also want maximum flexibility for the use of drugs financed by Medicaid. In Florida one of the large coalitions is the Clearinghouse on Human Services, run by Budd Bell, which meets every Monday morning at eight o'clock with about fifty people in attendance.

Then there are coalitions that cross "family" lines.[7] Perhaps the most visible of these strange bedfellows are business and labor. In many places, business and labor have formed the core of the coalition opposing the bottle bill. Indeed, they need one another in order to prevail on this issue. In Minnesota, where labor exercises substantial power, business makes a special effort to, in the words of one of its lobbyists, "get connections whenever we can." The motivation for business to link up with labor is somewhat less in other states.

Some companies manage to recruit as allies environmental and consumer groups, as unlikely as that may seem. Ordinarily, beer and environmental groups are at loggerheads. But in Florida the environmentalists supported beer's opposition to a seven-ounce packaging bill. The environmentalists did not want additional types of containers; neither did the beer wholesalers. Drug companies make their case in terms of "patient care," so their optimal coalition is one that includes doctors, pharmacists, and, whenever possible, patient groups.

Given the right circumstances, skillful lobbyists can recruit groups that will give a big boost to their client's cause. In one state builders were pushing a bill to allow them to dispose of waste materials on the construction site by digging a hole and burying them—a way for the industry to reduce costs. The lobbyist's client, a solid-waste-management group, would have been adversely affected. Because an environmental argument wielded by the solid-waste group would not have been heeded (the self-interest being too obvious), the lobbyist contacted the environmental groups and got them steamed up. He also appealed to the counties and municipalities that would have been responsible for regulating the builders under the proposed legislation. Although it had been moving through the legislature smoothly, the bill came to a screeching halt when this coalition was activated.

In another state, the natural gas industry, once an ally of the utilities, has lately become an adversary. In seeking additional markets, it sought legislation that would require utilities to use natural gas. The utilities naturally were opposed. Their lobbyist contacted consumer groups. "Have you looked at this?" he asked them. The coalition came together, with the consumer groups opposing the measure on the grounds that it would drive up prices and the utilities happily going along.

Not only does business turn to consumers and environmentalists for help, but it can also work the other way. The Colorado Public Interest Research Group (COPIRG) is taking the lead in exploring nontraditional coalitions. Four or five years ago, the big question at COPIRG was, "Should you have lunch with an industry lobbyist?" Since then, COPIRG has gotten involved in a coalition with ten businesses (including AT&T) to oppose reduction in the regulation of U.S. West Communications. Nontraditional coalitions such as this are very useful for public-interest groups. One benefit is that they open doors in the Republican-controlled legislature. COPIRG's lobbyist met the speaker of the Colorado house by working in such a coalition, achieving access that he might not otherwise have gotten.

Working Together

Cooperative action is frequently essential. But holding a coalition together is as tough as creating it in the first place. A Minnesota lobbyist for insurance interests described the tricks of his trade. His objective was to modify Minnesota's 1985 Superfund statute, which had made the cost of liability insurance for environmental impairment prohibitively high. But business groups and the insurance industry were divided, with "bickering, mistrust, suspicion, and dislike" among them. Their lobbyists agreed, however, that the St. Paul Area Chamber of Commerce would act as a facilitator of a coalition seeking to amend the Superfund law. In response to efforts by the insurance lobbyist, the governor established a task force composed of business leaders, insurance representatives, governmental agencies, and environmentalists to look into amending the statute. The business coalition was able to work with the task force as well as with legislative leaders. Near the end of the debate, however, the environmentalists balked. They would not support the coalition's amendment of the Superfund statute unless a victims' compensation fund was established. The business community could have fragmented at this point, but the coalition stood fast. Finally, their efforts succeeded because chief executive officers were involved in the debate and because lobbying, media, and internal business communications held together.[8]

The danger is that coalition members will pull away toward the end of the process. Even though they may agree on the general case, they can diverge on specifics. Some will drop out because their particular interests are being compromised or traded off. Some will make end runs to change an agreement or to cut their own deals. The moderates will be willing to make concessions while the militants will insist on holding firm.[9] An example of a coalition that fell apart occurred in California over oil-spill legislation. The oil industry supported the legislation proposed, but ARCO's position diverged because its crude oil came from Alaska by ship and the bill imposed a fee on oil imported by water. When ARCO's lobbyist succeeded in having the bill amended in the Senate Appropriations Committee, Shell and other companies attempted to restore the bill to its original form. The coalition disintegrated.

Lobbyists are responsible for leading and orchestrating their coalition's campaign. They have to keep members up-to-date, involve them in planning, assign tasks, and coordinate activities. Take as an example New Jersey's FAIR coalition, which was seeking changes in product liability and tort law. One of Trenton's major contract lobbyists played the lead role. He assigned coalition members tasks on the basis of who knew whom; who had greatest credibility and friendships; where facilities and plants were located; what types of experience groups had with legislators; and the expertise of various coalition lobbyists. He set up a task force of corporate CEOs, organized a grass-roots effort, and arranged for a public-information campaign. He also coordinated the direct lobbying activities of a platoon of professionals under contract to the coalition's member groups.

Grass-Roots Mobilization

During recent years Washington consultants have looked for business beyond the beltway to supplement their activities with Congress and federal departments and agencies (and to add to their revenues). Today, they are offering high-technology and grass-roots operations in place of the old-style lobbying that they disdain.[10] In part (but only in part) because of their efforts, lobbying in state capitals has been changing. Grass-roots lobbying is very much in vogue today, with environmental, business, professional, and governmental groups developing capacity and putting it to use. In 1986 a Public Affairs Council survey found that all six utility companies responding, eleven of fourteen nonmanufacturing firms, and thirty of thirty-five manufacturing companies had grass-roots programs involving employees, stockholders, retirees, and consumers.[11] But at about the same time, in a California survey asking lobbyists to rank several activities by importance, business lobbyists ranked "mobilizing constituency pressures" relatively low.[12]

The objective of a grass-roots campaign is to prove to legislators that their constituents are concerned about a particular issue. This kind of enterprise is referred to as "the constituency connection"[13] or "farming the membership." It is the equivalent of working the district for a legislator.[14] In the words of a Maryland lobbyist, "The old politics don't work anymore, you have to get back home where it really hurts." According to this line of reasoning, the legislator's district is where political power resides, and grass-roots lobbying puts legislators into contact with constituents who hold that power. It demonstrates vocal and tangible support (or opposition) for a measure. In a grass-roots campaign, constituents tell legislators how the measure will affect them instead of the lobbyist doing it. "Don't believe me," the lobbyist can say to the legislator, "just ask Charlie," a "key contact" from back home.

Grass-roots lobbying exists to support a direct lobbying effort in the legislature. A public-interest lobbyist in New Jersey saw the connection between grass-roots and direct lobbying clearly. The postcards and letters that voters write and the phone calls they make after a door-to-door canvass backs up the group's work in Trenton. She explained:

> When I go into a legislative committee meeting, I'm hoping that what they're looking at is not just me ... but they are also thinking about the fifty phone calls that came into the office last week or the six hundred postcards that we delivered at a press conference in their district the week before.

Grass-roots lobbying is an outside game, but it cannot occur independently of the inside one. The lobbyist therefore has to be involved in planning and coordinating a client's grass-roots effort.

Grass-Roots Capacity

Not every group is able to develop a grass-roots campaign. A group's potential in this regard depends on a number of factors. First, a group must have the resources to develop a field operation. Some cause groups operate on a shoestring. Grass-roots lobbying needs some money to launch a vigorous effort. Someone has to organize grass-roots efforts and keep them organized. Volunteers cannot do it; money is required to pay staff. Common Cause tried with volunteers. It established phone networks in one state; members agreed to call one another. But without someone to ride herd, the network atrophied. People were involved for a little while; then they walked away. Their lobbyist explained: "I would not hold a Common Cause day in [the state capital] because I don't think anybody would be impressed with thirty people." In Florida a lobbyist who represented farm workers had to obtain a grant to pay for the gas to bring some of her members to Tallahassee to meet with legislators. A more extended grass-roots campaign was completely out of her financial reach. When it comes to the legislature, local people do have power, but at least some money is required to mobilize it.

Second, a group's potential depends on its membership base. For instance, a Minnesota company recently downsized, going from thirty to ten local offices with correspondingly fewer employees. Although it became more economically efficient, it lost much of its political salience. It was without a grass-roots base. Oil companies in Florida, for example, have no plants, no refineries, and no employees. They are not even residents of Florida. They have no base there. In contrast, the jobbers are well distributed and strong throughout the state. They even have the potential to get a candidate to challenge an incumbent legislator. The Wine Institute has a base in California and New York, where wine is an important product, but elsewhere wine interests are weak. In contrast, beer has a wholesaling network throughout the nation. Not only the size but also the distribution of members throughout a state play a role. Realtors reside in all the legislative districts, and that is a source of their strength. By way of contrast, ophthalmologists tend to congregate in a few urban and suburban areas; and that limits them politically.

Third, a group's potential depends on its membership and/or product. Politics turns off many citizens, so it is extremely difficult to get them to participate in a grass-roots campaign. "Asking people to get involved in politics," says a consultant, "is like asking them to perform an unnatural act." [15]

Particular groups vary in their political dispositions. At one extreme are local elected government officials, who are already committed to politics. The Texas Municipal League, for instance, has its Grass-Roots Involvement Program (GRIP), the theme of which is "Get a grip on your

legislature." Also politically oriented and available for grass-roots activity
are trial lawyers. Not many teachers are natural political activists yet
large numbers can be galvanized by issues of salary and working
conditions that demonstrably affect them. The typical accountant is not
at all political; but a number of them are and do get involved in the
political work of a state society. A challenge for any lobbyist is Florida
farmworkers, some of whom only speak Spanish or Creole, or the
homeless, who are difficult to mobilize no matter how loud an action
alert.

The best grass-roots personnel, in the opinions of lobbyists, are
people who have the closest contact with legislators and in whom
legislators repose trust, although in a different domain. An auto mechanic
who services a legislator's car is an ideal constituent. So is the local
pharmacist, and particularly one in a rural area, who often is part of a
legislator's district network.

But organizations must obviously make do with the individuals
affiliated with them. Corporations have to rely on employees, stockholders, retirees, suppliers or vendors, and customers or clients. From time to
time they can get their top executives involved, but one state relations
director cautioned: "You can't play the big chips too often." [16] J.C.
Penney's grass-roots system is based on a network of about two thousand
store managers. American Cyanamid has business councils in six states,
which comprise all plant managers and other employees. Industrial Paper
is organized under regional managers, but the plant managers at the
company's 150 facilities are key.[17] Power and telephone utilities, as well
as other companies, use line management from plants in the district.[18]
Most companies, and particularly manufacturing companies, depend on
operating managers to play leading roles in grass-roots endeavors.[19]
Johnson & Johnson's grass-roots program illustrates one variation. Government task force meetings are held in each of J&J's target states—
California, Texas, Illinois, New Jersey, Georgia, and Florida. Members of
these task forces include plant managers, human resource personnel, and
finance personnel. Those teams, with the support of headquarters, are
responsible for grass-roots operations in particular jurisdictions.

Organizations range more widely in recruiting for grass-roots campaigns. The potential clientele depends on the group. The tobacco
industry has organized a "smokers' rights" network, using the marketing departments of several companies. Philip Morris USA began with a
list of a hundred thousand persons and now has twelve million names on
its computer as smokers.[20] Dayton Hudson, one of the principal corporations in Minnesota, awards grants through its foundation and calls on
its grant recipients for help when major issues arise that affect the
company. On recent legislation, designed to avert a takeover, the
message from the foundation was: "You have to save Dayton Hudson."

All the grantees, including a troupe of ballet dancers, signed on to help the company.

Public-interest groups in some states canvass door-to-door. New Jersey PIRG is an example of a group with impressive grass-roots capacity. It has two hundred members canvassing out of five offices around the state. They sign up members, get contributions, and push the issues PIRG is lobbying in Trenton. They circulate petitions or ask people to sign postcards (and to add a personal touch to the form card), and then PIRG delivers petitions or postcards to the legislators whose districts have been canvassed. On a recent campaign to promote clean-water legislation, PIRG had six organizers in eighteen targeted districts setting up local committees to have people get in touch with their legislators. PIRG's grass-roots organization can reach far and wide and generate a lot of activity.

Grass-Roots Organization

One of the outstanding grass-roots organizations is that of Anheuser-Busch, the manufacturer of Budweiser and Michelob beers, among other products. The structure and nature of the beer industry facilitate lobbying in general and grass-roots lobbying in particular. The industry projects an image of conviviality, having fun, and making friends. That goes with lobbying. It has a large customer base, which helps in grass-roots campaigns. Wine, by contrast, has an image of being more upscale and formal—even a little snobbish. It has a smaller customer base. Thus, with regard to grass-roots lobbying effects, beer is a natural, wine is not.[21] The difference in products also gives beer an advantage over wine. Beer has a short shelf life, so its wholesalers visit retailers more frequently. The beer-distribution system consists of many people with small territories to serve—the ideal situation for grass-roots organizing. In wine, there are fewer people serving larger territories—and communicating less often.

Anheuser-Busch employs more than forty thousand individuals, who can be activated at almost any time. They are assigned to legislative districts through a computer matching system. The company's strength is greatest in those states where it has plants—Virginia, Texas, Ohio, California, New Jersey, and Florida. (In New York, there is only a small brewery, but the president of the New York senate represents that district, so all is not lost.)

In addition to its immediate employees, A-B can call on its family of wholesalers, about 960 across the country, including 40 in Texas and 50 in California. These wholesalers have solid small businesses and are well positioned in their communities. Day-to-day they make contacts throughout their states since they are dealing with a total of almost five hundred thousand outlets in the nation. Every two weeks each person who holds a liquor license is visited by an A-B wholesaler, and these wholesalers receive the company's action alerts with support and briefing materials, as well as notification on the phone. A-B relies not only on employees and wholesalers (and, indirectly, retailers) but also on its suppliers. Barley growers in Montana and hops growers in Oregon can be mobilized, in addition to can companies and paperboard manufacturers. Finally, there is a third-party group, Beer Drinkers of America, with two hundred thousand members.

Another example of effective grass-roots organization is that of teachers. Education associations are apt to have a government relations committee or the like, with teacher representatives from around the state and local legislative action teams. The latter may be chaired by a member of the government relations committee, charged with grass-roots work, and staffed by headquarters professionals. In New Jersey these legislative action teams promote attendance at the NJEA Legislative Conference, at teacher lobby days in Trenton, at special rallies, and at legislative and political training seminars. Members of these teams are trained by NJEA's lobbying staff, and summer workshops train an additional twelve hundred teachers in political action techniques.

Teacher associations also possess excellent communications systems whereby they can inform and alert members. In both Colorado and Minnesota, for example, the associations have "action lines." Teachers can call in on a toll-free number and receive up-to-the-minute information, messages, and campaign instructions. The Texas State Teachers Association has more than thirty field offices linked by computer and a phone bank at its main office in Austin. Newsletters and legislative bulletins are also employed. Consider an NJEA two-page, back-to-back bulletin, dated April 6, 1990, as an example. It was headed "Crisis in State Aid" and called for a restoration of school funding. It asked that members reach out to legislators, that local and county presidents organize letter writing and telephone calls to legislators, and that local legislative action teams begin a letter-writing campaign to the chairpersons of the senate and assembly appropriations committees.

Grass-Roots Techniques

Michael Dunn's advice, as a consultant in the field, is that organizations should develop an ongoing grass-roots program rather than employ outsiders to run campaigns on an ad hoc basis.[22] Another consultant, Charles Mack, details the important elements of such a program, which include a network and a call to action that tells voters whom to write or call, the issue and bill number, the position to be expressed, and talking points (backed up whenever possible with personal experience). He stresses the importance of individual involvement, including visits to legislators, annual legislative dinners and receptions, and facility visits.[23]

Consultants in this field believe lobbyists ought to be intimately involved in the grass-roots enterprise. It is up to them to determine a strategy, select the most appropriate techniques, plan and coordinate activities, and see that things do not get out of hand. Involvement does not necessarily mean prominence, however. Lobbyists can work behind the scenes, with members and other constituents out front. "When I am doing my job best, I am invisible," is the way one professional saw his grass-roots role.

Among the variety of techniques in grass-roots campaigns, writing letters and making telephone calls are the most common. Some legislators question the efficacy of mass letter-writing efforts, saying they are unimpressed by postcards, preprinted letters, and letters drafted on the computer. Lobbyists, however, try to stay ahead of the legislators on the matter of mail. One contract lobbyist in New Jersey, for example, uses different grades of paper, various type styles, and computer letters with words misspelled in order to make the messages seem spontaneous rather than stimulated.

Lobbyists generally have confidence in the efficacy of letters and telephone calls. A cause lobbyist in California activates groups and members of his coalition, who in turn write and call. "It doesn't take many letters to get their attention," he pointed out. A legislative leader from Maine agreed: "Ten phone calls to a legislator is a groundswell." [24] The sheer weight of communications matters; the more, the better. A lobbyist for a professional association in California confessed that "when we decided not to use mail, they stuck it in our ear." Now his group errs on the side of writing. If a member warrants it, "blitz him" is that lobbyist's rule of thumb. It works: "When you blitz them, it's overwhelming."

Many organizations therefore devote substantial resources to phone and/or letter-writing activities. The Texas Civic Justice League, a coalition whose focus is product liability and tort reform, has forty phone-bank operators in a special facility in Austin to support its grass-roots operation. During one of its major campaigns, the league's staff went through every phone book in the state, identified businesses that would be interested, and made calls to thirty-five thousand of them. These businesses were sent materials and sample letters and asked to write to the legislature. Associated Industries of Florida has its own computer staff and software to send out action requests to which members will respond. Jon Shebel, the association's chief, claims that the group can put a thousand letters or telegrams from constituents on a legislator's desk with a twenty-four-hour turnaround.[25]

It is generally agreed that one of the most effective techniques is the use of key contacts. These are people who are members of the group who have some tie to a legislator in whose district they live. They know legislators, according to a Colorado lobbyist, "in settings other than asking them for something during the session." It might be someone from a manufacturing plant or facility. It might be an insurance broker who has the legislator as a client. The Colorado Association of Commerce and Industry relies on its 150-member board of directors, which includes 35 CEOs. All told, the association has at least ten people in each district who serve as key contacts.

The trial lawyers are diligent in this regard. In Texas they try to get members who have worked in a legislator's campaign. In Minnesota they have key contacts in every legislative district. Each one, of course, cannot ask for a legislator's help on every bill of concern to the group; but each may make an appeal once or twice during the session.

State societies of certified public accountants have developed key-contact networks and are trying to increase the number of members involved. The subject is a delicate one, however: some CPAs will not use their client relationship to try to advance the profession's goals. However, a number of them know legislators through a business or civic club or on some basis other than a client relationship. In any event, professional considerations do not hold the latter back. They are willing to use their relationships as long as the effort does not seem heavy-handed. Some state societies mail questionnaires out after each election asking every CPA who they know in the legislature. The staff takes it from there in recruiting new key contacts.

Associations of municipal and county officials are comprised of practically nothing but key contacts. Their members are elected public officials who are distributed geographically among the legislative districts of the state. They are people who know politics, possess political skill, and are likely to be well acquainted with the legislators in their districts. They are easily mobilized on issues affecting local government's interests. The Texas Municipal League is particularly impressive when it comes to key contacts in grass-roots campaigns. It begins by sending question-naires to all elected officials (and department heads, too) asking how well they know senators and representatives. That becomes part of the league's data base. Texas local officials do not often seek state legislative office, so they are not viewed as rivals or threats by legislators. That makes for a much smoother key-contact system.

Visiting with legislators in the capitol or in the district is also an effective technique, especially if the right people are involved. The "right people" are those who are connected in the legislature or affected by proposed legislation. They may testify, or simply make a cameo appear-ance, before a legislative committee. One lobbyist got the mother of a committee member to testify in favor of a particular bill. The member signed on as a sponsor as his mother was addressing him. In one legislature, a bill relating to crabbing on Sundays was at issue. On the day of the public hearing, the lobbyist appeared with a number of commercial crabbers wearing their work clothes—rubber boots, worn tee-shirts, and rough pants. These hulking men made a dramatic presence.[26] A lobbyist in the employ of the tobacco industry, to flesh out his argument against banning the sale of cigarettes in vending machines, brought fifty vending-machine truckers to the committee.

Many groups sponsor what are often called "lobby days" or "a day at the legislature." A few hundred business people visit their senators and representatives in the state capitol in St. Paul. Thirty or forty teachers roam through the halls of the capitol building in Austin. More than one hundred people, wearing stickers saying "Make Polluters Pay," seek out legislators on the four floors of the statehouse annex in Trenton.

A Florida lobbyist for farmworkers has made a special effort to have her clients and legislators meet face to face. She arranged for them to make a trip to the capitol to meet with legislators. They left their homes at 4 a.m. and drove in trucks and vans (some of which broke down) to Tallahassee. They visited legislators, presenting them with oranges and bell peppers as gifts. Then they had a soup-line lunch, with several legislators serving. That night they slept on the floors of local churches before returning home the following day. It was a moving event, one the lobbyist hoped would grab the legislature by its conscience.

On occasion, groups mobilize a large number of members in an effort to intimidate legislators. Florida's doctors turned out in the thousands for a 1986 visit to the capitol on tort reform. The New Jersey Education Association, in a 1982 attempt to get broad-based bargaining on non-wage-related issues, turned out twelve thousand teachers for a march on Trenton.[27] When the New Jersey legislature in 1990 debated a bill to restrict assault firearms, almost a thousand members of the Coalition of N.J. Sportsmen and the National Rifle Association held an aggressive demonstration in Trenton. One assemblywoman reacted: "Never in my life have I been subjected to the abuse, the verbal abuse, the vandalism of my office that occurred just this morning." A senator had a similar reaction: "I've never seen that kind of intimidation in sixteen years."[28] But the gun enthusiasts had certainly made their point and many legislators—like it or not—got the message.

Using tactics closer to home, the New Jersey Education Association hosts annual legislative dinners in each of the state's twenty-one counties, both to honor the legislators and to demonstrate organizational strength. It also arranges for small group meetings between members of the legislative action team and legislators in order to discuss one or two key issues. Colorado's teachers have receptions for legislators in their districts at least once or twice a year and in at least one locality breakfasts are held regularly throughout the session.

Business operates in a similar fashion. The New Jersey Business and Industry Association's employer-legislative committees in each county hold a monthly meeting to discuss issues of concern. Legislators from the area are invited and several show up. Companies in New Jersey bring legislators to their facilities to have lunch with workers, thus giving legislators a chance to meet with constituents and simultaneously building rapport for the company. Johnson & Johnson invites legislators to tour company plants and to meet with the chief executive officer; those on a health committee are brought in to meet with company researchers.

New Jersey PIRG also works along these lines. It organizes meetings of constituents and asks the delegation of legislators from the district to attend. When constituents, who have been chosen by PIRG, express their concerns, legislators feel the pressure. Sometimes, in fact, they commit publicly then and there. Other times, they agree to consider the PIRG position. If they do not attend at all, it can be considered a slap in the face to those constituents who care about the issue.

One way to convince legislators that their constituencies favor a certain measure is to make use of public-opinion polls. Statewide polls tell members very little about their own districts, but they still have an overall impact. If the results are unambiguous, they may serve to push fence sitters to one side or the other. For example, poll results made a difference in 1990 in getting full funding for abortions for low-income women in California. Choice had become an issue that year in determining elections, and the California Poll had found that 67 percent of Californians were prochoice and 59 percent supported abortion funding for poor women.[29] Florida's soft-drink and bottling industries, in opposing a "pop tax" in the legislature, took a statewide poll. Their poll showed that consumers disliked the idea of a tax on soft drinks by a margin of 62 to 36 percent.[30] Minnesota's leading corporation, Dayton Hudson, in its campaign to promote antitakeover legislation, hired a pollster to find out if Minnesotans from all over the state favored saving the company. They did.

It costs a lot of money to conduct polls in the districts of undecided legislators (i.e., those whose votes are still up for grabs). As a result, very few polls are taken in individual districts. But some are. On a bill regarding pensions for police officers in New Jersey, the knee-jerk reaction of a number of legislators was, "My constituents don't like this." So the lobbyist handling the issue commissioned a poll in several legislative districts and went to the skeptical legislators with the results. He explained the data to them and concluded: "You can believe what you want to believe, but here is as factual information as we can possibly provide."

On big issues, polls and focus groups are being used more frequently by lobbyists nowadays. Some results are conveyed to legislators, as part of a group's grass-roots effort, but these studies and analyses are primarily intended to help lobbyists shape their campaign strategies.

Does It Work?

Grass-roots campaigns are effective if they are applied to appropriate issues, employed with sensitivity, and kept under control. These conditions, however, are not always met. If the inside-lobbyist game works, there may be no need for outside strategies. Some contract lobbyists are completely sold on direct lobbying and apparently need little external support. They certainly prefer working their contacts. Bereano of Maryland, for example, is a one-man operation who depends on energy, knowledge of the process, and close relationships. A New Jersey lobbyist focuses primarily on leadership and sees little need for pressuring the rank-and-file with grass roots. "If the speaker puts the bill up," he concludes, "it's going to pass."

Certain issues, moreover, can be handled within the institution without stirring up the waters outside. A Minnesota association lobbyist pointed to one bill of importance to his industry. The public had little interest in the issue; the legislature had little more. On this issue, one-on-one lobbying was most appropriate. His association has not had "life-or-death" issues, or ones of much interest even to its members, during recent years. It has thus focused on the inside game and never considered a grass-roots effort.

On some issues, grass-roots campaigns simply will not work, not because members are uninterested, but because they are skittish. In New Jersey, when the legislature was deciding on an ethics bill for local government officials, the New Jersey League of Municipalities opposed it on the ground that, if enacted, such legislation would discourage talented and successful individuals from running for local office. But because mayors and city council members could hardly speak out against an ethics bill, the league could not generate grass-roots support. Elected officials could not run the political risk of taking a public position against a "motherhood" issue like this one.

There is no guarantee, however, that organizations will always be able to rely on an inside strategy. Issues change, as does the composition of the legislature. In earlier years Anheuser-Busch was able to prevail on tax issues by working within the legislatures. Taxes are still the major issue for the company, but nowadays grass-roots constituencies play a greater and more frequent role in the process. Fact sheets and white papers are prepared. Letters are sent out to wholesalers. Employees, retailers, and suppliers are alerted; displays are placed in bars; and delegations are advised to visit the capitol and talk taxes with legislators.

Grass-roots campaigns are not without risk. As a lobbyist for a Colorado governmental association summed up: "Grass roots can be great or it can be a disaster." This is particularly applicable in Colorado, where members of the General Assembly are adverse to outside pressure stimulated by interest groups. In the words of one lobbyist, "They don't like to see the pot stirred," especially if it does not have to be. One veteran legislator from Colorado warned a group of lobbyists: "You're attempting to intimidate me and overwhelm me when it may not even be an issue." His view was supported by a legislative leader from Maine, who admonished organizers of grass-roots campaigns: "If you don't do it right, you will be taken to the cleaners." [31] For these legislators, grass-roots campaigns are a last resort; they prefer direct-lobbying campaigns first.

One danger in grass-roots efforts is that the wrong legislators will be pressured. Appeals can be misdirected, having little effect on die-hard opponents and a boomerang effect on friends. Proper targeting is necessary. But rarely can individual participants throughout a state be adequately informed or closely controlled. A teachers association lobbyist recalled instances in which teachers (as part of a campaign) accused senators of being enemies of education when they were actually friends. Even if such mistakes are not made, there is the danger that certain legislators will always be hearing from the same people. Those who run campaigns must be selective; otherwise legislators will come to regard key contacts as the little boy who cried wolf.

Having the right members helps. According to a lobbyist for an association of local government officials, "If you have good, strong commissioners with knowledge, experience, and personality, it works well." But such people are hard to find, beyond perhaps the ranks of elected public officials. Few groups can afford to let their members loose in the capitol without some negative consequences. (It is true that the negatives might be outweighed by the positives.) Lawyers are politically attuned but "too damned smart," according to a lobbyist who works for them. His job, he says, is to ratchet them down to what a rural member of the legislature wants to know. Members of a Police Benevolent Association (PBA) may also know too much and go too far, according to a contract lobbyist who represented them: "Cops are great amateur lawyers. . . . They know their legislator. They have no fear and sometimes go right over the line. Tact is not something that they learned in the police academy." Many legislators regard the lobbying style of doctors as arrogant. They had their day at Florida's capitol, fighting for tort reform in 1986, declaring a doctors' holiday and traveling to Tallahassee in chartered jets and buses. A legislator recalled a delegation's visit to her office. "Let me give you some education about the medical field," was the way one of the doctors opened up the conversation with her. The legislator replied that she did not need the education he could give; she had been chairing the health committee of the house for years.[32]

"If it isn't carefully orchestrated, it can be dangerous," said a Colorado state government relations professional. Grass roots must be tightly managed to be effective and avoid embarrassment. But lobbyists cannot be certain of maintaining control when many people are involved. Just one loose cannon in a campaign can cost an organization dearly, as when a beer wholesaler called up a senator, told him he had given him a contribution, and declared: "Now, this is what I want you to do."

Not only are there the problems of maintaining control and the possibility that a campaign may veer off course.[33] Those managing the campaign can also make mistakes. Trial lawyers brought handicapped children to the New Jersey Legislature to demonstrate against tort reform. Some legislators resented this. New Hampshire legislators, it is reported, are in the habit of getting postcards with pictures of dead fetuses.[34] Such mail, apparently, does not predispose them to support the cause. In Florida, one organization tried to make its point on a bill by overwhelming legislators with phone calls. It managed to tie up all the capitol's lines, getting the sponsor of the bill so angry that he slipped in an amendment over the group's opposition during the final hours of the session.

When properly planned and executed, however, grass-roots campaigns can be a potent force. There are numerous examples, but a few will suffice. The New Jersey Cable Television Association, representing an industry that was under criticism for scrambled signals, poor service, and rising rates, was confronted early in 1990 by the prospect of a new telecommunications tax.[35] Within weeks after the release of the governor's budget message proposing the tax, the association's contract lobbyist, who also served as executive director, got a grass-roots campaign under way.[36] She took a proposal to her board of cable-company operators, the majority of whom wanted to flex their muscles. The lobbyist sent a packet to each NJCTA company, including sample letters, press releases, a position paper, a copy of the bill, and a list of legislators.

Also included were instructions as follows:

1. Order a thirty-second public-service announcement on the issue from NJCTA and air it often.
2. Write a letter to the editor of your local newspapers (sample enclosed).
3. Ask your employees to write their legislators (letter and list of legislators enclosed).
4. Distribute media release (sample enclosed).
5. Write letter from general manager to all legislators representing your franchise areas (sample enclosed).

6. Provide antitax postcards to your subscribers, employees, and walk-in customers (mechanical enclosed).

7. Record an antitax on-hold telephone message.

8. If your system has a news department, do commentary on the issue or interview your general manager (samples enclosed).

Each company determined for itself what it would do. The lobbyist received 150,000 postcards that she then had sorted and delivered to legislators. After holding a press conference, the lobbyist informed legislative leaders that the NJCTA grass-roots campaign was under way. Within a short time, the issue had been decided. Funds were found that would replace the $39 million in the budget from the tax on cable.

Public-interest groups have also used grass-roots campaigns with telling effect. Such groups cannot afford to rely on inside strategies, although they engage in direct lobbying along with everyone else. Their strength is pressure from outside the legislature, so public-interest groups work with the press and continuously recruit members and supporters. Take COPIRG in Colorado, for example. It canvasses out of Boulder in the winter and out of Boulder, Denver, and Colorado Springs in the summer (when the days are longer and more students are available). The board of directors, composed of students, decides at the beginning of the year what bills to get involved with. Then the canvassers raise their issues at people's doors, by way of soliciting members and stimulating involvement. In 1988 the COPIRG canvass was put to use in support of a safe-drinking-water bill. People were activated district by district, and hundreds of contacts were made with legislators. COPIRG won on this issue because legislators were sensitive to what their constituents thought. The operation was not as efficient as it might have been, however, so the organization resolved to spend additional energy on improving its grass-roots efforts.

The significance of grass roots extends beyond any single issue on which it may be decisive. An organization's ability to weigh in on critical issues is the important matter. Legislators may downplay the effectiveness of grass-roots tactics, but a lobbyist for a large association in California demurred: "Member contact really shakes them up." Hence we can conclude that legislators will develop greater sympathy for the goals of groups employing outside-pressure tactics. As one contract lobbyist in New Jersey puts it: "PIRG can have a thousand kids going door to door in a legislator's district. Those politics will carry the day."

The Media and Public Relations

One way to generate support is to place an emphasis on communications. The lobbyists' objective in managing the media and conducting public relations is to project their client's issues and image favorably to the public and public officials. The techniques that fall within this domain include newsletters, position papers, brochures, news releases, press conferences, television and radio interviews, editorial board meetings, advertising, community relations, and so forth.[37] Reaching the public and affecting the legislature through the media have become critical for groups that are not equipped or disposed to play an inside game. The cause groups and their lobbyists have considerable advantages here, while other groups are trying to counter them or catch up.

Common Cause lobbyists tend to be very adept with the media. They know that if legislators read about something in the press (or see it on television), they regard it as important. One Common Cause lobbyist cultivates the press, hangs out with reporters, and gives them information and a point of view. He will start off by sensitizing the press corps to an issue, such as campaign-finance reform. His objective is to supply reporters with both a context and the perception that the issue is appealing. Then, with data and statements—geared to the slower news days—he keeps the story alive. As the press takes hold, legislators cannot help but take notice.

When issues are featured in the media, they take on greater emotional content; that is the way stories are played. More and more groups are therefore tailoring their message to the media. A leading contract lobbyist in New Jersey recognizes that there is now a whole new side to lobbying not previously explored. He now uses videos, cable, talk shows, and other forums to help his client address the community. A communications strategy, he believes, is especially useful on emotional issues like incineration or packaging. "The more communication you have and the earlier communication is," he advises, "the less chance you have of it becoming an issue so dominated by one side versus the other side." In other words, business had better respond to environmentalist and consumer groups in the latter's language—that of the media.

The growing inclination of lobbyists and the organizations they represent is to use consultants to help with both issues and image. Public relations firms are being employed by groups to get into the press (and sometimes to keep out). Some now have a media consultant on retainer. The notion is that a good public relations campaign can soften the public and thus improve the climate for legislation desired by the client. One lobbyist known for his skills in PR and the media is Austin's George Christian, former press secretary to President Lyndon Johnson.

Dayton Hudson had an effective public-relations strategy in 1987, when it pressed the Minnesota legislature to pass a law that would prevent a hostile takeover. With the help of experienced media consultants, Dayton Hudson portrayed its struggle as one between a good corporate citizen of Minnesota and a raider from Washington, D.C. The company's campaign conjured up images of a cherished local employer of thirty thousand people on one side and Darth Vader on the other. "You can't come into my state and pillage" was the theme. Through meetings with capital reporters and editorial boards around the state, the large corporation got its homey message across.

Some issues have great appeal for the media, and groups that deal in these areas have special access. The media gives favorable coverage to environmental issues, growth management, consumer issues, and to ethics and campaign-finance reform. Although there obviously are exceptions, reporters in the state capitals generally regard the environmental and public-interest lobbyists as wearing the "white hats." Business lobbyists, in general, are not as well received and have a tougher time getting their stories across. In the middle are lobbyists for local government associations, also "white hats" as long as they are not opposing the environmentalists and taking the side of business.

A statehouse correspondent in New Jersey, in characterizing public interest groups, had this to say: "The media perception of these groups is more favorable. They are the first groups we will go to when we want the public's opinion on an issue." Thus, lobbyists for these groups generally have good rapport with the capitol press corps and the editors of the state's newspapers. The press, according to one Florida cause lobbyist, "has been sympathetic to our cause." But her group did not have sufficient resources or time to spend on press relations as she would have liked. She expressed disappointment in not being able to take full advantage of the opportunities before her.

It should be noted also that extreme groups—whether on the right or left—also get coverage, because of the newsworthiness of their stories. One lobbyist for conservative groups in Florida believes she gets press attention because no one else carries her message. The print press will always turn to her for a quote and television will invite her to appear on talk shows. All of this has helped make her known throughout the state (although her constituents, she reports, are not inclined to read the liberal press).

It is becoming more common for public interest, governmental, and business groups to arrange meetings with editorial boards seeking support. They contribute op-ed pieces. A Florida lobbyist for an association of local governments has sent a package of memos on a number of issues to twenty editorial boards. His thinking is that they will keep the materials on file. When they get around to an editorial on the subject, they will use what he has supplied and not have to rely on the wire service.

Press briefings and conferences are the preferred technique of cause groups. They do extremely well in appealing to the press. New Jersey PIRG is an example. Its lobbyists have an excellent sense of just what the press needs and when. The release of PIRG's studies naturally gets attention. Beyond that, PIRG lobbyists think in terms of events and "visuals." Press conferences are held at a "dangerous" or "contaminated" site. "Wanda the Fish" was used for clean-water legislation and a Ben Franklin character was used to sign a declaration of independence from toxic wastes. On Halloween PIRG went to Hoboken with people dressed in costumes as toxic avengers. They went door-to-door talking to residents about toxicity in the community. And, of course, PIRG held a press conference on this "scariest day of the year." The judgment of one of the group's lobbyists was that, "People like such an activity, the press reports it, and people read it." Timing is key, and relevant reporters are notified of an event a few days in advance. With a little experience, public interest and environmental lobbyists have learned how to talk in "quotes" for the print media and in "sound bites" for the electronic media.

There is no doubt that the press can be, and is, used in the process. Staged events and so-called media tours are important. Having the right sorts of issues is paramount. The effective lobbyist has all these in mind and develops the most appropriate bag of tricks for his or her particular needs. A lobbyist for one of Florida's cities knows, for example, that if a reporter attends a legislative committee meeting, it will help her cause. The presence of the press changes the dynamic. "I may even get their vote," she said, "or at least they'll shut up."

A group's public relations efforts reach further than its day-to-day attempts to manage the press. PR is a long-term endeavor and over time should contribute to a group's governmental goals.[38] The idea is to get on the side of the angels, build goodwill, and fashion the most positive image. For example, the dairy industry works on the following image: dairy products are portrayed as inexpensive and nutritionally beneficial; consumers are shown to benefit as a result; and the dairy industry is then depicted as being on the edge of chaos without governmental help.[39]

Community involvement is one means of achieving favorable public relations. For example, a Minnesota bank is involved in inner-city-neighborhood programs. It also sponsors a community home-buyers' program. Community activity proves, in the words of its lobbyist, that "the bank is willing to put its money where its mouth is." The bank thus gains credibility with inner-city legislators who can see things happening in their neighborhoods. There are other community projects as well, such as one in which bank employees adopt a high-rise building or a senior citizens' development and then work with the residents. In the lobbyist's opinion, community involvement pays off politically—as much as or more than financing political campaigns.

In part because of initiative battles, California probably has more experience than other states in using public-relations experts for legislative ends. Firms that once specialized in corporate public relations have turned toward political PR, and corporations have found that they need both lobbyists and PR experts. According to a consultant in a corporate and political public relations firm, there is a growing realization that "you just can't sell your issue to the legislature, you have to generate public acceptance for it." In more and more situations, the California legislature feels it needs public support for its position. "What used to be done in back rooms is now done by public consensus building," the PR specialist noted.[40]

An organization's image and standing can benefit from any number of public relations approaches. The institutional advertising of telephone companies has an impact. So do the television spots designed to enhance the image of teachers as caring and competent professionals. The athletic tournaments and other events sponsored by Avon, Pepsico, and Philip Morris also work. "They help us maintain an effective network of friends," says Avon's director of governmental affairs.[41] And full-page advertisements describe an industry's contribution to employment in the state. Currently the tobacco industry is waging a multimillion-dollar advertising campaign to discourage teen-agers from smoking.[42] An ad that appeared in *State Legislatures* magazine, which is sent to all of the country's legislators, asked: "What's the Tobacco Industry Doing to Discourage Youth Smoking?" It then responded by describing what appeared to be an impressive program. The tobacco industry paid for the ad, and it was their hope that legislators bought it.

The embattled alcoholic-beverage industry has recently undertaken an intense public-relations effort designed to improve its image. In creating the Century Council (an independent organization funded by beer, wine, and spirit companies), the industry was seeking to stem the tide of negative attitudes toward alcohol. The industry had never presented a united front, and the big-three beer companies (Anheuser-Busch, Coors, and Miller) were notably absent from the council. Nevertheless, this three-year, forty-million-dollar campaign (intended "to combat misuse of alcoholic-beverage products and to encourage responsible use among drinkers") appeared to have real potential for impressing citizens and, ultimately, legislators.[43]

Although the Century Council campaign did a great deal to improve the image of the alcoholic-beverage industry, another event may hold even greater promise. In the late summer of 1991 the study findings of researchers at the Harvard School of Public Health were announced in the national press. This study of 51,000 men found that, apart from its effects on other aspects of health, moderate drinking was actually good for one's heart. Men who consumed from one-half to two drinks a day were shown to have reduced their risk of heart disease by 26 percent compared with men who abstained from alcohol. And the beneficial effects for the heart increased with consumption (that is, two drinks were found to be more beneficial than just half a drink).

By confirming the results of several previous studies, the Harvard findings could not help but improve public attitudes toward alcohol, despite the personal health and public problems attributable to drinking. This news would not directly affect any votes in the nation's legislatures, but the indirect, longer-term effects on legislator attitudes toward the alcoholic-beverage industry might be substantial. Yet PR consultants, lobbyists, and the industry itself had nothing to do with the study. Not everything that affects the legislative process happens by plan or design.

Luck obviously helps any campaign. But hard work is also essential. If lobbyists tend to the business of coalition building, grass-roots mobilization, and the care and feeding of the electorate through the media and PR campaigns, they will be in an excellent position for the most critical task of all. Having laid the groundwork, they now have to make the case in the legislature and win on the issue in dispute.

Notes

1. John R. Wright, "Contributions, Lobbying, and Committee Voting in the U.S. House of Representatives," *American Political Science Review* 84 (June 1990): 422.
2. Bruce C. Wolpe, *Lobbying Congress: How the System Works* (Washington, D.C.: Congressional Quarterly, 1990), 35.
3. James Q. Wilson defines a coalition very differently—as "an enduring arrangement." And for him an alliance is a "temporary arrangement." *Political Organizations* (New York: Basic Books, 1973), 267, 277-278.
4. Sometimes, however, groups are intentionally excluded from a coalition because their identification with the cause might hurt rather than help.
5. Wolpe, *Lobbying Congress,* 35.
6. Kathleen Sylvester, "The Chastening of the Trial Lawyers," *Governing,* February 1991, 29.
7. Charles S. Mack, *Lobbying and Government Relations: A Guide for Executives* (New York: Quorum Books, 1989), 118-119.
8. Ralph J. Marlatt, "The Art of the Deal—Advanced Association Lobbying," unpublished paper, n.d.
9. Despite the problems of dissension, when Greenpeace joins in a coalition with the more moderate Audubon Society and Sierra Club, the former's radical postition enables the latter groups to get more.
10. W. John Moore, "Have Smarts, Will Travel," *National Journal,* November 28, 1987, 3023.
11. Public Affairs Council, *State Government Relations: Results of a Survey of 55 Corporations* (Washington, D.C.: The Council, 1986), 17-20.
12. Jerry Briscoe and Charles G. Bell, "Lobbyist—Committee Consultant Communications Patterns." (Paper prepared for the Annual Meeting of the

Western Political Science Association, Las Vegas, Nevada, March 28-30, 1985), 3.

13. See Jeffrey M. Berry, *The Interest Group Society* (Boston: Little, Brown, 1984), chap. 7.

14. Robert H. Salisbury, "Washington Lobbyists: A Collective Portrait," in *Interest Group Politics,* ed. Allan J. Cigler and Burdett A. Loomis. 2d ed. (Washington, D.C.: CQ Press, 1986), 149.

15. Michael Dunn, in remarks to State Government Relations Institute, New Brunswick, N.J., September 9, 1990.

16. Seymour Lusterman, *Managing Business-State Government Relations* (New York: The Conference Board, 1983), 24.

17. Ibid., 28-31.

18. Richard A. Armstrong, "Corporations and State Government Relations: An Overview," in *Leveraging State Government Relations,* ed. Wesley Pedersen (Washington, D.C.: Public Affairs Council, 1990), 10-11.

19. Public Affairs Council, *State Government Relations,* 21-22.

20. Kathleen Sylvester, "The Tobacco Industry Will Walk a Mile to Stop an Anti-Smoking Law," *Governing,* May 1989, 40.

21. My observation that beer interests are more effective than wine at grass-roots lobbying is, I believe, an empirical one. I must confess, however, to being a beer enthusiast who gets a headache from drinking wine.

22. Remarks to State Government Relations Institute, New Brunswick, N.J., July 9, 1990.

23. Mack, *Lobbying and Government Relations,* 131-136.

24. Rep. John Martin, speaker of the Maine house, in remarks to State Government Relations Institute, New Brunswick, N.J., July 9, 1990.

25. Rowland Stiteler, "Influence Peddling," *Florida Magazine, Orlando Sentinel,* May 29, 1988.

26. Kim Rogers Burdick, "A Folklorist Looks at Lobbyists" (College of Urban Affairs, University of Delaware, May 1990): 34-35.

27. Paul Feldman, "Those Who Can, Lobby," *New Jersey Reporter,* April 1983, 26-27.

28. *Star-Ledger,* May 18, 1990.

29. *The California NOW Activist* (September 1990).

30. *Miami Herald,* May 8, 1990.

31. Rep. Paul Schauer, Colorado house, and Rep. John Martin, speaker of the Maine house, remarks at State Government Relations Institute, New Brunswick, N.J., July 9, 1990.

32. Rep. Elaine Gordon, Florida house, remarks at State Government Relations Institute, New Brunswick, N.J., July 10, 1990.

33. Ronald J. Hrebenar and Ruth K. Scott, *Interest-Group Politics in America,* 2d ed. (Englewood Cliffs, N.J.: Prentice-Hall, 1990), 109.

34. *Boston Globe,* February 17, 1991.

35. See Ginger Gold, "Lobbyists: A Love Story" (Eagleton Institute of Politics, Rutgers University, May 14, 1990).

36. Similar campaigns had previously succeeded in Massachusetts and New York. See also Daniel Carson, "The Cable TV Tangle: A New Industry Learns the Legislative Ropes," *California Journal,* June 1988, 252-253, on the grass-

roots network of the cable industry in California.

37. Mack, *Lobbying and Government Relations,* 145-150.
38. Charles S. Mack, *The Executive's Handbook of Trade and Business Associations* (Westport, Conn.: Quorum Books, 1991), 87.
39. William P. Browne, "Issue Niches and the Limits of Interest Group Influence," in *Interest Group Politics,* ed. Allan J. Cigler and Burdett A. Loomis, 3d ed. (Washington, D.C.: CQ Press, 1991), 359.
40. Ann Bancroft, "The Consultant Is In," *California Journal,* September 1991, 411-412.
41. Lusterman, *Managing Business-State Government Relations,* 10.
42. See Eliza Newlin Carney, "Tobacco on Defensive," *National Journal,* March 7, 1992, 580-582.
43. Gordon Mott, "Leading the Charge," *Market Watch,* June 1991, 18-26.

CHAPTER 8

Making the Case

The outside game of building coalitions, mobilizing grass-roots support, and conducting media and PR campaigns is not only useful. For groups whose abilities to directly lobby the legislature are limited, the outside game is essential. These "outsider" tactics can be very effective. This is especially true for cause lobbyists, who are temperamentally and philosophically less disposed to compromise. As a lobbyist for a public-interest group in Texas notes, "As an outsider, you can stand up for principle and say what's right."

Many special-interest issues (such as those relating to taxes and jurisdiction and pertaining principally to business) require little outside action; an inside strategy normally suffices. An outside strategy, however, rarely stands alone. The public-interest lobbyist who noted that outsiders are freer to adhere to principle also observed that his outsider status was now being threatened. At the previous session of the Texas legislature, he had been invited to "sit at more tables to negotiate more deals." Admitting he may have been a bit uncomfortable, he nevertheless realized he and his client were better off. He could now play *both* games.

At some point, direct-lobbying techniques have to be employed if an organization is to make its case for or against a particular piece of legislation. By "direct lobbying," we mean forms of personal persuasion and involvement in the legislative process itself. Federal lobbyists surveyed in Washington, D.C., for example, said they testified at hearings (99 percent), contacted officials to present their point of view (98 percent), engaged in informal contact with officials (95 percent), and presented research results or technical information (92 percent).[1] Nearly everyone in Washington seems to engage in direct lobbying. The same is true in the states.

Direct lobbying involves numerous strategies and tactics. We shall explore below (1) the principles of direct lobbying; (2) the elements of defense and offense; (3) the targets in the process; (4) the role of information; and (5) negotiating results. Strategies and tactics differ from issue to issue and group to group.[2] "It depends," said a Colorado lobbyist, "There are no general rules." A Florida lobbyist agreed: "The strategy and tactics have to be tailored to each individual case." Two New Jersey lobbyists offered the following observations: "It's like a dance. You have to feel your way," and "You have to take advantage of the opportunities as they arise." Everyone involved seems to agree that generalizations do not apply to specific situations. Nevertheless, it is possible to cast greater light on what has previously been a shadowy area of direct lobbying.

The Principles of Direct Lobbying

When asked, "How do you lobby them?" an association lobbyist in Minnesota responded, "Carefully." The notion that lobbyists have to exercise care when dealing with legislators means different things to different people. It means, as we have explored earlier, forging and maintaining relationships. It also requires personal qualities such as credibility. Moreover, it means having respect for both legislators and the legislative process. All of these are by way of background characteristics. More in the foreground are several principles that many lobbyists observe.

1. *Be There.* Nothing can substitute for the lobbyist's presence. That is why contract lobbyists, who usually reside in or near the capital and belong to the capitol community, are believed to have an advantage over other lobbyists insofar as the legislative process is concerned. To be around all the time means being first to know about what is happening and who is up to what. A lobbyist cannot afford to go home early or get there late, particularly as the session nears its close. During the final week or so, something buried in committee can emerge or an amendment can pop up. If a lobbyist is on guard, with Patriot missiles armed and ready to go, the chances of an assault will diminish (at least somewhat). One of Tallahassee's leading contract lobbyists said that legislators have to know that a lobbyist is around—in committee, outside the chamber, or wherever. "You have to be there so they see you," he maintained.

2. *Stay with It.* Showing up may be 90 percent (or is it 80 percent?) of life for Woody Allen, but it is only the first step in effective lobbying. The persistent, single-minded lobbyist has the best chance of winning.

"Keep it up and keep it up and keep it up," advises one Florida lobbyist. "Keep on going, but don't become a pest." Another Florida lobbyist may have crossed the line; she bothers legislators constantly until she gets them. Does she go too far? She doesn't think so: "If I were a man, I would have been punched by now—but as a woman I can get away with more stuff." Guy Spearman of Florida exemplifies persistence. His intention was to get an amendment that would allow Sea World to import exotic snakes for a new display on dangerous sea animals. He got it on a house agriculture bill but lost three separate attempts to get senate approval. Still, he continued looking for another vehicle to accomplish his client's ends, and his efforts finally bore fruit.[3]

3. *Be Brief.* Although lobbyists should be persistent, they must be respectful of a legislator's time. One consultant follows the thirty-second rule; the message must be conveyed quickly.[4] A lobbyist in Maryland echoes this advice: "You can't take up a lot of their time. Get right to the point," she cautions, adding that lobbyists need to explain succinctly what a bill does and doesn't do. An Arkansas lobbyist recommends the following pitch to a legislator: "I have a client who is interested in this bill. The client's problem is this. The way to solve the client's problem is this. Here is the up side and the down side of it as far as you're concerned."[5] A Colorado lobbyist describes how he often spends more time discussing the down side, giving the legislator answers to questions opponents might have. For some clients, he prepares a one-page summary of the strengths and weaknesses of their case and leaves it in the legislator's office.[6] He then returns, and the legislators, who have yet to look at the summary, read it in front of him. This gives him further—if brief—opportunity to make his case.

4. *Take Nothing for Granted.* If there is no organized opposition, a lobbyist's bill will pass—except when it doesn't. Something unexpected can happen. A Colorado lobbyist found this out when he was carrying a bill for a professional association. He had gotten an influential legislator to sponsor the bill. The association's key-contact network had been activated. The chairman of the house committee having jurisdiction was on board. The state regulatory agency had announced its support. There was no organized opposition. All his ducks were in a row. But, unexpectedly, several house committee members voiced objections, adopting the attitude, "Let's make 'em fight for it." The lobbyist and his client had to redouble their efforts. Although they finally won, it was not without a struggle.

Legislators can be extraordinarily independent. A lobbyist and former legislative leader in Colorado pointed out how quickly the scenario can change. "You think you're in control, and then 'boom'." In the words of a Colorado lobbyist, "*Nothing* is a slam dunk." It can all fall apart at any moment because of the most trivial things. And because a lobbyist beats back a bill or amendment one time, this does not mean the opposition cannot resurrect it. With Florida's legislative session advancing to the second half, one veteran lobbyist uttered the pronouncement: "It's never safe, until they leave."

5. *It Is Necessary to Choose.*   Lobbyists and organizations cannot pursue everything on their agendas. They therefore need to set priorities. A contract lobbyist from Utah told the Pharmaceutical Manufacturers Association: "You can only go to the well so many times in one session." A contract lobbyist from Maryland gave similar counsel to PMA with respect to the issue of using animals in testing: "If we want other things to fall in line, we have to back off on that one." The problem for an association in particular is that because it has many members with different interests, it may take on too many issues. Similarly, contract lobbyists, who typically have multiple clients (each with its own issues), tend to present legislators with a large portfolio. Legislators will take on just so much work for any particular interest.

6. *Be Prepared to Lose.*   This principle is not intended to imply that a lobbyist should try to advance an obviously hopeless case. A lobbyist cannot afford to become identified with too many defeats. But both lobbyist and client must be willing, at least on occasion, to take a beating. No one involved in the process can expect to have his or her way all the time. Everyone will suffer losses, and how they are suffered is important. In the words of a Texas lobbyist, "You have to be able to lose with style and grace"—but not with frequency.

The Elements of Defense and Offense

Most lobbyists spend most of their time on the defense. A New Jersey contract lobbyist explained: "A great number of our clients, and obviously a great number of everybody's clients, want to be protected from the legislature. And they don't want bills to pass." A defensive position, everyone agrees, is easier to play. It is harder to push a bill through the legislative process than to stop one. One chief executive officer, who takes an interest in state government relations, observes that "trying to affect policy is like pushing a rope." [7] To move forward, a bill not only requires greater consensus but it must also overcome a series of obstacles as it moves from committee to caucus to floor in one house and then through the other. [8] It is said that one Colorado lobbyist, "can't pass things, but she can kill them in the senate." Anywhere along the line, the lobbyist has a shot at a bill.

Moreover, if there is doubt on any issue, it is simpler and safer for a legislator to vote no. A coalition can fall apart; the bill can pick up a gutting amendment; all sorts of things can happen to it. There are, in the words of a Colorado lobbyist, "a hundred ways to kill a bill and only one way to pass one." This particular lobbyist is said to have gone further, jokingly claiming that he and his colleague "couldn't pass Mother's Day, but we could defeat it."

In defending, lobbyists may pursue several paths. First, they may try to get the bill they oppose withdrawn or shunted aside. They will talk to the sponsor and ask that the bill not be pushed, or at least not pushed vigorously. Although the sponsor may refuse, there is a good chance that he or she will have been softened up. And perhaps the two sides will be able to get together and discuss a compromise. It is preferable, if possible, to leave the bill in the hands of a legislator with whom the lobbyist has close ties. A New Jersey lobbyist detailed his strategy:

> It is better, even if you oppose a bill, to have it in the hopper under a sponsor with whom you are reasonably friendly than to have it withdrawn ... because he or she will not move that bill. The strategy should be to keep it where I can see it, as opposed to where I don't have control over it.

Second, instead of opposing it head on, lobbyists may formulate an alternative bill. When presented with a problem, legislators usually ask for a solution. If lobbyists oppose a measure, what would they put in its stead? A lobbyist for the chemical industry, which has been under intense pressure from environmental groups in recent years, explained why it was necessary to be proactive: "We get beat every time we say no, particularly on emotional, high-charged issues." Associated Industries of Florida has developed a number of alternatives to proposals that it opposed. It even prepared a transaction tax on business, which would substitute for a sales tax on services were it again to be brought up in the Florida legislature.

Lobbyists for New Jersey business appreciate the importance of having an alternative when in opposition. For years they turned back public-interest groups and environmentalists who were trying to get a bottle bill enacted. Recycling was their alternative. In contrast, they opposed the "right to know" bill directly and lost a bruising battle. They learned their lesson. Recently, New Jersey industry has again come under assault, this time by the Hazard Elimination through Local Participation (HELP) bill. HELP would authorize local community and facility-based groups to conduct environmental and public-health inspections of plants where hazards might exist. The New Jersey Business and Industry Association, along with other groups, opposed the measure and prepared an alternative that would have authorized local emergency planning committees, formed on a county level, to conduct a specified number of on-site inspections. A good lobbyist is often able to have a bill amended so that it is not so injurious to his client.

Third, lobbyists may try to amend a bill to death by making it too costly, too encompassing, or too controversial. Frequently attempts are made to "poison pen" or "artificially sweeten" bills through amendments or committee substitutes that arouse the antagonism of other players or entail expenditures that are beyond the realm of political possibility. For many years a proposal to require seat belts in school buses was side-tracked in the New Jersey legislature. The lobbyist for the school bus owners was usually able to get a substitute bill that was so comprehensive and costly that it could not pass, and if it did the governor would have vetoed it.

Fourth, on occasions where a bill cannot be bottled up or a satisfactory compromise cannot be worked out, the lobbyist must launch an all-out fight on the floor of the house and/or senate, and possibly in the office of the governor.

When on the offense, a lobbyist's initial consideration is to recruit a legislative sponsor. The legislator who introduces the bill and then champions it will frequently play the key role in its enactment. If a lobbyist gets the wrong legislator as sponsor, no matter how good the arguments in its favor, the bill will go down in flames. The "author," as the person who introduces and carries the bill is called in California, is most critical in that state. If the author is seen as credible, he or she can get votes from other California legislators with few questions asked. The sponsor is also important in Colorado, where legislators are limited in the number of bills they can introduce. This makes it more difficult for lobbyists in Colorado to get sponsors. But they begin early, press their clients for a decision, and by the fall have sponsors lined up so that bills can be pre-filed before the December deadlines. If necessary, lobbyists can go to legislative leaders and obtain "late bill" status from them. Where there is a legislature, there is usually a way.

In choosing a sponsor or author, a number of factors are taken into account. The higher up in leadership, the more attractive the sponsor. Occasionally the speaker, president, or majority leader may agree to take on a lobbyist's bill. More frequently, the chairman of the committee with jurisdiction is approached and asked to act as sponsor. A Maryland lobbyist described the process. She went to the chairman and asked, "What do you think of this bill?" He responded, "I think I can support it." The lobbyist continued, "Will you be the sponsor?" She then explained that the concept was a good one, there was no opposition, and essentially no down side. "You do the homework," he replied, "I'll put my name on it." The first visit a California association lobbyist makes is to the staff consultants and chairman of the relevant committee. If, after discussion, the chairman says the proposal would be a great committee bill, then the matter is settled—from the lobbyist's point of view, settled in ideal fashion.

The advantages of having leaders sign on as sponsors are obvious. They exercise greater control over scheduling and other aspects of the process. They have status, power, and, usually, respect. Such sponsors are more inclined to stand firm when the going gets tough. If the chairman is unavailable, lobbyists will then seek out the "most powerful person in the business of passing that particular bill"—someone who, at the least, gets along with the chairman and other leaders. That tends to be a member of the majority party, particularly in a partisan legislature such as in California, Colorado, Minnesota, or New Jersey. A Colorado public-interest group, for example, routinely seeks Republican sponsors, even if they are conservative and not traditional allies of the group. They are the people with greatest influence there.

Other considerations relating to sponsorship involve whether legislators have shown an interest in the issue, whether they work hard (and, in some places, have staff that work hard), and whether they are looking for an issue to get publicity for reelection or a run for higher office. Many legislators, of course, take on bills because they believe in the issues. For some groups, such as those advocating a particular stance on abortion rights, potential sponsors are limited to the universe of true believers, maybe a half-dozen members in each house who would be willing to lead the fight.

Sometimes a group has no choice as to the sponsor. A prolife group in Pennsylvania would undoubtedly defer to Stephen Freind, a member of the house who has been the leading spokesman against a woman's right to abortion. Authors, in effect, may choose themselves. Legislators frequently initiate an action and then ask interest groups for their help. The leadership may also decide. According to a New Jersey public-interest-group lobbyist: "We may encourage a legislator to introduce a piece of legislation, but when they go in [to the leadership] with the idea, they may not necessarily get that bill. It may go to someone else." Once legislators agree to sponsor a bill, they can exercise as much control as they desire. Or they can delegate the managerial job to the lobbyists. In California the tendency is for authors to take control, steering the bill through each house. They are largely responsible for deciding which amendments to accept and which to reject. And the bill may take on a shape not originally intended by its lobbyist-advocates. One Colorado public-interest-group lobbyist advised:

> You have to act like it's their bill from the moment they put their name on it. The sponsor is the leader of the campaign who may defer to your advice. But you can't take the attitude that the sponsor is rubber-stamping your game plan. If you do, you'll get slapped down.

A public-interest-group lobbyist in New Jersey had similar feelings. He was taking orders, he said, from the senator whose name was on the bill. The senator had had to make changes with which the lobbyist disagreed; there was no alternative but to go along. The legislator was at the helm.

With a strong sponsor, therefore, the lobbyist takes on a supportive role. If the sponsor has other priorities—such as twenty or thirty bills he or she is pushing—then the lobbyist will have to manage the process. This is often the practice in Florida and New Jersey, where lobbyists negotiate on behalf of the sponsors. On occasion, moreover, "talk sheets" prepared by the lobbyist are used by sponsors when their bills are brought up on the floor. These sponsors are not overly familiar with the legislation that bears their name.

Targets in the Process

Once a bill is introduced, the process is formally under way, although, informally, much may have already been worked out. (Special attention will be given below to negotiating strategies and techniques.) It is not unusual, moreover, for the arguments to have been made and a consensus established by the time a bill is referred to committee. But often a sponsor (and his or her lobbyist allies) will try to rush a bill through—the theory being, says one Florida lobbyist that "the first pig out of the pen is the hardest one to catch." Known as a "ram job" in New Jersey (and otherwise elsewhere), speedy passage of a bill is, whenever possible, the lobbyist's objective. It should not be done at the risk, however, of annoying legislators of another persuasion.

One lobbyist described the campaign he waged on behalf of a professional association engaged in a turf battle with a rival. His client's bill had been kicking around for a while before he was hired. After spending six months laying the groundwork, he succeeded in getting the bill passed by both houses within two weeks. He had secured the committee chairman's agreement to hear it the first possible moment and then asked the presiding officer to post it right after the committee reported it out. The same schedule was being followed in the other house. The opposing group could do nothing at this point because the committee chairmen and leadership in both houses had agreed to support the measure. The element of surprise is critical, but "you really have to know what you're doing and with whom," cautioned this lobbyist, "and you must meet with all these people ahead of time."

Whatever the velocity of the process, lobbyists have a sense of the members with whom they have to deal. Who is in a key position? Who is respected? Where is the opposition? What about the committee? It always depends on the issue, but leaders, committees, and rank-and-file members—in one sequence or another—are the principal targets.

Leadership

Many lobbyists pursue a "top-down" strategy, concentrating on the presiding officers and committee chairmen. Such efforts account for about half of the work of many lobbyists, at least in those states where the legislative parties and leaders are still somewhat strong. The lobbyist for a California association focuses her energy on assembly speaker Willie Brown and senate president David Roberti. "There's no point in putting in a lot of time with a lot of members," she said, "when I can put in focused time with the decision makers." Not only do the leaders have the ability to influence members on issues, but they also exercise procedural control.

It is normally up to the presiding officers, with the assistance of staff, to refer a bill to committee. A bill can be drafted so that it comes within the jurisdiction of one committee or another, but leaders still have discretion—if they want to use it. A lobbyist wants his or her bill to go to a friendly committee (and an opponent's bill to be sent to an unfriendly one). It is not unusual for a lobbyist to ask a presiding officer to refer a bill to a particular committee and, according to a New Jersey lobbyist, "he will do it, if it's reasonable." But then, the lobbyist added, "You wouldn't ask him to do anything if it wasn't reasonable." Florida's lobbyists, it has been reported, routinely made recommendations to the senate president's staff regarding committee referrals, not only about which one but also how many. In some cases they asked that their bills be sent to as few committees as possible; in other cases they requested multiple referrals.[9]

The presiding officers can also decide, either directly or through rules committees, when, and if, a bill will be taken up (calendared, posted) on the floor of the chamber. In Florida, for example, many of the bills that are favorably reported by committees and take their places on the house or senate calendars never get considered. A bill has to be placed by the rules committee on the special-order calendar in order for the presiding officer to get around to it. And the speaker's or president's top lieutenant chairs the rules committee. The question every lobbyist asks, therefore, is "How do I get my bill on the special-order calendar?" Toward the end of Florida's session, when leaders are beleaguered by such requests, the lobbyist who has a connection can get three minutes with the rules chairman or five minutes with the staff director and a special-order placement or two.

In some instances, lobbyists also attend to executive leaders—the governor and his or her staff and department heads. This can be an important part of lobbying, although we touch on it only briefly here. On environmental issues, the governor and the environmental department usually play a leadership role. For a county or city, support may have to be lined up in the department of community affairs. On taxes or budget issues, the administration is generally out in front. If a lobbyist's client is concerned with finances or an appropriation, the place to start is with the agency's budget request. After that, the governor's budget office needs to be lobbied.

Whatever the issue, if lobbyists are attempting to get a bill passed, they will want to make sure that the governor signs it. There is always the possibility of a veto. It is therefore customary for them to check with the governor's office before a bill's introduction, during the legislative process, or after its enactment. And lobbyists who fail to defeat legislation they oppose have as a final resort the veto. There is little to be lost in making a last-ditch effort in the governor's office.

Committees

The standing committee is, perhaps, the lobbyists' principal focus. If a lobbyist is advocating legislation, it has to be reported out of committee favorably in both houses (although in some states, bills may not be referred to committee in the second house). When the chairman and committee members vote for a bill, they will ordinarily do some work to have it pass on the floor. The committee has acquired a stake in the legislation by virtue of its favorable action, even though in some places the author or sponsor manages the bill. If a lobbyist is opposing legislation, it takes only a few votes, and perhaps only the chairman's, to kill it at this stage. If the bill gets to the floor, however, many more votes are required to defeat it; a substantial effort is required to overcome the committee's recommendation. Bills are rarely defeated on the floor, although a number are amended there. One Washington-based lobbyist for an association has made it a practice of developing relationships with committee chairmen in a number of states. "If I'm doing my job well," he commented, "I never have to deal with leadership." The issue does not get that far; he has managed to stop things in the committee.

The lobbyist's primary target is the committee chairman. If the chairman (or even a majority-party member of the committee) is sponsoring the bill, it has a very good chance at the committee level and, thus, a good chance in at least one house. Committee members will ordinarily defer to the chairman and to one another, just as house members generally follow the recommendations of their committees. What happens in the other chamber, however, may be a different story. Chairmen in most states have virtual life-and-death power over bills referred to their committees. So, if a lobbyist wants to stop something, the chairman is the one to do it. Except in a few legislatures, such as Colorado's, the chairman may choose not to schedule a bill for consideration. Without the chairman's assent, that bill is unlikely to be reported out, although it may be reincarnated later in the form of an amendment.

As much as anything else, therefore, a lobbyist wants the chairman's support. Sometimes the chairman is an old ally. Occasionally he or she has agreed to this one piece of legislation. Frequently he or she is sympathetic, but a compromise still has to be negotiated. The chairman may say that he or she cannot vote for the bill unless a change is made. More than likely, the lobbyist will accede to the request. Or the chairman may simply refuse to vote for a bill. However, the chairman can be helpful in other ways, such as by not showing up the day the bill is on the committee calendar.

Whether the chairman is on board or not, lobbyists rarely stop there. Most will also work committee members, one by one. Nothing can be left to chance. A Maryland lobbyist recalls legislation she was promoting. The chairwoman of the committee had introduced the bill. So the lobbyist thought it was a done deal. There was no organized opposition. One member of the committee objected, however. The bill almost died because, as the lobbyist admits, "I read it wrong. I should have worked the bill."

The lobbying of members starts before the bill is heard. This is the time when grass-roots key contacts are used and when lobbyists (if there are more than one on a side) divide up members according to who has the closest ties. A Minnesota lobbyist points out that people can change their minds and that no one should be written off. "I don't think you ignore anyone on a committee, even if you know they're on the other side," he observed.

An important aspect of the committee process is the hearing, at which proponents and opponents testify. A committee hearing brings out every lobbyist on the issue. They sit in the audience, often with witnesses for their case. Yet many view such testimony as a "show and tell" exercise. Although a witness may present absolutely compelling testimony on an issue, the position being advocated can still lose overwhelmingly. That is because the other side has been hard at work, having rounded up the votes before the hearing.[10] It is widely believed that testimony at hearings seldom changes votes. But hearings allow a group's position to become part of the record, attract media attention, transmit information to legislators, and—last but not least—impress a group's membership.[11]

Lobbyists and the groups they represent do more at committee hearings than present their specific case. They present themselves, and this matters for longer-term relationships. The Pharmaceutical Manufacturers Association, for instance, takes advantage of hearings to have physicians and scientists make the more general case for the industry. A lobbyist will take great care to instruct his clients on their demeanor before committees. One counseled doctors scheduled to testify: "Don't be condescending. Don't give them the impression that you think you're wasting your time here but should instead be treating patients."

Hearings not only offer groups an opportunity to be seen and heard, but they also give legislators a chance to take the measure of lobbyists. How a lobbyist responds to questioning can help to determine his or her future treatment at the hands of legislators. A Colorado lobbyist described how committee members work new lobbyists over: "The cowboys want to see if you'll run away. They may kill your bill again, but they'll do it with less vigor if you behave well." Good behavior is imperative for the lead lobbyist of a coalition in Texas. After their bill is heard, instead of walking out of the room, as is the prevailing custom, lobbyists on the coalition team remain at the meeting until the entire agenda is completed and the meeting ends. On their part, it is a sign of respect for the committee.

Staff

A former staff member of the California assembly has detailed the decisive role he played in the legislative process. According to his account, staff would frequently meet with lobbyists to obtain support for what staff had already decided on. They would bargain with the lobbyists, offering to include or delete certain provisions of a bill in return for backing from groups with political strength. As group after group signed on, staff would then make use of their lobbyists to influence legislators they knew.[12]

This may not be the normal process, even in California. But there is little question that such influence exists in legislatures with substantial staffs. In states such as California, Florida, New Jersey, and Texas, staffs cannot be circumvented. Lobbyists must work with them. As a New Jersey lobbyist put it, "We need to deal with staff because legislators rely on them."

Although lobbyist-staff interaction depends on the issue, many lobbyists spend considerable time on staff. In California, they are reported to spend more time with professional staff than with legislators themselves.[13] Elsewhere they work with a member's staff and/or with committee consultants, particularly on the details of legislation and amendments to bills. Some staffs will assume responsibility for the work if their member or their committee favors the legislation. Others will let the lobbyist do all the work, according to the preference of the legislator principal. Even where a legislature has relatively little staff support, as in Colorado, staff can play a role. Before a legislator sponsors a lobbyist's bill, he or she may ask a bill drafter on the central staff to work on a bill with a lobbyist.

Florida's staffers—especially the chiefs of staff for the presiding officers and the staff directors of the standing committees (particularly the rules committees)—are seldom bypassed. Their involvement can be critical in shaping compromises that can achieve consensus. In New Jersey it may be someone on the partisan staff or a legislative service agency professional, both of whom are staffing the committee. The lobbyist's contact will vary, but some staffer is likely to be targeted. "My approach," said a Trenton contract lobbyist, "is to not ignore anyone associated with the issue." At the initial stage, this generally means committee members and their staff. The approach is essentially the same in Texas, where lobbyists do a lot of visiting with staff of the leader, committee, and individual members.

Members

Even if lobbyists have won in committee and have leadership on their side, they cannot afford to neglect the larger membership. Votes count, especially on controversial issues (lobbyists must be able to count, too). This is not to suggest that lobbyists have to buttonhole every legislator; they may choose to pass over those who are clearly adversaries. "As the saying goes," counsels one experienced professional, "never try to teach a pig how to sing. It wastes your time and annoys the pig." [14] An early study on lobbying confirms this adage: lobbyists rarely attempt to change an opponent's mind, and such efforts constitute a very small part of the lobbying process. [15] Lobbyists concentrate their efforts instead on the fence sitters—the legislators who can be won over. [16]

On a few issues legislators may be committed to a lobbyist's cause by virtue of conscience, constituency, or consistency (that is, one's previous record). On a few, legislators may belong to a group a lobbyist represents. Trial lawyers who serve in the legislature are apt to carry the trial lawyers' case. Teachers who serve in the legislature tend to sympathize with the teachers' case. In Alabama, as was mentioned earlier, many teachers or former teachers are in the legislature. If a vote directly affects education, lobbying them helps but is not vital: "the huge bloc of legislators with teaching backgrounds doesn't need to be told what to do." [17] Legislators may have some other characteristic that will impinge somehow on a client's case. Being a smoker or nonsmoker may matter. One lobbyist who represented tobacco interests complained that in the particular state he was working, only 1 out of 40 members of the senate smoked and only about 10 out of 120 in the house did.

Most members hang loose on many issues that concern interest groups. Neither their fealty nor their enmity can be relied on. Therefore, lobbyists tend to cast a wide net, approaching as many members as they, or their colleagues, can. The case can best be made member to member, but lobbyists nevertheless reach out to whomever they can—with the obvious exception of those leading the charge against them. Although lobbyists will not approach implacable opponents, they will try not to alienate them. "You can't get their votes," said a Florida lobbyist, "but you may be able to keep them from killing you." Another Florida lobbyist said that although he would not "waste his time" with a particular senator, he does send someone else to cover him "so he can't say we didn't come by." No gain can be derived from a legislator who feels ignored, as was the case in California where business associations had neglected personal contact. "I can't actually remember," says one legislator, "when I was personally lobbied on a bill by someone representing the CMA or the Chamber." [18] It is important for lobbyists to come by and visit even with those legislators who are not especially friendly to their issue or to their clients. Nothing can be taken for granted on the current issue; moreover, the visit may help a lobbyist on the next issue.

If the lobbyist needs votes to pass or defeat a bill or, more likely, to adopt or stave off an amendment on the floor, then there can be no substitute for working the members. "Work every son of a bitch in the legislature," advises a Florida lobbyist, "Then, go back and see them again. And again. If you get them to commit three times, you have them." Lobbyists spend much of their time trying to discover where legislators stand and asking them to make a commitment. They are constantly taking vote counts, carrying tally sheets or notebooks that list legislators who can then be checked off according to their positions on the issue at hand.

Getting legislators to commit themselves before they actually have to may be among a lobbyist's toughest jobs. Legislators often try to cooperate with both sides because they see merits on one hand and also on the other. They also have regard for lobbyists in both camps and do not want to alienate anyone unless they have no alternative. A legislator may therefore be kind, agreeable, and encouraging. The lobbyist should interpret none of this, however, as a sign of commitment. [19] The lobbyist must therefore not only make the rounds of rank-and-file, but also identify the solid supporters, the definite nos, and the question marks in between.

The crucial final stages of the persuasion process may be in caucus, on the floor, or later in a conference committee. In New Jersey, if a bill survives the majority-party caucus, there is little chance of it being reversed or revised on the floor. But when legislators are meeting in caucus, events are harder to predict. This is extremely frustrating for lobbyists. In Minnesota and Texas conference committees settle many issues, so lobbyists make their last-ditch efforts there. It is critical, for example, for Texas lobbyists to have at least one of "their" people on the ten-member conference committee—"someone who will carry your water," says one lobbyist in Austin, "and can get other votes." "Someone on the inside," he explains, "can keep you informed."

Every lobbyist hopes to have things worked out well in advance of floor consideration. Many do, but they cannot be sure that they will. "If you have a floor fight," commented a California lobbyist, "you haven't done your job in the legislature." At least, that is the way it used to be in California. Today, the lobbyist cannot afford to wander far from the floor. Often it is the job of lobbyists to quarterback their side, when the bill is on second or third reading. A Colorado lobbyist had a major bill on the house floor. She and her colleagues stood behind the glass at the rear of the chamber. As amendments were introduced, legislator allies would carry them back to her. She and the others would read the amendments (the last one had not even been printed), make quick decisions, and signal which way to vote to legislators in the chamber.

There are stories about powerful lobbyists who sit in the gallery of the chamber, signaling thumbs up or down to members. This is often the case when amendments are coming fast and furious and members have had little chance to read, let alone make sense of, them. The signals are often given by legislative leaders or members who sponsored and are carrying the bills. They are necessary cues for members.

Lobbyists face their greatest tactical challenges during the final days of a session. On the one hand, they must enact bills that may have died, or even been rejected, in committee. Their bills may have emerged from committee but not been taken off the calendar. This is the last chance, furthermore, for lobbyists to insert words, phrases, or additional language into someone else's bill as a way of getting their own measure enacted into law. What they need is a "vehicle," the title of which is broad enough to encompass their amendment.

Two Texas lobbyists, known as the "Booze Brothers" (one represents whiskey and wine, the other beer), are particularly adept during these closing hours. According to one lobbyist, a frequent victim of their successful tactics, "they wait until the very last minute, put their entire legislative package in one bill, and [then] run it through the legislature." [20] The liquor code is so complicated that few legislators understand it or realize what is happening until it is too late.

Lobbyists must also keep amendments *off* their own bills and prevent hostile bills from slipping through as amendments to other measures. The last few days of the session in Florida are especially hectic. One lobbyist compared it to a basketball game, with the ball going up and down the court. Lobbyists have to ascertain who is in control. Key staff members therefore have to be identified at this stage in order for lobbyists to be able to find out as quickly as possible what is happening and who is planning to do what. Lobbyists will have "watchers," who scan the process for them, pick up amendments filed with the clerk, and just hang out, hoping to pick up bits and pieces of vital information from members and other legislative creatures. Without timely intelligence, it is difficult for lobbyists to figure out how to react. There is little time to think.

Education and Information

Today's lobbyist will almost invariably have to make an argument on the merits. Personal relationships still count, as do grass-roots efforts and political campaigns, but lobbyists also have to present a reasonable case. A Florida lawyer-lobbyist maintained that, before, it was more "who you knew," but, today, it is more "what you know." A lobbyist can no longer rely simply on approaching a legislator friend and saying, "I need this." On most issues today, the weight of the argument is what matters.

A Minnesota lobbyist described how lobbying in his state was "merit and substance based," although some folks still did the job old-style. "Effective lobbying is taking a reasonable position," he explains, "supporting it with facts, selling the idea from legislator to legislator, and being there all the time so that when the decision is about to be made, you're around." Merit and substance may play a slightly larger role in states like Minnesota than in Florida or New Jersey, but everywhere lobbyists have to present legislators with information and educate them as to their clients' positions. Public interest and other cause lobbyists, in particular, spend considerable energy in this regard. They present their facts, argue the merits, and often put an emotional spin on the whole package.

Providing Information

About twenty years ago a study of lobbying in Massachusetts, North Carolina, Oregon, and Utah inquired into how dependent legislators were on lobbyists for information. Forty-one to 83 percent of the legislators in these states replied that they depended on lobbyist information a good deal or some of the time; 55 to 88 percent answered that they had a lot or quite a bit of confidence in the information; and 28 percent to 61 percent replied that they found all or most of the information helpful.[21]

Today, with more staff and other sources of information available and with lobbying under fire from the press, it is unlikely that legislators would respond as positively to questions such as those noted above. Nonetheless, they still seek information from lobbyists and lobbyists still seek to provide it. Legislators tend to be overwhelmed by communications, newsletters, reports, and data of every kind. But they are constantly on the search for information, which is essentially data that have been manipulated, interpreted, and packaged. Lobbyists can furnish such information—processed, understandable, and politically and policy relevant. What a lobbyist does, therefore, is to provide basic information—quickly and intelligibly.[22] Moreover, it reaches legislators about when they need it, not too early and not too late. In the words of a New Jersey contract lobbyist, timing is crucial: "Getting the right information to the right people at the right time.... It's a home run to make that combination work." The supply of information ideally should match legislator demand—helping members do what is right; making friends, allies, and constituents happy; and protecting significant interests in their district.[23]

To be sought out by legislators for information, lobbyists themselves must be knowledgeable. According to an observer: "Profound knowledge of an issue is an advantage a lobbyist carries into battle." [24] A lawyer-lobbyist, who is an expert on land use, is much in demand by members of the Florida legislature. A lobbyist for the chemical industry has developed the reputation in California of furnishing reliable information, which is especially useful for the record. Trustworthiness is also essential. Legislators must trust the lobbyist in order to rely on his or her information. "People trust us," is a comment many lobbyists offer about why legislators use their information. A Florida lobbyist, for instance, has spent his entire career in the field of alcoholic beverages, including a stint as director of the division of alcoholic law in a previous gubernatorial administration. He is a trusted source of information on such issues. A Minnesota lobbyist is an expert on insurance, and on such issues legislators turn to him.

Lobbyists are indispensable when it comes to providing legislators with what is primarily political, rather than substantive, information. Most important, because they represent their clients, they can communicate what their positions are and how intensely they are held. That is vital information. In addition, they can tell legislators how other actors might be affected by a measure being considered. They also try to give legislators an idea of how their districts would fare if a bill were enacted. A number of lobbyists are in the habit of preparing position papers on issues. They also try to tailor their arguments to individual legislators. A member with strong business ties will be presented one argument; a member with strong union ties will hear another.

Lobbyists also provide substantive or technical information. They conduct research and issue reports. California business associations, for instance, are known for the research papers their lobbyists write in their particular areas of responsibility.[25] Common Cause, in New Jersey and

Florida among other places, acquires and reports considerable information on the subject of campaign finances. And legislators inevitably use it. In the past five to ten years, too, policy and fiscal analyses have gained great currency. Some explore the actual effects of ongoing programs and policies. Others challenge policies that are proposed. In Florida, for instance, the governor wanted to increase environmental fees. Lobbyist Wade Hopping responded with an analysis, however, that demonstrated that the fees were excessive. As a result, the increases were scaled back.[26]

In view of their declared rationale, public-interest research groups in the states naturally devote substantial energy to research and its dissemination. New Jersey PIRG, for instance, usually leads off a major campaign for legislation with a research report on an environmental or consumer issue. In addition to analysis, the report will make recommendations on legislation, regulation, or enforcement. One such report, issued early in 1988, entitled "Polluters' Playground—An Investigation of Water Pollution Violations in New Jersey," focused on permit violations and the government's response. In virtually every area of study, PIRG found "a pattern of corporate and municipal violation" that was "coupled with government action which can best be described as lethargic." PIRG recommended stiffer penalties and less discretionary authority. Reports like these are aimed as much at the press and the public as they are at legislators themselves. In the ensuing battle, legislators sympathetic to environmental causes did not fail to use PIRG's research.

In addition to research and reports, lobbyists and their clients deliver experts, who testify before committees and even speak to members one on one. A lobbyist for a government association in Maryland set up a panel of finance and budget experts to explain at two hearings just what a proposed tax-collection bill would do. This resulted in a study group being appointed to explore the matter further. Or take the issue of whether industrial laboratories should be permitted to use animals in their research. This is an emotional issue to the public, and one that the pharmaceutical industry feels strongly about. A lobbyist explained the approach that his company took:

> You try to get people who are involved with that issue in the legislature to meet with people who are involved in your research and have them share all the information as to why we need to have animals—not because it's something that we want to do, but because it's something we think we have to do.

Arguments furnished by experts and technicians can be persuasive.

Arguing the Merits

The fact is that, in many cases, lobbyists represent special interests that are seeking sanction or advantage from government action. The contestants are mainly self-serving in these disputes, although they also believe that what benefits them is also good public policy. And this is the argument they make. Such an argument must be made today; it is practically a requisite for success.[27] One of Tallahassee's major lobbyists (before taking a position with the Chiles administration) was not one to besiege the legislature with a bunch of statistics. He nevertheless admitted "you like to know that what you are arguing makes some good policy sense and has some strength to it."[28]

The public-policy rhetoric used by lobbyists varies from issue to issue, but some general examples are in order. Most, but not all of them, are defensive.

1. *"It isn't fair."* The tobacco and alcoholic-beverage industries rely heavily on the "it isn't fair" argument to combat tax increases and stiffer regulations. A Florida bill that would disallow business expenses for promotion is "unfair," according to industry lobbyists. Taxes on tobacco and/or alcohol to fund health care and social programs are also opposed for the same reasons. These programs, the industries maintain, should be funded out of general revenues and not by earmarked monies derived from a tax on a few products. Recently, tobacco has effectively used the fairness issue, enacting legislation in a number of states that prohibits employers from discriminating against candidates for employment who smoke. The issues involved were hiring practices, smoking in the workplace, and telling employees what they could or could not do. Even though legislators had been in the habit of kicking tobacco around, the fairness argument was telling.

2. *"It won't work."* Frequently lobbyists will argue that, whatever the merits of a proposal, it does not make sense in practice. This is presented as one of several arguments. The pollution of New Jersey's beaches with debris led to a bill that would prohibit the sale of tampon devices that used a disposable applicator made of plastic or other nonbiodegradable materials. Playtex, a manufacturer of tampons, produced a study that showed that plastic applicators represented less than .4 percent of beach debris in the state.[29] What was the point of the ban if debris would not be substantially reduced!

3. *"It can be done in other ways."* Lobbyists try to persuade legislators that there are other, less hurtful, ways to skin the cat. The main line of defense against the bottle bill is that recycling offers a better method of cleaning up. Moreover, now that recycling programs are in operation, lobbyists for beer, soft drinks, glass, retailers, and recyclers

argue that a bottle bill would kill recycling by taking the profits out of the solid-waste stream. They have a point. The tobacco industry and restaurant associations oppose legislation requiring restaurants to set up smoking and nonsmoking sections. They argue that restaurants are already providing these sections on a voluntary basis, and the system is working.

4. *"It is too costly."* Especially if the tab has to be picked up by the state, the cost argument can be powerful, and more so in times of budget stringency. Business lobbyists usually maintain that environmental measures are too costly and will harm not only business but also consumers and taxpayers. Lobbyists for municipalities will argue that a particular measure would cost the cities $300 million, and impact heavily on local taxpayers.

5. *"It will help consumers."* Lobbyists and their clients justify many special-interest measures in terms of how they would benefit consumers. When a group seeks to become licensed by the state, for example, its rationale is to protect the public. For example, occupational therapists desire state regulation, maintaining that a law would prevent unqualified individuals from claiming they are professionals. Regulation would serve to protect the elderly people and other populations that need therapists. In the case of the so-called car wars, lobbyists for Hertz and Avis charged that Alamo's collision-damage-waiver practices constituted unfair competition and therefore hurt consumers. Alamo rejected the charge and argued that consumers should have the right to decide. New Jersey is one of only two states where self-service gasoline stations are banned. The oil industry, advocating self-service in addition to full-service, justified its position in terms of consumer choice. The New Jersey Gasoline Retailers Association, supporting the ban, maintained that choice would raise the price of gas for consumers. (It also argued that self-service stations would inconvenience the elderly and disabled and could pose safety problems.)

6. *"It will hurt the public."* Professions that are resisting encroachment on their turf will often argue—and not without some justification—the health and welfare of the public. Ophthalmologists, who have opposed legislation to allow specially trained optometrists to prescribe certain drugs, maintain that it would authorize nonphysicians to practice medicine. They suggest that there might be serious consequences. In their testimony before health committees, ophthalmologists may tell of patients who became blind after optometrists failed to diagnose diabetes. Veterinarians, who resist the efforts of pet groomers to get authorization to brush animals' teeth, use a similar argument. Veterinary dentistry, they maintain, is a medical procedure. Veterinarians, they maintain, have to undergo a licensing procedure and demonstrate clinical competency in an examination in order to protect the

public from incompetence. When a veterinarian examines an animal's teeth, he or she will look for a disease of the mouth, malocclusion, cavities, tooth fractures, tumors, wounds, and so forth. By contrast, groomers have a purely cosmetic objective.

7. *"It will hurt the industry."* Before a company moves into a state, it has bargaining power. Chase Manhattan and Citicorp were successful in getting a bill through the Delaware legislature by promising to locate in the state and provide jobs. American Express has also used economic-development rhetoric to advance its legislative priorities in a state where it may locate a facility. But once an industry is located within a state, its economic-development argument is much weaker. A California lobbyist for business pointed out that damage to an industry and loss of jobs is no longer the argument it used to be. "We lose a thousand jobs, we'll create another thousand." A New Jersey lobbyist for business went further: "Legislators don't want to hear that you are going to move out of the state. They've heard it too many times in the past, and nothing happened." It is not sufficient, therefore, to base the case on harm to industry. It is preferable to argue other merits, as is done by the pharmaceutical industry. Access to quality health care, patient care, the doctor's ability to prescribe the best drug, cost effectiveness—these are the merits on which pharmaceuticals rest their case. A lobbyist for a major firm describes how he presents things: "This, we believe, is in the best interest of our company, our industry, the health care of individuals, and the whole health-care delivery system." That is a tough combination to beat.

Among the information that counts heavily are two types—(1) what other states are doing and (2) what difference a measure has made. A bill authorizing New Jersey's physician assistants to practice was signed into law early in 1992. Its passage through the legislature was helped considerably by the group's argument that every other state in the nation had already passed similar legislation. And New Jersey optometrists, arguing for their bill, told their legislators that similar laws were in effect in twenty-seven states. No damage had been done, they claimed, as evidenced by the fact that malpractice insurance premiums for optometrists had not gone up.

Statistics, it should be noted, can be extremely helpful to a group's case. They played a key role in 1991 legislation to require motorcyclists to wear helmets. Proponents of the legislation including the insurance industry, showed that 76 percent of those injured and 83 percent of those killed in California were not wearing helmets. Based on data from other states, they argued that the toll in California would go down if cyclists wore helmets. The legislature passed the helmet law and Governor Pete Wilson signed it.

Putting on Spin

Sometimes lobbyists have to do more than simply provide information. They may also have to doctor it or put on some spin. At the least, they have to get legislators' attention. Thus, one of the lobbyist's roles is "illuminating" the issue. For a state government relations professional in Washington, D.C., this entails "making the light so bright that they are overwhelmed."

For a New Jersey contract lobbyist the challenge was to get the attention of legislators who did not quite grasp the issue. The weekend before his bill was to be considered, he still had not been able to get them to appreciate the significant savings his measure was going to achieve. How could he make the numbers he had for each legislative district look real? The answer was to have checks printed up, on heavy blue paper, with "Pay to the order of Taxpayers in [with the number of legislative district]" and numbers ranging up to four million dollars typed out. The idea was that legislators would realize that their districts would get a refund if the measure was enacted. The facsimile checks were put in window envelopes and given by the lobbyist to legislators in the halls of the New Jersey State House annex. Legislators thanked the lobbyist, stuck the checks in their pockets, and walked around the corner, pulled out the envelope, and opened it up. The lobbyist had devised a clever way of getting their attention, although some legislators might have been a trifle disappointed in discovering that the check was a promotional gimmick and not a campaign contribution.

One way lobbyists get their points across is by labeling. What a bill is titled can matter enormously. One contract lobbyist recalled that he could not get occupational therapists the licensing bill they wanted. The title of their bill would arouse every doctor in the state. "They can have what they want," he explained, "if they just call it something different." That way, there would be little opposition at all. Thus, frequently "the name is the game." [30]

The environmental movement has a distinct advantage in that virtually every legislator wants to be perceived as an environmentalist. Environmentalists maximize their advantage by the most artful labeling. They structure the issue first, label it second, and release it to the press with fanfare third. "The Clean Water Act," "The Safe Drinking Water Act," "The Clean Air Act," "The Right-to-Know Act," and "HELP." The wording implies that these will all benefit the public. Labeling, of course, works both ways. In the battle over restricting smoking in public places, the proponents of the ban referred to the bill as "The Clean Indoor Air Bill," while the opponents called it "The Smoking Restriction Bill." [31]

Another way that lobbyists seek to get their message across is by personalizing it. "I try to translate it into real people for members—

welfare lines, the homeless," is how a lobbyist for one of Florida's cities described her approach. Another Florida lobbyist pointed out the personalization in the outdoor advertising association's campaign to restrict the ability of cities to regulate billboards. The association did not argue the interests of the billboard industry, but rather those of poor old Mom and Pop, who own one sign that Coca Cola rents from them. Regulation would put Mom and Pop out of business.

A New Jersey lobbyist, who opposed a proposed tax on plastic containers, figured out that this would apply to milk cartons and the milk that children buy in school. In testifying before the committee, he brought a half-pint milk carton (which would have been taxed the same as a one-gallon carton) and asked the assembled legislators if they were going to hurt the children in school by taxing their milk. The legislators responded that they did not intend to do anything like that. The bill died and the children went on drinking their milk at the same prices.

Public-interest lobbyists are especially adept at personalizing their issues. They frequently see a tactical advantage in identifying a villain. Often, too, because of ideology and/or strategy, they portray the struggle as one between good and evil.[32] "If you're against us on this bill, you're against the environment" is what they often contend. For most other lobbyists, this might be a high-risk strategy, and therefore unacceptable. Yet it fits the overall posture of those lobbying for a cause.

Related to this personalization of an issue is imbuing it with a lot of emotion. This can be done in practically any fashion. For instance, in 1987 Colorado passed a bill authorizing dental hygienists to set up shop independently of dentists. Dentists opposed the bill, while the hygienists were not a real political force. But the bill became a women's issue because hygienists were women, as are many of Colorado legislators.[33] Cause lobbyists have emotionally laden issues to begin with, and they can be made even more so. When that occurs, it is difficult for those on the other side, usually representatives of business, to counter the argument and hold their ground.

One contract lobbyist was resisting a measure advanced by a public-interest group requiring dealers to display warnings about hazardous toys. Representing a toy manufacturer, the lobbyist was fighting the odds. All he could do was sit down with legislators and argue that such a requirement would affect only those companies in the state, not companies in other states. So it would not solve the problem. He further maintained it was a federal problem, adding a gentle threat: why should his client, who wants to expand in the state, be penalized and thus not be able to go forward with his expansion plans. At the same time, he explained to legislators that his client did not want to market a toy that children would choke on because it would quickly put him out of business. Lastly, he tried to convince the legislators to visit with his client and listen to his side of the story. All of this did little good, and he knew it early on. "You take your shot that way and you know you are not going to win," he concluded. He was not mistaken. In October 1991, the governor signed the bill surrounded by children at a local day-care center.

The Functions of Information

One lobbyist declared that "information is still power in Colorado," adding, "You can win no matter who you're up against." Conversely, another lobbyist observed that "policy arguments have to be made in Minnesota, but they don't necessarily win out." Both lobbyists are right. Information is but one among many sources of influence. If the lobbyist has not only solid information but also a compelling public-policy argument and a good delivery system, his case has a marked advantage.

Information makes legislators more knowledgeable on the specific measures under consideration.[34] Without relevant information, on many issues legislators might be entirely in the dark. One lobbyist allows that legislators know something about a lot of things, but so many matters are beyond their ken:

> They have bills to decide on the release of helium balloons. Come on, these guys don't know about helium balloons! All they know about helium balloons is that you have them at your rally. You can't fault them for not knowing. But sooner or later, somebody manages to get the bill in the position where these guys have to make a life-or-death decision on helium balloons.

What legislator would have ever imagined that he or she would be deciding on balloons! Beyond the immediate issue, information can serve to educate the legislator along a variety of more general lines—about a policy area, a segment of the population, or an industry.

As important as anything else is the reassurance that information (provided by a lobbyist) can bring. Legislators need a justification or a rationale for their decisions. Therefore, one of the lobbyist's essential tasks is "to make it as easy as possible for a legislator to support an issue or request."[35] And even if they are going to vote against a lobbyist, they still want the information he or she can furnish—so there will be no surprises.

The Art of Compromise

Negotiating is one of the most important phases of the legislative process. Negotiations are constantly going on among legislators, among lobbyists, and among members of groups on both sides of an issue. Most of these sessions are informal, occurring in the offices of legislators and lobbyists, in conference rooms, restaurants, and dozens of other locations. In state legislatures, just as in Congress, formal, open committee sessions are being supplemented by informal gatherings. Legislators, like U.S. representatives, now convene in open session—in committee, on the floor, and sometimes in caucus—"to ratify," writes Bruce Wolpe, "what has been previously decided in private." [36]

The primary objective of negotiating is to arrive at an agreement on legislation among the concerned parties. This will almost always entail compromise by each side. On most issues handled by a legislature, compromise (sometimes referred to as the "vaseline" of the legislative process) is critical to moving things along. A lobbyist for an influential association in Minnesota acknowledged that one side or the other can never get all that it wants. "If you pass a bill," she said, "there is always some give and take."

What's in It for Lobbyists

According to Ralph Haben, a Florida lobbyist and former speaker, lobbyists have a choice: they can work with others to smooth out disagreements or try to run them over.[37] Part of what lobbyists do is to try to kill bills, another part of their effort is to work things out, and yet another, perhaps the smallest, part is to try to get one's own bill passed in its original and pristine form. Lobbyists, particularly the insiders with many clients, are usually willing to negotiate and compromise. There are a number of reasons for this.

First, they are in business for the long run, so they have adopted a "live and let live" philosophy. The idea it to keep everybody happy and make nobody mad. Furthermore, in the view of a Texas lobbyist, "It goes against human nature to say no all the time." Second, lobbyists want to be able to show a client something for their efforts. They cannot stand to lose everything or win nothing; the risks of refusing to compromise can be high. Third, as we shall discuss below, legislators prefer for opposing sides to work it out rather than fight it out. Lobbyists are more than inclined to go along with what legislators want.

Fourth, if possible, it is better not to vigorously oppose a bill sponsored by legislators. They may hold it against the lobbyist and his or her client in the future. One lobbyist pointed out that his organization had been fighting a particular bill sponsored by a senator and pushed by a public-interest group. His organization was also opposed to several other bills before the committee the senator chaired. The lobbyist thought the chairman had stacked the hearings on these bills in favor of proponents. The message, in the lobbyist's opinion, was: "I'm going to make life miserable for you until you support my bill." After a compromise was hammered out on the disputed bill, the lobbyist's organization began to get wonderful treatment at the hearings on the other legislation. "There was never anything said," the lobbyist concluded, "but it was abundantly clear."

Fifth, sometimes lobbyists have to cut their losses. The best they can do on a bill is to reduce the damage to their client. In Minnesota, legislators are in front of the curve in imposing strict environmental standards. Minnesota business, which has the reputation of being progressive and socially responsible, still objects to particular environmental measures. But because of the legislature's orientation, business can seldom win; it has to compromise. Business in New Jersey faced a similar situation in 1990-1991, particularly with Democratic governor Jim Florio, a Democratic legislature, and a strong environmental lobby. It could not win in the contest over the Clean Water Enforcement Act of 1989. It proposed amendments, however, ensuring that those innocent of real environmental harm would not be punished, capping legal fees stemming from lawsuits, and delaying implementation of the act to allow a phase-in period. After Republicans won both legislative houses in 1991, business interests could breathe somewhat easier for a while.

When the votes for one's side are simply not there, a modifying amendment is by far the best that one can get. "If a steamroller is coming down the mountain," a New Jersey lobbyist explained, "why should I stand in front of it and get squashed." A cause lobbyist on the liberal side can count on twenty-five friends in the Florida house and about twelve in the senate—far from a majority. A lobbyist for a conservative cause can count on no more in the Florida house. The latter had to deal with a sex-education bill opposed by her organization. She worked out some problems with amendments, improving the bill somewhat from her point of view. She nonetheless continued to oppose the measure.

Sixth, if both sides want something and if the balance of power is equal, they have to compromise if they want to accomplish anything. This was essentially the case in California when George Deukmejian was governor. Environmentalists were not willing to compromise with industry unless they had to; but because Deukmejian backed industry, they were forced to, and several compromises were effected as a result.

Lobbyists are not always disposed to compromise, however, particularly if they have a "slam-dunk" measure and have little reason to negotiate with their opponents. To pass a bill in Colorado, it takes eighteen (of thirty-five) votes in the senate and thirty-three (of sixty-five) votes in the house. One lobbyist commented, "If you have thirty-three and eighteen, let's roll with it; otherwise, let's talk." Even then, if problems arise and the other side is reasonable, a lobbyist will normally try to work things out. If an influential legislator wants something, lobbyists will consider compromise, even when the votes are almost certainly theirs. Rarely do groups have such a lock on the legislature, moreover, that they do not have to negotiate at all.

On occasion, lobbyists may be forced to go for broke because their clients insist on it. A contract lobbyist can be dealing with an organizational leadership that decides, "Win or lose, we're going to the mat." Especially on an issue that becomes emotional and where a grassroots campaign has been launched, the attitude may be, "Even if we go down the tubes, we should not compromise." A lobbyist will usually try to persuade a client to ease up, but he or she does not always succeed.

Groups that rely largely on outside strategies—mobilizing grassroots support and cultivating the press—are somewhat less inclined to settle out of court. After all, the best way to get on TV is not to negotiate but rather to take an extreme position. "You don't get a lot of coverage from sitting down with people and working out problems," observes Sara Vickerman of the Defenders of Wildlife.[38] Thus, cause lobbyists often prefer to stand firm rather than compromise their principles. Prochoice and prolife groups, for example, tend to be doctrinaire and therefore not very flexible when it comes to negotiating and compromising. In view of the issues involved and their constituencies, however, it may be difficult for them to do so. Cause groups also feel that they have to get as much as possible out of legislation they are proposing because they will not get another opportunity for quite a while. Once the legislature has dealt with an issue, it has little desire to revisit old problems.

When public-interest lobbyists choose to play an inside game, they have no choice but to negotiate and compromise. There are dangers in sitting down at the table and participating in the drafting of amendments. Moral-principle lobbying becomes tougher and lobbyists risk being co-opted. They have to be especially alert so that they do not go too far. A Colorado public-interest lobbyist admits to negotiating but insists that "you cannot compromise beyond a certain point. You must know where to draw the line." A public-interest lobbyist in Texas recently started playing an insider role and had a seat at the table. After negotiations, he says there was always the question: "Could we have gotten more if we pushed harder?" That question inevitably arises, but it cannot be answered. Moreover, once public-interest lobbyists take a place at the table and become part of the bargaining process, they forfeit their ability to criticize the results later on.

What's in It for Legislators

John Martin, the speaker of the Maine house, counseled a national meeting of lobbyists: "If you want to have a slug out, you must win. If you don't win, your effectiveness is gone—and you might as well find yourself another legislature to work in." [39] That is because legislators far prefer compromise to conflict. They do not want to be caught between competing special interest groups, so they will ask the groups' lobbyists to reach a compromise. By insisting that conflicting groups work out their differences, the legislature can minimize the cross pressures it faces.[40] A New Jersey lobbyist described the dilemma:

> One thing the legislator hates is to get caught between two friends on the opposite sides. Instead, he looks for the conciliatory way out. He really does not wait to get caught making the hard decision whether to go with, for example, the mortgage bankers rather than the realtors.

Why displease one side when it is possible to satisfy both sides!

If a settlement cannot be reached, the possibility of legislation passing is much diminished. Take the car-rental dispute, which we have mentioned before. In New Jersey, a proposed bill, backed by Hertz and Avis, would have prohibited the selling of collision-damage waivers under certain circumstances. Proponents argued that CDW forced consumers to pay for unnecessary duplicate protection, because nearly 60 percent of auto insurance policies provide coverage to rental cars. Alamo's lobbyist offered a compromise: no ban, but a requirement that consumers be furnished specific information about their options with respect to CDW (as was required by law in thirteen other states). The proponents balked at the offer. Because the two sides could not get together, the legislature did nothing.

Apart from increasing their own comfort levels, legislators have other incentives for wanting groups to reach an agreement. If everyone can live with a bill, it is, first, more likely to be enacted into law and, second, more likely to work in practice. Parties on both sides of an issue have "bought in"; they now have a stake in a measure's success. Furthermore, sometimes legislators do not realize the down side of a measure until the opposition has begun to lobby. The negatives can be eliminated or reduced if the concerned parties can get together.

Therefore, legislators will usually ask lobbyists if they have worked matters out with groups and lobbyists on the opposite side. If not, legislators will suggest that they do so. Often, the committee chairman encourages negotiations. The encouragement typically sounds like the following: "This guy wants this. Sit down and figure out what you can live with. If you come to an agreement, fine. If not, you don't get a bill." The lobbyist will then negotiate and return to the chairman with, "Here's the deal." If an influential legislator asks lobbyists to negotiate a compromise, the request will seldom be turned down. The understanding is, compromise or lose.

Negotiations can take place with or without the participation of legislators. If the various parties go off and reach an agreement, the legislative committee and legislature are almost certain to ratify it. Frequently, however, the committee chairman, bill sponsor, and legislative staff will play a major role in negotiations. This has been a practice in Florida, where leaders and committee chairmen over the years have initiated the negotiating process. On a variety of issues they would get everyone into a room and mediate an agreement. Nowhere has this negotiating process been more in evidence than in the area of growth management. Cities, counties, large and small developers, the environmental community, and state officials each year would meet to try to work out legislation. Leadership by legislators in these efforts has been critical.

Working Things Out

An important objective for most lobbyists is getting into the room where the fine points are being negotiated and a deal is being made. Addressing a groups of lobbyists representing opposing clients at a legislative committee meeting, the chairman will declare: "We're going to work this out." He will point to three of the lobbyists to whom he will entrust the final negotiations: "You, you, and you." Lobbyists want to be in the position to be chosen for the job of crafting agreed-on language in a bill. "Everyone can play," says one Florida lobbyist, "but not everyone can get invited into the speaker's conference room behind the chamber." The back room is the place to be, because the moment of truth is in the negotiation of details.

Especially when compromises are being fashioned, details can make a difference. To be accomplished as a lobbyist, therefore, one must master more than the substance of the issue at hand. One must also be technically proficient and skilled in negotiating the fine points of legislation. A Minnesota lobbyist warned: "If you don't draft it, watch out." He knows that agreements can be reached in principle, but legislation has to be drafted in detail. The bottom line is how the agreement in principle is resolved in statutory language. If the lobbyist has a seat at the table and helps to draft amendments, he or she has greater control of the process. "You try to control the process as much as you can—by wielding the pen or the word processor," commented a Minnesota lobbyist.

Negotiations go on throughout the process. They may, in fact, have begun even before a bill is introduced. Recognizing that the legislature is likely to go along if they can get together, the two camps will try to agree on a draft. Lobbyists will seek points of agreement, identify disputed areas, and seek solutions acceptable to all parties. Anything that can be negotiated ahead of time brings tremendous relief to lobbyists. But if one party thinks it will have an edge, it may put off negotiations until later when it will be able to get more. As the process proceeds from preintroduction to introduction to committee to floor and then to the second chamber, things obviously change, and the settlements differ accordingly.

Negotiating processes do not always succeed. The parties involved are too far apart or they are not inclined to give. A Texas lobbyist was blunt: "Sometimes you can't work it out. You just have to kill shit." Sometimes even though several issues can be resolved, others remain, and the parties in dispute wind up in battle. Sometimes, too, one side appears willing to compromise but does so mainly to stall the process so that the proposal dies along the way. No battle is waged openly—the warfare is surreptitious. Frequently, however, the process works. The contestants sign off on a compromise, legislators accept the settlement, and battle is avoided.

Oil-spill legislation in California is a classic case of compromise. Legislation was introduced in response to the Exxon-*Valdez* and British Petroleum oil spills. The environmentalists lined up on one side, the oil industry on the other. One of the industry's lobbyists approached the author of the bill and his staff and offered technical assistance in shaping a bill that "will satisfy the needs of California and still be a bill we can live with." His client was not happy. But the industry had a choice: it could oppose the bill outright or try to make it better. It decided to work toward a compromise. The process got under way, with staff of the governor, the assembly speaker, and the senate president meeting repeatedly with representatives of the Sierra Club, Natural Resources Defense Council, and the trade association for oil. As agreements were reached, they were ratified in committee and finally a bill was passed and signed by the governor. It satisfied everyone—at least to some extent. The negotiating process had worked.

Notes

1. Kay Lehman Schlozman and John T. Tierney, *Organized Interests and American Democracy* (New York: Harper and Row, 1986), 150. The authors conducted a survey in which they asked federal lobbyists about twenty-seven techniques of exercising influence.
2. Jeffrey M. Berry, *The Interest Group Society* (Boston: Little, Brown, 1984),

205-206.
3. *St. Petersburg Times,* May 1, 1991.
4. Larry Landry, "The Art of State Government Relations," in *Leveraging State Government Relations,* ed. Wesley Pederson (Washington, D.C.: Public Affairs Council, 1990), 94.
5. *Arkansas Democrat,* June 24, 1990.
6. One expert has called this the "one-page rule," whereby a lobbyist should confine any written document to a single page (perhaps accompanied by longer documents that staff can read). Landry, "Art of State Government Relations," 94.
7. Andrew Baker, MetPath. (Remarks to the State Government Relations Institute, New Brunswick, N.J., July 12, 1990.)
8. Schlozman and Tierney, *Organized Interests,* 314-315; Bruce C. Wolpe, *Lobbying Congress: How the System Works* (Washington, D.C.: Congressional Quarterly Inc., 1990), 50-51.
9. *St. Petersburg Times,* October 18, 1990.
10. Landry, "Art of State Government Relations," 9.
11. Ronald J. Hrebenar and Ruth K. Scott, *Interest Group Politics in America,* 2d ed. (Englewood Cliffs, N.J.: Prentice Hall, 1990), 96; also Harmon Zeigler and Michael A. Baer, *Lobbying: Interaction and Influence in American State Legislatures* (Belmont, Calif.: Wadsworth, 1969), 162.
12. Michael J. BeVier, *Politics Backstage: Inside the California Legislature* (Philadelphia: Temple University Press, 1979), 74-76.
13. Jerry B. Briscoe and Charles G. Bell, "The New Sacramento Lobbying Corps," *California Data Brief* 9 (Fall 1986): 2.
14. Paul Hollrah, "Lobbying State Capitols: Rules for a New Game," *State Policy,* January 1984, 5.
15. Zeigler and Baer, *Lobbying,* 132-133.
16. Schlozman and Tierney, *Organized Interests,* 292.
17. Alan Ehrenhalt, "In Alabama Politics, the Teachers Are Sitting at the Head of the Class," *Governing,* December 1988, 27.
18. Max Boot, "Business Associations—Big Names, Less Clout," *California Journal,* October 1988, 454.
19. Bruce C. Wolpe, *Lobbying Congress,* 10-12; also Landry, "Art of State Government Relations," 88; and Alan Rosenthal, "The Fine Art of Saying 'No'," *State Legislatures,* January 1986, 24-26.
20. *Dallas Morning News,* May 26, 1991.
21. Michael Baer, "Legislative Lobbying: In Washington and the States," *Georgia Political Science Association Journal* 2 (1974): 26.
22. William K. Muir, Jr., *Legislature: California's School for Politics* (Chicago: University of Chicago Press, 1982), 19.
23. Landry, "Art of State Government Relations," 89.
24. Berry, *Interest Group Society,* 103.
25. Boot, "Business Associations," 456.
26. *Florida Times Union,* April 15, 1991.
27. Wolpe, *Lobbying Congress,* 24-25.
28. *Miami Herald,* May 8, 1990.
29. Ginger Gold, "Lobbyists: A Love Story," Eagleton Institute of Politics,

Rutgers University, May 14, 1990.
30. Landry, "Art of State Government Relations," 90-91.
31. Kathleen Sylvester, "The Tobacco Industry Will Walk a Mile to Stop an Anti-Smoking Law," *Governing,* May 1989, 34.
32. Berry, *Interest Group Society,* 121.
33. Alan Ehrenhalt, *The United States of Ambition* (New York: Times Books, 1991), 205.
34. Muir, *Legislature,* 19.
35. Wolpe, *Lobbying Congress,* 6.
36. Ibid., 4.
37. Randy Welch, "Lobbyists, Lobbyists All Over the Lot," *State Legislatures,* February 1989, 19.
38. *Boston Globe,* March 29, 1992.
39. State Government Relations Institute, New Brunswick, N.J., July 9, 1990.
40. Malcolm E. Jewell and Penny M. Miller, *The Kentucky Legislature: Two Decades of Change* (Lexington: The University Press of Kentucky, 1988), 276.

CHAPTER 9

Power and Representation

Anyone who pays attention to policy making in the states will acknowledge that lobbyists are integral to the legislative process. One or another of them is involved at just about every stage of nearly every issue addressed by the legislature. Few if any legislators remain untouched by some lobbyist on any issue at hand. They are out there advocating their clients' positions, forging relationships with legislators, providing political and policy information, establishing coalitions, orchestrating grass-roots campaigns, playing electoral politics, and bargaining and negotiating throughout. It is difficult to conceive of a legislature and its processes without them.

Lobbyists play an important role in the drama of legislation. But how much influence do they actually have, and under what circumstances? Does their influence derive mainly from the power of those whom they represent? Given the activity of lobbyists and their principals, what about those who are not represented? Is the system fair to them? Is it fair overall?

The Influence of Lobbyists

"How good is he?" "Is she doing the job?" "What can we expect?" Clients wonder if their lobbyists are effective. But these questions are not easy to answer. Take an in-house lobbyist. On what basis can top management evaluate the performance of its state governmental relations staff? Some companies count the numbers of bills their lobbyists draft and have introduced and how often they testify at hearings. Some operate their state governmental relations departments as cost centers, calculating the dollars saved (or lost) as a result of bills enacted, defeated, or modified.[1] Much of this, however, would appear to be misleading. The director of state relations for a drug company agrees: "The difficulty is in judging how important your influence was. There are so many imponderables that affect legislative decisions and votes."[2]

Yet it should be possible to make a judgment. The chief executive officer of one company reflected on how he would evaluate his state relations director. He could not quantify his performance but would, instead, rely in part on what others thought of the lobbyist and in part on his own gut feelings. It would take time, but he felt he could do it.[3] Most in-house lobbyists have a number of issues in their portfolio. So they usually have some accomplishment to show top management. If enough issues are at stake, a lobbyist is unlikely to be shut out. As one Minnesota association lobbyist says, "I'll always get something to bring home." If he fails to get anything, however, his members will undoubtedly express their dissatisfaction.

In the case of contract lobbyists, their clients want to know whether influence is being exercised on their behalf. Because contract lobbyists have multiple clients, one client can never be absolutely certain that his or her interests are being represented most effectively or more effectively than another client's. Many of those who employ contract lobbyists, moreover, know little about legislative politics and are not always able to hold their lobbyists accountable. In such instances, it is possible for lobbyists to create activity and give the impression that their intervention had saved a client from the most baneful legislation. This happens, although it is probably not a common practice.

Most contract lobbyists have to show clients something for their money. A Maryland lobbyist, for instance, feels he has to succeed at a variety of tasks in order to keep his clients satisfied. Not only does he have to defend and advance their interests, but, when asked, he also must deliver the house speaker or senate president to address their groups. Other lobbyists also have to produce results, or their regular clients will surely leave them. Most are able to do so.

Lobbyists tend to exaggerate their own influence. A New Jersey lobbyist compared the influence of some of the "power" lobbyists to that of legislators. Even those legislators in good standing, he said, "do not have the influence and the clout with the presiding officers that a handful of lobbyists have." Like officeholders, lobbyists cannot afford to be overly modest in public. Their practice, after all, depends largely on their reputation for influence. A survey of lobbyists in Washington, D.C., is illustrative. The survey, which asked about the relative importance of resources at their disposal, showed that lobbyists tended to assign greater importance to their own qualities than to those of their organizations.

Four out of five mentioned that a reputation for being credible and trustworthy was most important; one out of four mentioned a wide circle of contacts. In contrast, only one out of five mentioned a large membership, one out of seven an appealing cause, and one out of thirty a large budget.[4]

What counts, as far as influence is concerned, is how people perceive lobbyists. This explains why few lobbyists object to press stories that charge them with dominating the legislative process or wielding too much power. They prefer to be seen in that light than to be considered ineffectual. They know that the *perception* of influence matters as much as anything else, for in the world of lobbying perception is reality. Jon Shebel of Associated Industries of Florida (who is also president of the Florida League of Professional Lobbyists) had this to say: "Power is actually just the perception of your power on the part of the people you deal with. If they think you have power, then you've got it."[5] It is in the interests of contract lobbyists, therefore, to give legislators, clients, the press, and the public the impression that they are indeed influential. If that means cultivating a myth or two, so be it.

Top lobbyists at the state level are hard to identify, especially in view of the variety who operate. But, again, perception serves to discriminate. How lobbyists are regarded by their colleagues and by legislators is what matters. In each state capital certain lobbyists are reputed to be the most influential, just as certain groups are known as the most powerful. Often lobbyists with the most clients and the highest incomes are thought to be the most influential. Similarly, the groups with the largest memberships and the largest PACs are frequently considered the most powerful. For example, a Gallup survey of ninety-three New Jersey legislators found that thirty-three rated the New Jersey Education Association, as "most effective" in advancing their interests. The New Jersey Business and Industry Association was named by twelve legislators, and contract-lobbyist Harold Hodes and his firm, Public Strategies, were mentioned by ten. The associations of dentists, builders, and trial lawyers each received three mentions. Legislators in Florida perceived Harry Landrum, Jon Shebel, Wade Hopping, and Ken Plante to be the most influential lobbyists.[6]

Having read about lobbyists at work in the preceding pages, readers should have little doubt that lobbyists provide substantial assistance to their clients, and conclude that those without lobbyists must be at a disadvantage. To some extent, such a conclusion may derive in part from my particular approach, which relies heavily on information provided by lobbyists themselves. Moreover, I have intentionally written this book from a lobbying perspective. Consequently, it is especially important for us to not exaggerate the influence of lobbyists. Lobbyists may do so, and the press surely does in the interests of presenting a lively story. Yet it should be stressed that whatever the influence of lobbyists, it is only one among a number of factors that play a decisive role in the legislative process.

The lobbyist's client needs to be factored in. Some distinction must be made between the effects of the lobbyist on the one hand and the independent effects of the interest group itself on the other. A state government relations professional for a large pharmaceutical company expressed the view of many of those who work for large corporations:

> The lobbyist would like to think that it's the lobbyist that has the most influence. I believe that that's secondary. I think it's the organization that the lobbyist represents that lends most credibility to an issue. A company such as _____, that has an outstanding record in the quality of its products, in the way it treats its employees, and in its contribution to its community in a social-investment way, speaks much better than any lobbyist could.

It is much easier, he pointed out, to visit a legislator and say that he represented _____ than to say that he represented some chemical company that was polluting the environment. "I don't care how good he is," he added, "that lobbyist has his hands full."

The success of in-house lobbyists (in contrast to contract lobbyists) is far more likely to hinge on their clients' identity and standing. Contract lobbyists have many clients and therefore cannot be identified by legislators with any single client. Thus, it is difficult to directly compare the influence of in-house and contract lobbyists.

The nature of the issue is very significant. In writing about organizations, James Q. Wilson observes that effectiveness can be traced, first, to the organization's characteristics and, second to the issues it has to confront.[7] Similarly, the influence of lobbyists depends on both the individual and the principal, but it also varies with the issues. The legislative process deals with very different arrays of issues.

Governors and legislators commit themselves and their leadership to broad policy initiatives on education, employment, economic development, and taxes. Groups have lesser weight in these arenas. They can furnish leadership, however, where causes are concerned—for example, the environment, homelessness, and abortion rights. These issues tend to have considerable public significance, and they arouse more than a little passion.

The identities of some lobbyists are linked, not so much to a client, but rather to a cause. They do not lack individual skill or resources, but their influence nevertheless derives mostly from the popularity of their cause. Thus, a highly regarded lobbyist in Florida could admit that most of his success in the process derived from his touting the environment and not from any special talents on his own part.

Finally, there are the essentially special-interest issues that are of concern to economic, professional, and occupational groups vying for protection or advantage. Although participants on both sides will argue the public-policy and public-interest merits of their case, these issues arouse little concern on the parts of either the public or its representatives. If neither the public's nor the legislator's interest is aroused, the role and influence of the lobbyist can be critical.

With lobbyists scurrying here, there, and everywhere, it is possible to discount the power of legislators. Yet their role and their importance should not be overlooked. The conception that legislators are putty in the hands of lobbyists is way off the mark. Legislators have their own ideas, interests, and intentions. They are advocates, exercising leadership and seeking support from groups and lobbyists, not simply responding to pleas and pressures. They initiate. In dealings between legislators and lobbyists, the legislator is almost always the dominant party. Each party needs the other, but lobbyists are far needier.

Legislators act in response to many forces, not only those generated by lobbyists and groups. Constituency is one of the more obvious and more potent of them. As Guy Spearman, a Florida contract lobbyist, said: "A legislator is going to listen to his own constituents any day over me." [8] No matter how close the friendship between lobbyist and legislator, the latter will never go against the district's interests. A legislator's convictions, principles, or values also matter. They matter not only on broad issues like capital punishment, choice in education, and welfare but also on the narrower, special-interest issues. The minds of some legislators are practically made up before lobbyists get to work on a particular issue. In Florida, for instance, a number of lawmakers had had an annoying personal experience with boats speeding by them on the St. Johns River near Tallahassee. They had made up their minds on the need for further regulation of pleasure craft, and they proceeded along those lines. Lobbying did not affect them. In states where the car wars were fought, some legislators lined up against Alamo because they had been given a hard sell or paid more for a rental than they had expected or thought proper. No matter who the Alamo lobbyist was, they knew Alamo firsthand and were not to be won over.

In a number of instances legislators look at an issue with virtually no preconceptions. They may then decide according to what they regard as the merits. One story that circulates in statehouses is about the lobbyist who asked a legislator (with whom he had a good relationship and to whose campaign his client has contributed) for his support on a bill. "I can't vote for that bill," said the legislator, "It's a bad bill." "Of course, it's a bad bill," the lobbyist replied. "I wouldn't need your help if it were a good bill." However special or specialized, some bills are not deemed worthy of support, and nothing a lobbyist does will turn legislators around. They will not support what they believe to be bad bills.

In addition to the factors mentioned above, there are so many more that help to shape the process. "Regardless of how hard they [lobbyists] work, policy outcomes will often be determined by factors mostly out of their control." [9] If the economy is in recession and the state budget is in crisis, legislators, in the words of one lobbyist, tend to "grab at anything and everything." At such a time, it is difficult to fight tax increases on business. A New Jersey lobbyist pointed out that her organization opposed, but did not lobby hard against, the increase in sales taxes proposed in 1990 by the Florio administration. To do so would have been fruitless. Lobbyists and their groups were helpless; it was clear to all of them that the higher taxes were going through.

What happens elsewhere also has effects, and the best lobbyist will not be able to control them. If practically every other state adopts a measure, as was noted in chapter 8, the logic may become irresistible. One lobbyist, who represented ophthalmologists in their struggle with optometrists, managed to stave off the assault for ten years. But he finally lost the battle because practically every other state had passed legislation giving optometrists the right to apply eyedrops. Legislators came up to him and said, "Come on! No one has gone blind yet in all those other states." The lobbyist had no way to rebut the argument or buck such a trend.

With all the other factors at work, it may now appear that little room exists for lobbyists to exercise influence. By no means. They still have ample room to bring their talents to bear. On the many issues that state legislatures handle, such as those where private interests compete, or where only one interest is heard from, or where the public interest is very difficult to discern, or where most of one's constituents are unconcerned, lobbyists can and do play an important role. No matter what the rhetoric employed, these are essentially special-interest issues of narrow scope, with little salience to the broader state community. This is where lobbyists can earn their spurs. Thus, the less important the issue, the more important the lobbyist. Or as Zeigler and Baer observed two decades ago: "In general, the narrower the scope of a piece of legislation, the greater the opportunity for a lobbyist to intervene in the decision-making process." [10]

For example, the Greater Miami Opera spent nearly $200,000 on lobbyists in the period from 1987 to 1990. The return on its investment was $2 million in state appropriations. Previous to 1987 the Greater Miami Opera got very little money from the state of Florida. Opera is a narrow issue, and lobbyists made a difference. Yet lobbyists are not the only ones who weigh in. Discovery Center, a new museum in Ft. Lauderdale, had no lobbyist, yet it was written into the 1990 state budget for $427,000. Tom Gustafson, the house speaker that year, was a board member of the Discovery Center. [11] The speaker undoubtedly made a difference, as do a number of legislators when it comes to getting "turkeys" for their districts.

Narrow issues that concern special interests constitute a large part of the legislative process, although not the part most visible to the press and the public. Association, company, and contract lobbyists will almost always be involved in such issues. Lobbyists for county and local governments involve themselves sporadically, and cause lobbyists, by the very nature of their issues, seldom engage in special-interest battles.

On these issues, it is usually not necessary, nor advisable, to go outside. The inside game tends to dominate here. The relationships lobbyists have cultivated, the clients they are representing, and the way they make their cases count heavily. Relationships are the primary vehicle of influence for the contract lobbyist. For the in-house lobbyist, the client's standing is the primary means of influence. On many of these special-interest issues legislators may take cues from their leaders, committee chairmen, colleagues, and staff. They may also listen to lobbyists and their principals, depending on how much trust they place in them, how credible they appear, and the reputations they bear. On most special- interest issues, lobbyists provide most of the cues. Insofar as they can, they enlist legislators on their side and encourage them to work their colleagues.

A number of issues are not so narrowly focused. Often a government agency, a legislator, or a group espousing a cause seeks a change in law. Changes in the law typically affect someone's interests adversely. Such issues are usually of scope. Conventional wisdom suggests that lobbyists exercise less influence here. As the former executive director of California Common Cause points out, "When the issue is highly visible, the persuasiveness of the lobbyist does not make much difference." [12] Two political scientists agree, arguing that the impact of lobbyists is: "likely to be less substantial on highly visible issues that engage public passions or media coverage and on issues in which there are strong competing ideological, partisan, or constituency pressures." [13]

The outside game is much more important when these kinds of issues are involved. No longer are relationships or connections sufficient. Teacher organizations, for instance, make extensive use of grass-roots techniques and campaign activity. Cause lobbyists rely heavily on the media to transmit their messages both to the public and to public officeholders. To some extent, as has been noted, a group's resource base affects its strategy and tactics.[14] To some extent, too, the issue and the group itself will determine the adoption of an inside or an outside strategy. The latter expands the audience of an issue and raises its salience for legislators.

Given the likely involvement on broad and visible issues of a legislator's values, emotions, constituents, or prior record, the lobbyist's impact may be reduced. Yet it is by no means negligible. Those lobbying on behalf of teachers for example, have something to win or something to lose. Management of the campaign is in the hands not of teachers but of their lobbyists. Cause lobbyists, too, have to prove themselves. However popular their cause and involved the legislators, their achievements depend partly on their skills and efforts. And those who are lobbying for status-quo groups, trying to resist what may appear to be popular tides, can also contribute substantially to the outcomes. They may not be able to win, but just how well they hold the line and to what extent they reduce their losses is largely in their hands.

On important issues the influence of lobbyists may be at the margins. But the margins are where many important outcomes can be located. Seldom, as has been pointed out earlier, does one side win, while the other loses. Outcomes are more mixed than that. The question is, rather, how much does each side win or lose. The answers come from lobbyists, who are engaged in the hard work of negotiation and compromise.

Arriving at settlements with which each side can live is one of the major objectives of legislators. It cannot always be achieved, but when it is, the inside game of lobbyists is much in evidence. Outside strategies and tactics provide groups with favorable or unfavorable position. But lobbyists, sitting around the table agreeing to amendments and to specific language, are among the players who finally convert advantages or disadvantages into actual outcomes. They are among a handful of people who control the details. And the details, as we have seen, can be very important. Such influence is not readily observable (partly because few look in this area), but it does exist.

On minor issues, the lobbyist's influence is likely to be central, and may in fact carry the day. On major issues, other factors play a much greater role, and a lobbyist's influence is likely to be marginal. But it matters, nevertheless. In either case, lobbyists can, and often do, make a substantial difference.

Clients and Causes

A lot rides on the lobbyist making the case. On narrow issues the lobbyist may bear responsibility for whether a client wins or loses. On broader issues the lobbyist may bear responsibility for the precise terms of the settlement. In addition, a lot also rides with the case itself and the client in whose behalf the case is being made.

Those groups that are perceived to be influential have standing in the political universe. Legislators take them seriously. Political scientists studying interest groups have generally found that business organizations, labor unions, lawyers, and teachers tend to be effective or influential in a number of states.[15] Other analyses, relying on the perceptions of legislators, identified roughly the same interests, depending on the state. Labor, teachers, and public employees are regarded as most effective in Minnesota, while in Florida realtors, business, trial lawyers, and insurance interests are perceived to be influential.[16] This is not the place to try to assess the influence of various groups or causes state by state. Most studies of interest-group influence neglect to specify the scope of influence, that is, the issue area to which influence is directed. Different groups care about different domains, and thus their influence may not be directly comparable.[17]

Suffice it to say that group influence is a complex phenomenon, and as such does not lend itself to reputational analysis. A reputational approach casts such a broad net that those groups rated to be influential are usually the ones with traditional or conventional resources. Such groups are likely to have a large membership that is distributed widely among legislative districts. Or they may have wealth and/or an economic position important to the state, or possibly status.[18] These groups often tend to be seen as influential, whether or not they are achieving their policy objectives.

Business associations and large companies are among the groups possessing these conventional resources. Business has money, sometimes jobs in a district, PACs, and capable lobbyists. There is no denying, for example, the influence wielded by the New Jersey Food Council, which represents the second-largest industry in the state, has grass-roots capability, and runs one of the largest PACs. In Texas the chemical industry, which accounts for almost one-third of the state's overall economy, cannot be overlooked when the question is one of influence. It is true, too, that business and industry generally are well positioned in Colorado, where the Colorado Association of Commerce and Industry (CACI) has clout. But it is influential because, according to one veteran legislator, "its values coincide with those of the Republican party." [19] And the Republican party has controlled both houses of the legislature for some time. IBM in Minnesota gets, at the very least, a sympathetic hearing in the legislature because it is a major employer and a leading member of the brain-power industry that Minnesota wants to keep. The company also has star quality. That all helps, as does IBM's network of relationships with legislators. Despite the standing of some companies, however, business in Minnesota is fragmented and has little clout. It is not enough in tune with the Democrats who control the legislature.

The present exploration of lobbying suggests that business is far from monolithic and, overall, its influence is thereby limited. Business rarely speaks with a single voice and, until recently, it has been less than adept at politics. For instance, despite its strength in Colorado, business is often divided. Large banks compete with small banks and savings and loan associations compete with banks.[20] It should also be remembered that business has assumed a defensive posture. When confronted with a number of demands (for example, on taxes, the environment, consumer protection, and occupational safety), business has had to give ground. It would seem that business in many instances has either had to bow to contemporary political movements or at least engage in measured retreat. As one lobbyist put it, "You win when you don't get taxed or get taxed less than expected." If that constitutes victory, then business has certainly had its share of defeats.

No matter how formidable a group may seem, its influence is checked if its issues arouse opposition from another formidable group. Nowadays, the competition among groups is intense. In Washington, D.C., there is the paradox of more interest groups and more lobbyists wielding less influence over policy results. With integrative institutions becoming weaker, demand making is on the rise and single-issue groups are in the ascendency.[21] There are so many interests and so much pressure in the statehouses that only a few demands go unopposed. Policy making in many places is more pluralistic than before, and any single interest is less likely to dominate. If groups are relatively equal in strength, the influence of each will be curtailed in a competitive situation. If one group is weak, and thus the opposition is negligible, the stronger will likely prevail. The possible lineups are numerous.

A recent study suggested that instead of trying to measure the relative strength of interest groups, it would be better to focus on how well specific interests are served by public policy.[22] Along these lines, consider state societies of certified public accountants. Few legislators would consider them to be at all powerful. CPAs do not get everything, but they get much of what they want. They do not have the enemies doctors or trial lawyers have. And nearly every legislator can support them on most issues. If, or when, the profession becomes involved in more contentious matters, legislators will be less inclined to endorse the positions the CPAs take. So if the question is, "have the accountants been influential?" the answer has to be "yes." It helps, then, to have little opposition and needs that arouse little controversy.

As opposition to a group widens and intensifies, however, its interests will almost inevitably suffer. The trial lawyers illustrate the point. They are believed to be powerful, and they probably are. But when just about everybody lines up against them, as has been happening, they too can lose.[23] The proof is that since 1986 tort reform efforts in more than half the states have overcome the opposition of trial lawyers and infringed on their practices to some extent. But neither business on the one side nor the trial lawyers on the other have won total victories or suffered utter defeats.

Some groups, in fact, appear powerful, yet their power is like the emperor's new clothes. The insurance industry is embattled practically everywhere, except in Hartford, the insurance capital of the country. Once an issue becomes politicized, as frequently happens today, insurance finds itself at a great disadvantage. It is not well received in state legislatures. On a measure it wants to achieve, insurance will keep a low profile and hide behind other groups. Its identification with an issue could be the kiss of death.

Oil provides another example. It is an industry that is more powerful at the national level than at the state level. The image we have is of Big Oil. Yet, outside of a few states, oil is not a potent force. It has no local refining base and thus no local roots. And when a refinery or two is located in a state, the benefit of one thousand to two thousand employees does not compensate for the liability oil assumes in producing pollutants. Politically, oil is on weak ground. Moreover, the industry has little cohesion and major and minor companies all pursue their separate ways. An oil lobbyist from one state commented, "Breaking even is a victory; if we don't lose ground, it's a win." A lobbyist from another state said: "No one will listen to us because we represent big oil." Public interest groups, environmentalists, and farmers are not reluctant to pick fights with the industry because oil is such an easy target. Industry's response, as indicated by one lobbyist, is, "We don't lock horns with these people. We can't win." The industry feels beset even in Louisiana, a large oil producer. Whenever the state needs revenues, it turns to oil for taxes. It is hard to think of oil as being bullied, but that is the way its lobbyists feel.

Another industry on the defensive, and steadily losing ground, is tobacco. Despite its wealth, its campaign contributions, and the talents of the power-broker lobbyists it employs, the tobacco industry faces stiff opposition from the American Heart Association, the American Lung Association, the American Cancer Society, and the American Medical Association. Since 1964, when the first surgeon general's report warned of health dangers from smoking and since 1982 when "second-hand smoking" was labeled a risk, the antismoking movement has been forging ahead.[24] As of now, for instance, all but six states have imposed limitations of some sort on smoking in public places and workplaces. Tobacco has fared better in a few places than in others. Its power in the California legislature has been substantial until very recently, but then the tide began to shift.[25]

Tobacco interests have naturally been more successful in North Carolina and Virginia, the nation's largest tobacco producers. But even in these states they have had a fight on their hands. In 1989, in resisting an antismoking bill in Virginia, tobacco had thirteen lobbyists arrayed against the executive director of the state's chapter of GASP (Group to

Alleviate Smoking in Public), a volunteer, and a part-time paid lobbyist, who worked for the American Heart Association and the American Lung Association. The sides were as unequal as they could be. Moreover, despite the fact that the industry provided thirty-two thousand jobs and the state's economy depends heavily on tobacco, a bill mandating restrictions on smoking in public places almost passed.[26] If tobacco is not safe in Virginia, then indeed the mighty have fallen.

One group that nearly always makes the list of the most powerful in a state are the teachers. This group is perceived to have influence, and it does. A recent study of interest groups in fifty states indicated that teacher organizations were considered more effective than any other group, ranking as most effective in forty-three states and at a second level of effectiveness in five others.[27]

The 1987 Gallup survey of New Jersey legislators showed teachers at the top of the rankings of effectiveness. The legislators claimed that the New Jersey Education Association earned its reputation by being on top of the issues and knowledgeable, by providing information, by having a large and vocal constituency, and by its commitment.[28] The teachers have been among the strongest groups in New Jersey for some time, and over the years, NJEA has unquestionably grown stronger. Its grass-roots capacity has increased, its PAC has become larger, and its campaign activities have grown more effective. But while the association has grown stronger internally, its overall influence has probably declined. That is because the NJEA now operates in a more pluralistic environment. The New Jersey School Boards Association has emerged as a competing force, school enrollments have declined, and, most recently, state revenues have not kept pace with state expenditures.[29] Given the many competing needs in the state, it is difficult nowadays for NJEA to achieve many of its programmatic goals. Yet it maintains its veto power. The situation, as mentioned by one lobbyist, is that: "NJEA can't get everything it wants, but it can certainly stop what it doesn't want."

Like the New Jersey association, teacher organizations elsewhere may have less influence than earlier, but they still manage to get something of what they want and block much of what they do not want. Their resources continue to be considerable and are effectively used. Teachers benefit from having a relatively large and well distributed membership. Teachers are politically aware, cohesive, and can be mobilized for political action. These are substantial advantages. Teachers contribute money and people to political campaigns. And their associations are well organized, well led, and staffed by skillful lobbyists—nearly all of whom have classroom experience. The potential of teachers for influence is high; their actual exercise of influence, however, will depend on the issue, the state's economy, the mood, the political alignment, and the circumstances at the time.

Just as reputedly powerful groups may be weaker than they appear, those groups not usually considered powerful may be stronger than most people think. Public-interest and environmental groups are seldom cited in the top ranks of influential interests.[30] Yet they have had a substantial impact on policy in many places. Their resource base is different from that of business and professional groups. Entertainment and campaign contributions are not their stock in trade. Nor do these groups retain contract lobbyists who pride themselves on having close relationships with key legislators. The influence of these cause groups is based on other factors. The popularity of the issues they advocate, the attention and support they receive from the press, their grass-roots canvassing, the strategic and tactical skills of their staffs, and the alliances they have with both executive officials and legislators all contribute to their influence. One lobbyist declared, "We have the issues and the press—and, for the most part, the staff."

Most important, these groups are not perceived as advocating special interests. Instead, they are taken at their word and accepted as representatives of the public interest, leading the charge against selfish interests. An environmental lobbyist in Florida observed that "when an executive agency and citizen groups are together, we're practically unbeatable." No lobbyist wants to take on groups like the Sierra Club, the Audubon Society, or Common Cause. And certainly not when they have substantial sympathy in both the executive and legislative branches.

The New Jersey Public Interest Research Group exemplifies the power of a relatively new kid on the block, one who behaves differently from the older kids. PIRG has had a full-time presence in Trenton since 1984. It took the group a while to get on the political map, but by 1990 it had achieved some big wins and was recognized as a major player. One of the group's lobbyists described how legislators were now "checking with PIRG, seeking our approval, wanting us to work on their issues, and siding with us." Legislators, he asserted, were trying to enhance their political images by identifying with a number of PIRG's issues. Whatever their motivations, legislators did not want to be viewed as opponents of PIRG on environmental or consumer issues.

Other groups have also been able to exercise influence because of the issues they were promoting and the energy and dedication of their members. These groups may not be perceived as being powerful; but within a circumscribed area they are extremely important. The groups on either side of the abortion issue are illustrative. Prochoice groups have had an effect in the 1989 political campaign in Virginia and New Jersey as well as in the 1990 California campaigns.[31] Right-to-life groups influenced the outcome of elections in Michigan and Pennsylvania. The groups not only helped the candidates they endorsed but also pushed other candidates to adopt their views, whether for or against abortion rights, in the state and/or district. The influence of the abortion groups has washed over legislatures, which have become battlegrounds since the Supreme Court's decision in *Webster v. Missouri*. In Pennsylvania, Utah, Louisiana, and Idaho, prolife forces have come out ahead in the legislature, although the governor of Idaho vetoed a bill that would have virtually banned abortion. In Connecticut, Maryland, and New Hampshire, prochoice groups have come out ahead in the legislature, although the governor of New Hampshire vetoed a liberal abortion bill. In other places, the issue was either compromised or left unresolved. But without leadership by groups on either side of this explosive issue the situation would have been quite different. The agenda has largely been theirs and, for the most part, legislators have been conscripted into battle.

Representing Interests

Finally, we need to address the question of how the system of lobbying and interest group politics affects the public interest. Who prospers? Who suffers? Is the overall public good served or subverted? On the large, visible issues—those on gubernatorial or legislative agendas—public preferences and interests are somehow taken into account. On the narrower, special-interest issues, legislators assume that, if on the one hand no one objects or on the other all parties agree, the public interest will be served, or at least not undermined. The interest-group systems that operate in the states, however, do not necessarily safeguard the public interest, even though each special interest maintains that its agenda will promote the public good.

In those instances where a group is pushing a measure to which no other group voices objection and where there are no direct costs to the state, the legislature will usually go along. It has to deal with enough conflict and does not want to encourage conflict where none has to exist. Why not say yes, and make some group of voters and its lobbyists happy! These are the consensual issues that offer concentrated benefits at no cost, or with very dispersed costs. No one gets hurt as a result. A group— say, one seeking licensing for its occupation—may benefit, while no one suffers except for, possibly, a larger, more diffuse public.[32] Legislative staff members have little time to focus on these narrow issues and few incentives to do so; legislators are not apt to dally over staff arguments when they want to settle something peaceably and move on.

On many special-interest issues two sides do come into conflict. Contradictory arguments are expressed, and legislators can choose between them. In these instances, as we saw in chapter 8, unqualified victories are rare, and compromise is the probable outcome.[33] Legislators encourage the disputants to negotiate and resolve their differences.

Legislators may even play a role as mediators or contestants; above all, they are motivated to reach a settlement with which everyone can live. Lobbyists are similarly inclined, realizing that they benefit if fewer legislators have to choose sides and fewer line up against them. The issues in dispute may be complex, and it is often difficult to determine which group got the better of a particular compromise. One contestant may win more than the other, but neither ordinarily loses too much; both may actually come out ahead.

Although a settlement is reached in many of the disputes involving special interests, there can be no assurance that the broader public benefits from the outcome. Conflict and debate do not necessarily promote the public interest. Some legislators will try to examine the issues from the perspective of the general public, but many will align themselves with one group or the other, and most will want things worked out with minimal bloodshed. Furthermore, the legislators' assumption is that if they keep interests in a reasonable state of balance, the public interest will be approximated.

In addition, legislators appreciate that whatever the legislative outcome of such special-interest issues, the governor stands as another line of defense. If indeed a particular interest is overreaching or several interests are dividing up the pie to the detriment of the people of the state, the governor can be expected to exercise the veto. The governor has a broader perspective. The governor and the governor's office are more insulated from lobbyists and the interests they represent; they can both afford and are more inclined to say "no." If the review done by gubernatorial staff is different from that done by legislative staff, it is because the two have dissimilar roles on these issues.

The interest-group system, as it operates today, will also lead to stalemate or deadlock in some important areas. Both Congress and state legislatures are strongly criticized for failing to address or decide key problems facing the nation and the states. Take California, for example. During the tenure of Governor George Deukmejian and a Democratic-controlled legislature, it was commonly held that critical issues were gridlocked. The governor did not want to have anything done and the legislature lacked the courage to take the lead. According to an article in the *California Journal*, titled "Special Interests Dominate Legislative Session," many insiders believe that

> There has long been a cause-and-effect relationship between fund raising and policy paralysis. Law-makers were unwilling to bite the hands that fed them. Donations did not necessarily buy a bill but donations could purchase a stand-off.[34]

Whether campaign contributions were at the root of the problem is disputable. A conservative Republican governor, such as George

Deukmejian, and a liberal Democratic legislature could be expected to deadlock on a number of key issues. They had different political philosophies and were responsive to different interests. Moreover, in California as elsewhere, building a consensus is scarcely manageable on issues where groups are polarized. Again, if we assume that the public clearly needs and obviously desires a measure, then there may be a "correct" outcome. But such an assumption rests on one's values and one's interests.

One example offered to prove that special interests triumph over the public interest is the bottle bill. Although deposit laws have been enacted by nine states, such measures have been blocked in a number of others. Public-interest groups point to the bottle bill as a clear-cut case of the will of the people being defeated by a powerful lobby. While public opinion polls may show a majority of voters favoring such a measure, the opposition of the retailers, bottlers, liquor distributors, and the like proves to be decisive. In New Jersey, for example, beverage-container-deposit legislation was bottled up in committee for seven years without being heard. Finally, the bill was given a hearing late in 1991. On that occasion, two legislator sponsors of the proposal deserted the cause, arguing (along with business) that a deposit law would hinder New Jersey's objective of achieving a 60 percent recycling rate. Meanwhile, proponents of the bill maintained that despite the success of the state's mandatory recycling law, New Jersey would not reach its objective without a deposit law.[35] New Jersey legislators had reason to wonder which path to pursue—one that would burden retailers, hurt the glass industry, and possibly undermine a recycling program that was well under way or one that offered promise of further environmental gains.

Public-interest groups, along with many members of the statehouse press corps, portray government as being of the special interests, by the special interests, and for the special interests. Most citizens nowadays agree. John Gardner, the founding chairman of Common Cause, expressed the widespread feeling that "in the Special Interest State that we have forged, every well-organized interest 'owns a piece of the rock'." [36]

If special interests seem to dominate, one reason is that although people today vote less, they participate more. They participate either directly or indirectly through narrow-gauge groups. Some years ago, a state senator in Texas, in responding to an interviewer's question declared: "They accuse me of being a tool of the special interests. And I plead guilty. Every son of a bitch in my district has one special interest or another." Contemporary America is fragmented into racial, ethnic, social, and interest groups. Practically every one of these groups is organized for political action. While citizens may not participate actively, pay dues, or carry cards, their views—if they have them—are represented before legislative bodies.

When citizens do not hold views on a subject, as on so many issues before the legislature, they must rely for representation on elected public officials. Even when citizens are unconcerned, they have representatives who are disposed to be responsive. But their representatives cannot express views that are not held, so they must decide on other bases. Such bases are provided by interest groups as well as a lawmaker's constituents, convictions, prior record, party affiliations, and relationships.

The interest-group systems that operate in Washington, D.C., and in the state capitals are taken to task on several grounds. In the first place, it is argued, the proliferation and strength of special interests have led us to lose sight of a more general interest, that is, the public interest.[37] The concept of the "public interest" has been examined and critiqued by pluralists for years. The arguments need not be repeated here. Suffice it to say that the notion of the public interest rests on the assumption that the citizens of this country and of the fifty states constitute homogeneous bodies with common interests that transcend narrow group concerns. Is there, in fact, such a unitary and discernible public interest beyond the various factional interests that are articulated?[38] Perhaps, but its existence has yet to be persuasively demonstrated. The public interest is not necessarily the same as the distribution of responses to questions in a poll. Nor is it necessarily what associations designated as "public-interest groups" say it is. Each of us has his or her own notion of what it is in some area of public policy, but we do not always agree with each other.

The idea of the public interest lacks empirical reality. It is a myth, albeit a useful one. It needs to be taken into account by public officials; indeed, it should weigh heavily in the decisions they make. On the big issues, it does, to one degree or another, but it is mediated by other potent factors. Governors, legislative leaders, and legislators actually believe in the concept "public interest," and they pay more than lip service to it.

Another criticism is that the interest-group systems do not offer everyone equal access to the arena of decision making. Although no one is completely shut out, some citizens and some groups are relatively advantaged while others are relatively disadvantaged. Representation has broadened of late, but upper- and middle-class interests are still better represented.[39] However, it is not easy to get people to agree on which specific groups come out ahead and which come out behind. In a survey of Kansas legislators, for instance, the members were asked to identify underrepresented groups and groups that were overrepresented in the legislative process. Three-quarters of them responded that, yes, some groups were underrepresented. Half of them named the "average citizen," and one out of five mentioned the poor. Three-fifths of the legislators said that, yes, some groups were overrepresented. But there was no agreement, the researchers found, on which specific groups and, hence,

"no general perception that any particular interests are disproportion-
ately influential." [40]

It is generally believed that interests with money also have influence.
Money, no doubt, gives additional weight to people's preferences. It costs
money to employ contract lobbyists with connections. It is expensive to
pay for entertainment that helps develop or buttress relationships
between legislators and lobbyists. Political campaigns require money.
Most important, money is needed to maintain a basic organization and to
mobilize grass-roots support. Without some semblance of organization,
an interest can hardly make its own case, although the case may be made
for it.

Those who have money also have an edge, other things being equal.
This is more likely to occur on the narrow, special-interest issues. Other
things are less likely to be equal on broader issues, where legislators'
values and district interests come into play. As a Colorado business
lobbyist pointed out: "All the PAC money in the world will not persuade
a legislator to go against his own or his district's interests."

Money is certainly an important resource in interest-group politics,
but it is by no means the only or the most important resource. Some
monetary base is requisite, but beyond that it is only one commodity in
the marketplace of competing interests. James Q. Wilson discusses the
organizational representation and interest-bargaining system of today.
This pluralistic system assures that organized, affected parties will be
heard and that their preferences will be taken into account. Unorganized
groups were previously neglected by such politics, but that is no longer
the case. Nowadays, the mobilization of new groups, grass-roots appeals,
and the role of the media have widened the arena of conflict, placed new
issues on the agenda, and challenged traditional institutional arrangements.[41] What we have is neither a closed system nor one in which every
participant is equal. Just how participants weigh in depends on who they
are. It also depends on the particular issue in contest, the politics of the
time, the people in government, and more immediate circumstances.

Lobbyists are an integral part of all this. Just as few people would
think of appealing to the courts without the benefit of counsel, few people
would consider dealing with government without the benefit of a lobbyist.
Lobbyists have access and influence that the average citizen lacks
because they are experienced, expert, and work full-time at the job. They
naturally help the clients and causes they represent. That is what they
are paid to do. But they also contribute—albeit imperfectly—to the
legislative process in the states and to the pluralistic interest-group
system that prevails in the nation.

Notes

1. Robert E. Wood, "Measuring Performance: The Critical Factors," in *Leveraging State Government Relations,* ed. Wesley Pedersen (Washington, D.C.: Public Affairs Council, 1990), 50-51.
2. Seymour Lusterman, *Managing Business-State Government Relations* (New York: The Conference Board, 1983), 13.
3. Andrew Baker, MetPath. (Remarks at the State Government Relations Institute, New Brunswick, N.J., July 12, 1990.)
4. The survey is reported in Kay Lehman Schlozman and John T. Tierney, *Organized Interests in American Democracy* (New York: Harper and Row, 1986), 104.
5. Rowland Stiteler, "Influence Peddling," *Florida Magazine, Orlando Sentinel,* May 29, 1988.
6. Gallup Organization, "The 1987 Gallup Survey of the New Jersey State Legislature" (Princeton, N.J.: Gallup, 1987), 2; Anne E. Kelley and Ella L. Taylor, "Florida: The Changing Patterns of Power," in *Interest Groups in the Southern States,* ed. Ronald J. Hrebenar and Clive S. Thomas (Tuscaloosa: University of Alabama Press, forthcoming).
7. James Q. Wilson, *Political Organizations* (New York: Basic Books, 1973), 308.
8. Stiteler, "Influence Peddling."
9. Jeffrey M. Berry, *The Interest Group Society* (Boston: Little, Brown, 1984), 118.
10. Harmon Zeigler and Michael A. Baer, *Lobbying: Interaction and Influence in American State Legislatures* (Belmont, Calif.: Wadsworth, 1969), 133.
11. *Miami Herald,* December 11, 1990.
12. W. John Moore, "Have Smarts, Will Travel," *National Journal,* November 28, 1987, 3023.
13. Schlozman and Tierney, *Organized Interests,* 314.
14. Michael T. Hayes, *Lobbyists and Legislators* (New Brunswick, N.J.: Rutgers University Press, 1981), 74-75, 76-77.
15. Clive S. Thomas and Ronald J. Hrebenar, "Interest Groups in the States," in *Politics in the American States,* ed. Virginia Gray, Herbert Jacob, and Robert B. Albritton, 5th ed. (Glenview, Ill.: Scott, Foresman/Little, Brown Higher Education, 1990), 144-145.
16. See, for instance, Gallup, "1987 Gallup Survey of the New Jersey State Legislature," 6-7; Craig Grau, "Minnesota: Labor and Business in an Issue-Oriented State," in *Interest Groups in the Midwestern States,* ed Ronald J. Hrebenar and Clive S. Thomas (Ames: Iowa State University Press, forthcoming).
17. Harold Wolman and Fred Teitelbaum, "Interest Groups and the Reagan Presidency," in *The Reagan Presidency and the Governing of America,* ed. Lester M. Salamon and Michael S. Lund (Washington, D.C.: Urban Institute Press, 1985), 323. The failure to specify the scope of influence is one reason why, when some legislators are asked which groups are most effective, many different groups are nominated, although realtors, trial lawyers, and doctors

may come out somewhat ahead. See Keith E. Hamm and Charles W. Wiggins, "Texas: The Transformation from Personal to Informational Lobbying," in *Interest Group Politics in the Southern States* (Tuscaloosa: University of Alabama Press, forthcoming).

18. Sarah McCally Morehouse, *State Politics, Parties and Policy* (New York: Holt, Rinehart, and Winston, 1981), 103-104. The difficulty of assessing the power of special interests is acknowledged by Allan J. Cigler and Dwight C. Kiel, who surveyed lobbyists and legislators in Kansas, *The Changing Nature of Interest Group Politics in Kansas* (Topeka: Capitol Complex Center, University of Kansas, June 1988), 19-20.

19. John A. Straayer, *The Colorado General Assembly* (Niwot, Colo.: University Press of Colorado, 1990), 179-181.

20. Paul Brace and John A. Straayer, "Colorado: PACs, Political Candidates, and Conservatism," in *Interest Groups in the American West*, ed. Ronald J. Hrebenar and Clive S. Thomas (Salt Lake City: University of Utah Press, 1987), 56.

21. Robert H. Salisbury, "The Paradox of Interest Groups in Washington—More Groups, Less Clout"; and Aaron Wildavsky, "A World of Difference—The Public Philosophies and Political Behaviors of Rival American Cultures," in *The New American Political System*, ed. Anthony King, 2d version (Washington, D.C.: AEI Press, 1990), 203-229 and 263-286.

22. Wolman and Teitelbaum, "Interest Groups," 324.

23. Kathleen Sylvester, "The Chastening of the Trial Lawyers," *Governing*, February 1991, 30.

24. Kathleen Sylvester, "The Tobacco Industry Will Walk a Mile to Stop an Anti-Smoking Law," *Governing*, May 1989, 36.

25. Charles M. Price, "How Tobacco Courts California," *California Journal*, August 1991, 345.

26. Sylvester, "Tobacco Industry," 34.

27. General business organizations were just below teachers in the rankings of most effective interest groups in thirty-one states. Thomas and Hrebenar, "Interest Groups," 144-145.

28. Gallup, "1987 Gallup Survey of the New Jersey State Legislature," 3, 6-7.

29. Paul Feldman, "Those Who Can, Lobby," *New Jersey Reporter*, April 1983, 24.

30. But see Kelley and Taylor, "Florida: The Changing Patterns of Power," who point to the increasing influence of public-interest and citizen groups, special-issue groups, and local governments.

31. See Debra L. Dodson and Lauren D. Burnbauer, *Election 1989: The Abortion Issue in New Jersey and Virginia* (New Brunswick, N.J.: Eagleton Institute of Politics, Rutgers University, 1990).

32. Diane M. Evans, "PAC Contributions and Roll-Call Voting," in *Interest Group Politics*, ed. Allan J. Cigler and Burdett A. Loomis, 2d ed. (Washington, D.C.: CQ Press, 1986), 116.

33. Schlozman and Tierney, *Organized Interests*, 312-313.

34. James Richardson, "Special Interests Dominate Legislative Session," *California Journal*, November 1990, 528.

35. *Star-Ledger*, September 24, 1991.

36. Quoted in Common Cause, "Lobbying Law Reform in the States," unpublished paper dated September 1988, 2.
37. See, for instance, Ronald J. Hrebenar and Ruth K. Scott, *Interest Group Politics in America*, 2d ed. (Englewood Cliffs, N.J.: Prentice-Hall, 1990), 305.
38. James A. Morone, *The Democratic Wish* (New York: Basic Books, 1990), 6, 126.
39. Berry, *Interest Group Society*, 219.
40. Cigler and Kiel, *Changing Nature of Interest Group Politics in Kansas*, 16-18.
41. James Q. Wilson, *Political Organizations* (New York: Basic Books, 1973), 345.

SELECTED BIBLIOGRAPHY

The following books and articles are among the most informative scholarly and applied work on lobbying and lobbyists, with emphasis on the states.

Ambrosius, Margery M., and Susan Welch. "State Legislators' Perceptions of Business and Labor Interests." *Legislative Studies Quarterly* 13 (May 1988): 199-209.

Berry, Jeffrey M. *The Interest Group Society.* Boston: Little, Brown, 1984.

BeVier, Michael J. *Politics Backstage: Inside the California Legislature.* Philadelphia: Temple University Press, 1979.

Cigler, Allan J., and Dwight C. Kiel, *The Changing Nature of Interest Group Politics in Kansas.* Topeka: Capitol Complex Center, University of Kansas, June 1988.

Cigler, Allan J., and Burdett A. Loomis. *Interest Group Politics,* 2d ed. Washington, D.C.: CQ Press, 1986.

———. *Interest Group Politics,* 3d ed. Washington, D.C.: CQ Press, 1991.

Crawford, Kenneth Gale. *The Pressure Boys: The Inside Story of Lobbying in America.* New York: Arno Press, 1974.

Deakin, James. *The Lobbyists.* Washington, D.C.: Public Affairs Press, 1966.

Ehrenhalt, Alan. *The United States of Ambition.* New York: Times Books, 1991.

Elazar, Daniel J. *American Federalism: A View from the States,* 2d ed. New York: Thomas Y. Crowell, 1972.

Haley, Martin Ryan, and James M. Kiss. "Larger Stakes in Statehouse Lobbying." *Harvard Business Review* 52 (January-February 1984): 125-135.

Hall, Richard L., and Frank W. Wayman. "Buying Time: Moneyed Interests and the Mobilization of Bias in Congressional Committees." *American Political Science Review* 84 (September 1990): 797-820.

Hayes, Michael T. *Lobbyists and Legislators.* New Brunswick, N.J.: Rutgers University Press, 1981.

Hrebenar, Ronald J., and Ruth K. Scott. *Interest Group Politics in America,* 2d ed. Englewood Cliffs, N.J.: Prentice-Hall, 1990.

Hrebenar, Ronald J., and Clive S. Thomas, eds. *Interest Group Politics in the American West.* Salt Lake City: University of Utah Press, 1987.

———. *Interest Group Politics in the Southern States.* Tuscaloosa: University of Alabama Press, forthcoming.

———. *Interest Group Politics in the Midwestern States.* Ames: Iowa State University Press, forthcoming.

Jewell, Malcolm E., and Penny M. Miller. *The Kentucky Legislature: Two Decades of Change.* Lexington: The University Press of Kentucky, 1988.

230 *Selected Bibliography*

Jones, Ruth S., and Thomas J. Borris. "Strategic Contributing in Legislative Campaigns: The Case of Minnesota." *Legislative Studies Quarterly* 10 (February 1985): 89-105.

Josephson Institute of Ethics, *Actual and Apparent Impropriety: A Report on Ethical Norms and Attitudes in State Legislatures.* The Institute: Marina del Rey, Calif., January 1992.

King, Anthony, ed. *The New American Political System,* 2d version, Washington, D.C.: AEI Press, 1990.

Lusterman, Seymour. *Managing Business-State Government Relations.* New York: The Conference Board, 1983.

Mack, Charles S. *The Executive's Handbook of Trade and Business Associations.* Westport, Conn.: Quorum Books, 1991.

———. *Lobbying and Government Relations: A Guide for Executives.* Westport, Conn.: Quorum Books, 1989.

Magleby, David B., and Candice J. Nelson. *The Money Chase: Congressional Campaign Finance Reform.* Washington, D.C.: Brookings, 1990.

Milbrath, Lester W. *The Washington Lobbyists.* Chicago: Rand McNally, 1963.

Morehouse, Sarah McCally. *State Politics, Parties, and Policy.* New York: Holt, Rinehart, and Winston, 1981.

Morgan, David R., Robert E. England, and George G. Humphreys, *Oklahoma Politics and Policies: Governing the Sooner State.* Lincoln: University of Nebraska Press, 1991.

Muir, William K., Jr. *Legislature: California's School for Politics.* Chicago: University of Chicago Press, 1982.

Pedersen, Wesley, ed. *Leveraging State Government Relations.* Washington, D.C.: Public Affairs Council, 1990.

Public Affairs Council. *State Government Relations: Results of a Survey of 55 Corporations.* Washington, D.C.: Public Affairs Council, 1986.

———. *The Third House: An Informal Survey of Corporate Lobbying at the State Level.* Washington, D.C.: Public Affairs Council, 1973.

Public Affairs Research Group. *Public Affairs Offices and Their Functions.* Boston: School of Management, Boston University, 1981.

Salisbury, Robert H. "Interest Representation: The Dominance of Institutions." *American Political Science Review* 78 (March 1984): 64-76.

Salisbury, Robert H., et al. "Who You Know Versus What You Know: The Uses of Government Experience for Washington Lobbyists." *American Journal of Political Science* 33 (February 1989): 175-195.

———. "Who Works With Who? Interest Group Alliances and Opposition." *American Political Science Review* 81 (December 1987): 1217-1233.

Schlozman, Kay Lehman, and John T. Tierney. *Organized Interests and American Democracy.* New York: Harper and Row, 1986.

Straayer, John A. *The Colorado General Assembly.* Niwot, Colo.: University Press of Colorado, 1990.

Thomas, Clive S., and Ronald J. Hrebenar. "Interest Groups in the States," in *Politics in the American States,* edited by Virginia Gray, Herbert Jacob, and Robert B. Albritton, 5th edition. Glenview, Ill.: Scott, Foresman/Little, Brown Higher Education, 1990.

Walker, Jack L., Jr. *Mobilizing Interest Groups in America.* Ann Arbor: University of Michigan Press, 1991.

———. "The Origin and Maintenance of Interest Groups in America." *American Political Science Review* 77 (June 1983): 390-406.

Wiggins, Charles W., and William P. Browne. "Interest Groups and Public Policy within a Legislative Setting." *Polity* 15 (Spring 1982): 548-558.

Wilson, James Q. *Political Organizations.* New York: BasicBooks, 1973.

Wolpe, Bruce C. *Lobbying Congress: How the System Works.* Washington, D.C.: Congressional Quarterly Inc., 1990.

Wright, John R. "Contributions, Lobbying, and Committee Voting in the U.S. House of Representatives." *American Political Science Review* 84 (June 1990): 417-438.

Zeigler, Harmon, and Michael A. Baer. *Lobbying: Interaction and Influence in American State Legislatures.* Belmont, Calif.: Wadsworth, 1969.

INDEX